CONSTRUCTIVISM:
THEORY, PERSPECTIVES,
AND PRACTICE

SECOND EDITION

CONSTRUCTIVISM:
THEORY, PERSPECTIVES, AND PRACTICE

SECOND EDITION

Catherine Twomey Fosnot

EDITOR

Teachers College, Columbia University
New York and London

Published by Teachers College Press, 1234 Amsterdam Avenue, New York, NY 10027

Library of Congress Cataloging-in-Publication Data

Constructivism : theory, perspectives, and practice / Catherine Twomey Fosnot, editor.— 2nd ed.
    p.   cm.
    Includes bibliographical references and index.
    ISBN 0-8077-4570-7 (pbk. : alk. paper)
    1. Constructivism (Education)   I. Fosnot, Catherine Twomey.
  LB1590.3.C676 2004
  370.15′2—dc22

        2004062139

ISBN 0-8077-4570-7 (paper)

Printed on acid-free paper

Manufactured in the United States of America

12 11 10 9 8 7 6 5   8 7 6 5 4 3 2 1

To Eileen and Gerald
In deep gratitude for their parenting

Contents

Preface

Constructivism is a theory about knowledge and learning; it describes both what "knowing" is and how one "comes to know." Based on work in psychology, philosophy, science, and biology, the theory describes knowledge not as truths to be transmitted or discovered, but as emergent, developmental, nonobjective, viable constructed explanations by humans engaged in meaning-making in cultural and social communities of discourse. Learning from this perspective is viewed as a self-regulatory process of struggling with the conflict between existing personal models of the world and discrepant new insights, constructing new representations and models of reality as a human meaning-making venture with culturally developed tools and symbols, and further negotiating such meaning through cooperative social activity, discourse, and debate in communities of practice.

Although constructivism is not a theory of teaching, it suggests taking a radically different approach to instruction from that used in most schools. Teachers who base their practice on constructivism reject the notions that meaning can be passed on to learners via symbols and transmission, that learners can incorporate exact copies of teachers' understanding for their own use, that whole concepts can be broken into discrete subskills, and that concepts can be taught out of context. In contrast, a constructivist view of learning suggests an approach to teaching that gives learners the opportunity for concrete, contextually meaningful experience through which they can search for patterns; raise questions; and model, interpret, and defend their strategies and ideas. The classroom in this model is seen as a mini-society, a community of learners engaged in activity, discourse, interpretation, justification, and reflection. The traditional hierarchy of teacher as the autocratic knower, and learner as the unknowing, controlled subject studying and practicing what the teacher knows, begins to dissipate as teachers assume more of a facilitator's role and learners take on more ownership of the ideas. Indeed, autonomy, mutual reciprocity of social relations, and empowerment become the goals.

Too often in the past, reforms in practice were not grounded in theory and thus took on a "cookbook" faddism. We again run the risk of short-lived reform, or "fuzzy-based" practice unless educators understand the theory, the connections across the disciplines of the reforms, and the major restructuring that is needed in schools and teacher preparation programs if we are to take constructivism seriously.

When this book was initially conceived, it was intended as a reader for educators who cared to go beneath the surface reforms and look at the deeper questions and issues related to teaching and learning. My hope was that readers would gain from the book new images of classrooms, visions of schools and universities as they could be, and the theory to argue and defend the needed reforms to policy makers and parents who must support our efforts. Ten years after the first edition, the theory is no longer controversial. Most contemporary neurobiologists and cognitive scientists agree: knowledge is actively constructed. The implications of constructivism for *education*, however, remain very controversial. In the last decade, schools have been engaged in a flurry of reform initiatives encompassing new curricula, new forms of assessment, new standards, and professional development. But various interpretations of constructivism still abound, often confusing it with "hands-on" learning, discovery, and a host of pedagogical strategies—confusion and misinterpretation that has resulted in public attacks by the media, by parents, and even at times by various groups in the academic community.

In this revised edition, written almost 10 years later than the first, I have tried to update the theory section with further contemporary biological evidence—to go beyond the theories of Piaget and Vygotsky. To accomplish this, I asked Randall Stewart Perry, an astrobiologist whose work is in early evolution, to join me in an attempt to develop a biological model of epistemology—a more contemporary framework for a psychological theory of learning. Chapter 2 reflects those revisions. At the same time, I have added two new chapters in the practice section, and a new epilogue section, to reflect the school-based reforms that have occurred since the writing of the first edition. These chapters most specifically address the changes in math education and teacher education, but also included is a new chapter on social studies, authored by Catherine Franklin. Lastly, D. Kim Reid and Jan Valle graciously agreed to co-author a chapter from the perspective of the emerging field of Disability Studies. They begin by addressing the issue of why people in general (not just teachers) who work with disabled students have not embraced constructivism and they describe the social construction of disabled people (i.e., as other and as incapable, needing direction, a burden on society, etc.) and show how these students are positioned by beliefs and sociocultural practices within schools. Their chapter ends with a critique that unmasks these practices and assumptions as ones that serve the orderliness of schools, rather than students and their families. They review the research—some of it by hard-core traditionalists—revealing that when we give kids a chance, they can and do learn just like the rest of us through progressive structuring and restructuring of knowledge/experience.

As with the first edition, there are many ways to read this book. Cover to cover in a linear fashion is of course one, but readers are encouraged to read with their own questions in mind. Those interested in practice might start with the last section. With appetites having been whetted, the theory can be studied next, followed by the perspectives. Those who have a particular content interest may choose instead to read across the sections; for example, readers interested in language arts might begin with Chapter 6, move to Chapter 11, and then turn to the theory behind the reforms.

Books, like trees, may appear on the surface to be discrete entities; but their roots go deep, and the growth pattern and eventual form taken are affected by many sources. Special acknowledgement is due to the contributors of this volume. Except for Chapters 3, 10, and 15, all the chapters were written specifically for this volume. I owe special gratitude to each author for the multiple drafts and revisions many produced as we all worked to make this volume a cohesive, theoretically consistent whole. Five colleagues whose chapters do not appear in this volume must also be acknowledged. Bill Doll from Louisiana State University, Barry Wadsworth from Mt. Holyoke College, Sue Holloway from Connecticut State University, and Roger Anderson from Columbia University engaged in long conversations with me about the first edition, and in the initial writing of chapters for that edition, and then graciously agreed to have their chapters cut as the book took a new form. Jill Lester from Mt. Holyoke College, who had a chapter in the first edition (about the work we had done together 10 years ago when I was part of the Summermath for Teachers project), was exceptionally understanding when I suggested that I replace her chapter in the second edition with a chapter I coauthored with Maarten Dolk on the more recent math work I have been doing with the Freudenthal Institute in New York City. For this I have deep gratitude and recognition of their support and professionalism. Along the way, many colleagues at City College read versions of Chapter 2 and provided insightful comments and support, most specifically Gary Benenson, Ed Farrell, Irvin Schonfeld, and Ed Wall. The work described in the epilogue chapter and in Chapter 10 could not have been written without the support and insights of my Mathematics in the City colleagues and staff, most specifically Maarten Dolk, Toni Cameron, Sherrin Hersch, Dawn Selnes, Herbert Seignoret, and Pablo Carvajal. I gratefully acknowledge Mathematics in the City's funding sources as well, the National Science Foundation, and the New York City and New Rochelle Boards of Education. My previous students and colleagues at the Center for Constructivist Teaching at Southern Connecticut were all instrumental in the original edition and in the compilation of data for Chapter 15. Special thanks are due Kathleen Scott, Maria Clark, June Gould, and Sue Holloway, as well as our funding source for that project: Federal Funds for Innovation in Education. And lastly, a very special thank you is due Brian Ellerbeck at Teachers College Press, who worked patiently with me, stretching me both to reformulate and revise the text through its various stages and editions.

June 1, 2004

PART I
Theory

CHAPTER 1

Introduction: Aspects of Constructivism

Ernst von Glasersfeld

The key idea that sets constructivism apart from other theories of cognition was launched about 60 years ago by Jean Piaget. It was the idea that what we call knowledge does not and cannot have the purpose of producing representations of an independent reality, but instead has an adaptive function. This changed assessment of cognitive activity entails an irrevocable break with the generally accepted epistemological tradition of Western civilization, according to which the knower must strive to attain a picture of the real world. While the revolutions in the physical sciences in this century have led to the realization that such a picture seems impossible even according to physical theory, most philosophers hang on to the belief that the progress of science will somehow lead to an approximation of the ultimate truth.

Throughout the ages, however, there have been thinkers who did not share such a belief.[1] Indeed, since the beginning of our history of ideas, the skeptics have formulated logically irrefutable arguments showing that if true knowledge is to represent a real world, it could not be attained. Although they provided constant irritation to the philosophical establishment, it was always easy to make their arguments seem absurd by mentioning some of the wonderful things human knowledge had achieved. In ancient times one could point to the accurate predictions concerning eclipses and the movement of celestial bodies in general, and in our days there are not only the miracles of technology we use in everyday life but also the overwhelming fact that a man was able to land on the moon. In the face of such successes, it would, indeed, be ridiculous to question the validity of knowledge.

Constructivism: Theory, Perspectives, and Practice (Second Edition). Copyright © 2005 by Teachers College, Columbia University. All rights reserved. ISBN 0-8077-4570-0 (paper). Prior to photocopying items for classroom use, please contact the Copyright Clearance Center, Customer Service, 222 Rosewood Drive, Danvers, MA 01923, USA, telephone (978) 750-8400.

ADAPTATION INSTEAD OF REPRESENTATION

Yet in spite of their power on the commonsense level, the achievements of science and technology do not actually resolve the fundamental problem of knowledge. In order to appreciate this, one has to become aware of the fact that validity in our experiential world is not the same as truth in the philosopher's absolute or ontological sense. It was, indeed, the skeptics themselves who helped to obscure this distinction. Their error did not lie in the logic of their arguments, which are, in fact, irrefutable. But they failed to question the way in which what we know should be related to reality. It is here that Piaget's use of the notion of adaptation opens a path that makes it possible to accept the skeptics' logical conclusion without diminishing the obvious value of knowledge.

The concept of adaptation stems from biology, and it indicates a particular relationship between living organisms or species and their environment. To say that they are adapted means no less but also no more than that they have been able to survive given the conditions and the constraints of the world in which they happen to be living. In other words, they have managed to evolve a fit or, as I prefer to say, their physical characteristics and their ways of behaving have so far proven viable in their environment.

Piaget took the notion of adaptation out of the biological context and turned it into the cornerstone of his genetic epistemology. He had realized early on that whatever knowledge was, it was not a copy of reality. The relationship of viable biological organisms to their environment provided a means to reformulate the relationship between the cognitive subject's conceptual structures and that subject's experiential world. Knowledge, then, could be treated not as a more or less accurate representation of external things, situations, and events, but rather as a mapping of actions and conceptual operations that had proven viable in the knowing subject's experience.

The use Piaget makes of the notion of adaptation is therefore not the same as that suggested by the contemporary school of thought that goes by the name of evolutionary epistemology. Unlike this school, which formed around the work of Konrad Lorenz, in Piaget's constructivist theory one cannot draw conclusions about the character of the real world from an organism's adaptedness or the viability of schemes of action. In his view, what we see, hear, and feel—that is, our sensory world—is the result of our own perceptual activities and therefore specific to our ways of perceiving and conceiving. Knowledge, for him, arises from actions and the agent's reflection on them. The actions take place in an environment and are grounded in and directed at objects that constitute the organism's experiential world, not things in themselves that have an independent existence. Hence, when Piaget speaks of interaction, this does not imply an organism that interacts with objects as they really are, but rather a cognitive subject that is dealing with previously constructed perceptual and conceptual structures.

THE CONCEPT OF ENVIRONMENT

From this point of view, the notion of environment is obviously not the ordinary one. In the commonsense description of our world, the environment is what surrounds all of us; we think of it as existing as such, whether we happen to be in it or not. In the constructivist model, environment has two quite distinct meanings. On the one hand, when we speak of ourselves, environment refers to the totality of permanent objects and their relations that we have abstracted from the flow of our experience. On the other, whenever we focus our attention on a particular item, environment refers to the surroundings of the item we have isolated, and we tend to forget that both the item and its surroundings are parts of our own experiential field, not an observer-independent objective world.

This, I believe, is a crucial aspect to consider if we want to approach teaching and education from the constructivist position. Too often teaching strategies and procedures seem to spring from the naive assumption that what we ourselves perceive and infer from our perceptions is there, ready-made, for the students to pick up, if only they had the will to do so. This overlooks the basic point that the way we segment the flow of our experience, and the way we relate the pieces we have isolated, is and necessarily remains an essentially subjective matter. Hence, when we intend to stimulate and enhance a student's learning, we cannot afford to forget that knowledge does not exist outside a person's mind.

This issue has recently been somewhat confused by talk of shared knowledge and shared meanings. Such talk is often misleading because there are strikingly different ways of sharing. If two people share a room, there is one room and both live in it. If they share a bowl of cherries, none of the cherries is eaten by both persons. This is an important difference, and it must be borne in mind when one speaks of shared meanings. The conceptual structures that constitute meanings or knowledge are not entities that could be used alternatively by different individuals. They are constructs that each user has to build up for him- or herself. And because they are individual constructs, one can never say whether or not two people have produced the same construct. At best one may observe that in a given number of situations their constructs seem to function in the same way, that is, they seem compatible.

That is why those who are stressing the social dimension of language and knowledge would do well to use Paul Cobb's expression "taken-as-shared" (Cobb, 1991), which accentuates the subjective aspect of the situation. For it is one thing to assert that, as far as one's experience goes, the meaning others attribute to a word seems to be compatible with one's own, but quite another to assume that it *has* to be the same.

THE CONSTRUCTION OF MEANING

The mutual compatibility in our use of words and language is, of course, the result of social interaction. The process that leads to such compatibility, however, is not one of giving, taking, or sharing meanings as an existing commodity, but rather one of gradual accommodation that achieves a relative fit. Any observer of a child acquiring new items of vocabulary will notice that the meaning the child attributes to a new word is idiosyncratic in the sense that it comprises either more or less than the adult speaker of the language intends. Only repeated use and failures to achieve the desired response will bring about adjustments.

As I have said many times, the need to adjust what one considers the correct meanings of the words one uses does not end with childhood. Over and over again we discover, after many years of successfully using a given word, that we use it in a situation where the meaning we have attributed to it does not seem compatible with the meaning it appears to have for other users of the language. A dictionary will in many cases resolve the problem— and, in doing so, confirm the illusion that meanings are, after all, fixed entities that do not depend on individual usage. But a moment's thought on how anyone acquires the meaning of a word would reveal that this is an illusion. The dictionary presents definitions and examples that invariably consist of other words, which give rise to meanings only insofar as the reader interprets them. Such interpretation can be done only in terms of the chunks of perceptual and conceptual experience the individual reader has associated with the dictionary's words. Hence, no matter how one looks at it, an analysis of meanings always leads to individual experience and the social process of accommodating the links between words and chunks of that experience until the individual deems they are compatible with the usage and the linguistic and behavioral responses of others.

CONCLUSION

Without going into the details of the radical change of epistemological perspective inherent in the move to constructivism, I want to suggest that there are certain circumscribed areas in which a constructivist orientation can modify a teacher's attitude. It could, for instance, bring home the realization that students perceive their environment in ways that may be very different from those intended by the educators. And this environment includes curricula, textbooks, didactic props including computer programs and micro worlds, tasks they are given, and, of course, the teachers. This emphasizes the teacher's need to construct a hypothetical model of the particular conceptual worlds of the students they are facing. One can hope to induce changes in their ways of thinking only if one has some inkling as to the domains of experience, the concepts, and the conceptual relations the students possess at the moment (cf. von Glasersfeld & Steffe, 1991).

Similarly, the consideration of how meanings are constituted, and how, consequently, linguistic communication works, would dismantle the still widespread notion that conceptual knowledge can be transferred from teacher to student by the means of words. This is not to say that language is not important. In fact, it is the most powerful tool available to the teacher, but it does not transport meanings or concepts. Language enables the teacher to orient the student's conceptual construction by precluding certain pathways and making others more likely.

These are only two facets of the constructivist model, but they go a long way toward establishing the fundamental principle that learning is a constructive activity that the students themselves have to carry out. From this point of view, then, the task of the educator is not to dispense knowledge but to provide students with opportunities and incentives to build it up.

NOTE

1. An extensive review of this history can be found in Chapter 1 of von Glasersfeld (1995).

REFERENCES

Cobb, P. (1991). Reconstructing elementary school mathematics. *Focus on Learning Problems in Mathematics, 13*(2), 3–22.

von Glasersfeld, E. (1995). *Radical constructivism: A way of knowing and learning.* London: Falmer.

von Glasersfeld, E., & Steffe, L. P. (1991). Conceptual models in educational research and practice. *Journal of Educational Thought, 25*(2), 91–103.

CHAPTER 2

Constructivism: A Psychological Theory of Learning

Catherine Twomey Fosnot and Randall Stewart Perry

Psychology—the way learning is defined, studied, and understood—underlies much of the curricular and instructional decision-making that occurs in education. Constructivism, perhaps the most current psychology of learning, is no exception. Initially based on the work of Jean Piaget and Lev Vygotsky, and then supported and extended by contemporary biologists and cognitive scientists as they studied complexity and emergence, it is having major ramifications on the goals that teachers set for the learners with whom they work, the instructional strategies teachers employ in working toward these goals, and the methods of assessment used by school personnel to document genuine learning. What is this theory of learning and development that is the basis of the current reform movement and how is it different from other models of psychology?

INTRODUCTION: THEORIES OF LEARNING

Behaviorism

Behaviorism is the doctrine that regards psychology as a scientific study of behavior and explains learning as a system of behavioral responses to physical stimuli. Psychologists working within this theory of learning are interested in the effect of reinforcement, practice, and external motivation on a network of associations and learned behaviors. Educators using such a behaviorist framework preplan a curriculum by breaking a content area (usually seen as a finite body of predetermined knowledge) into assumed component parts—"skills"—and then sequencing these parts into a hierarchy ranging from simple to more complex. Assumptions are made that observation, listening to explanations from teachers who communicate clearly, or engaging in experiences, activities, or practice sessions with feedback will result in learning; and that proficient skills will quantify to produce the whole, or more encompassing concept (Bloom, 1956; Gagne, 1965). Further, learners are viewed as passive, in need of external motivation, and affected by reinforcement (Skinner, 1953); thus, educators spend their time developing a sequenced, well-structured curriculum and determining how they will assess, motivate, reinforce, and evaluate the learner. The learner is simply tested to see where he or she falls on the curriculum continuum and then expected to progress in a linear, quantitative fashion as long as clear communication and appropriate motivation, practice, and reinforcement are provided. Progress by learners is assessed by measuring observable outcomes—namely, behaviors on predetermined tasks. The mastery learning model (Bloom, 1976) is a case in point. This model makes the assumption that wholes can be broken into parts, that skills can be broken into subskills, and that these skills can be sequenced in a "learning line." Learners are diagnosed in terms of deficiencies, called "needs," then taught until "mastery"—defined as behavioral competence—is achieved at each of the sequenced levels. Further, it is assumed that if mastery is achieved at each level then the more general concept (defined by the accumulation of the skills) has also been taught. It is important to note the use of the term "skill" here as the outcome of learning and the goal of teaching. The term itself is derived from the notion of behavioral competence. Although few schools today use the mastery learning model rigidly, much of the prevalent traditional educational practice still in place stems from this behaviorist psychology. Behaviorist theory may have implications for changing behavior, but it offers little in the way of explaining cognitive change—a structural change in understanding.

Maturationism

In contrast, maturationism is a theory that describes conceptual knowledge as dependent on the developmental stage of the learner, which in turn is the result of a natural unfolding of innate biological programming. From this perspective learners are viewed as active meaning-makers, interpreting experience with cognitive structures that are the result of maturation; thus, age norms for these cognitive maturations are important as predictors of behavior. Psychologists working within this paradigm focused on delineating stages of growth and behaviors characteristic of each stage. For example,

Erikson (1950) studied the development of the concept of identity and proposed eight stages, each having a developmental crisis which he felt needed to be worked through for a healthy self-image to result; and Gesell (1940; Gesell & Ilg, 1946; Gesell et al., 1956), working with his colleagues Ilg and Ames, studied children at different ages and characterized their behaviors into age-dependent stages. The educator's role, from this perspective, is to prepare an enriched, developmentally appropriate environment. Learners are assessed in relation to developmental milestones, such as conservation tasks or Gesellian-based kindergarten screening tasks. Further, the curriculum is analyzed for its cognitive requirements on learners, and then matched to the learner's stage of development. Early attempts to apply Piaget's theory to education were based on this theory. His stage theory was misinterpreted as a maturationist theory, thus learners were assessed with a battery of tasks to ascertain whether they were preoperational, concrete-operational, or formal-operational. These global stages were seen as hierarchical and used as delimiters and/or goals of curriculum, and instructional methods were prescribed in relation to the stages in generalities such as "learners need concrete materials when they are in the concrete-operational stage." Models of teaching commonly known as "developmentally appropriate practice" evolved from this theory, as depicted in the 1988 position statement written by the National Association for the Education of Young Children:

> Between 6 and 9 years of age, children begin to acquire the mental ability to think about and solve problems in their heads because they can then manipulate objects symbolically—no longer always having to touch or move them. This is a major cognitive achievement for children that extends their ability to solve problems. While they can symbolically or mentally manipulate, it will be some time before they can mentally manipulate symbols, for example, to solve mathematical problems such as missing addends or to grasp algebra. For this reason, primary age children still need real things to think about . . . in addition, appropriate schools recognize that some thinking skills, such as understanding mathematical place value and "borrowing" in subtraction, are beyond the cognitive capacity of children who are developing concrete operational thinking and so do not introduce these skills to most children until they are 8 or 9 years of age. (1988, pp. 65–66)

Constructivism

As pointed out by von Glasersfeld in Chapter 1, constructivism is fundamentally nonpositivist and as such it stands on completely new ground, often in direct opposition to both behaviorism and maturationism. Rather than behaviors or skills as the goal of instruction, *cognitive development* and *deep understanding* are the foci; rather than stages being the result of maturation, they are understood as *constructions of active learner reorganization.* Rather than viewing learning as a linear process, it is understood to be *complex* and fundamentally *nonlinear* in nature. Constructivism, as a psychological theory, stems from the burgeoning field of cognitive science, particularly the later work of Jean Piaget just prior to his death in 1980, the sociohistorical work of Lev Vygotsky and his followers, and the work of Jerome Bruner, Howard Gardner, and Nelson Goodman, among others who have studied the role of representation in learning. It also has roots in biology and evolution—the logical outcome of the work of contemporary scientists such as Ilya Prigogine, Humberto Maturana, Francisco Varela, Ernst Mayr, Murray Gell-Man, Wolfgang Krumbein, Betsy Dyer, Lynn Margulis, Stuart Kauffman, and Per Bak (among others), as attempts were made to unify physics with biology. The remainder of this chapter will present a description of the work of these scientists and then a synthesis will be developed to describe and define constructivism as a psychological theory of evolution and development.

THE BIOLOGICAL LANDSCAPE OF LEARNING: EVOLUTIONARY SYSTEMS

Knowing and cognitive processes are rooted in our biological structure. The mechanisms by which life evolved—from chemical beginnings to cognizing human beings—are central to understanding the psychological basis of learning. We are the product of an evolutionary process and it is the mechanisms inherent in this process that offer the most probable explanations to how we think and learn.

Environmental Equivalence

Life evolved from the chemicals and substrates on early Earth. Complex inorganic- and carbon-based chemicals coevolved with their environment. One cannot separate one from the other any more than we can separate the construction of knowledge from its environment. We introduce the term "environmental equivalence" to emphasize the importance of the idea of equivalence—the active interplay of the surround (environment), to evolution *and* to learning. The environment of an organism is composed of itself (and its neurological events), the population of other organisms, and the physical nature of its surround. Organisms create their environment and are created by their environment. Thus, "The environment itself has about the equivalent power and influence as the biota and both communicate with each other in equilibrated and successful ways to keep the total system going" (Krumbein & Dyer, 1985, p. 150). Neither the organism nor learners are passive objects to their change, a point also made by Piaget when he suggested that both Lamarckian and Darwinian models of evolution were too extreme.

Biological Equilibration

Although Piaget's writings appeared over a 50-year span, it is the work done in the 10 to 15 years prior to his death that serves as a beginning point for the psychological basis of constructivism. During this time period, rather than discussing global stages as descriptive of learning as he had done in his earlier writings, he and his colleagues focused on the mechanism of learning. Rather than labeling the type of logic used by learners, that is, preoperational, concrete, or formal (as they had done in their earlier work), they focused on the *process* that enabled new constructions—new perspectives—to come about. Piaget had proposed equilibration as the mechanism to explain development very early in his career, but it was in the last 15 years of his life that he returned to this study, delineating it further and even eventually reformulating his model. In order to understand fully the mechanism of equilibration, a discussion of Piaget's early work as a biologist studying snails is important. Piaget's fascination centered on the variability of the snail's adaptation. He studied three separate groups of Limnaea stagnalis: those that live in still, tranquil clear waters (habitat A); those that live in mildly disturbed waters agitated by waves (habitat B); and those that live in severely disturbed waters agitated by high winds and waves (habitat C). While the shape of the snail in calm water was elongated, the shapes of the snails in both types of agitated water were the same—globular and curved. See Figure 2.1.

Piaget believed that the globular shape was due to the activity of the snails. The animal in the course of its growth attaches itself to its solid support, which dilates the opening. At the same time and even because of this, it draws on the muscle that attaches it to its shell, and this tends to shorten the spine, that is, the upper part of the spiral shell (Gallagher & Reid, 1982, p. 22). Piaget noticed that the globular snails of habitat B that had globular offspring in habitat B, when removed and placed in an aquarium (habitat A) had offspring that were elongated. This showed that the change in structure was only a phenotypic change, not a permanent genetic change. In contrast the snails of habitat C, although they looked exactly like the snails in habitat B, showed no change even when they were left in an aquarium for 16 years, and their offspring were globular. In other words, the snails in habitat C were distinctly different, having a different genotype. From these observations, as well as from observations of plant growth, Piaget proposed a middle ground

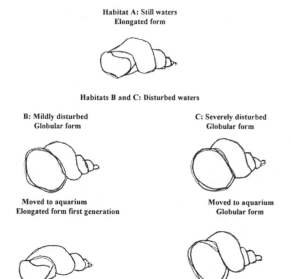

FIGURE 2.1. Pond snail (*Limnaea stagnalis*) as an example of biological equilibration.

position between the commonly held theories of that time—Lamarck's and Darwin's. Lamarck (1809) had proposed that evolution was a result of the organism's adjustment or accommodation to the environment's pressure; for a species to survive in a changing environment it made structural, genetic changes, acquired changes as a result of behaviors that were adaptive in nature. Darwin (1859) took a different view. He proposed that evolution was due to chance mutations, a method for selection generated by the organism, and that the mutations more suited to the environment would be carried on—a survival of the fittest, so to speak. Piaget criticized both Lamarck's and Darwin's theories as being too extreme—the former as mechanistic, the latter as purposeless (Doll, 1993). In contrast, Piaget took the position that the activity of the organism drives the evolution of new structures because the development of new behavior more or less causes an imbalance in the genome, the regulatory system of the genetic structure. This perturbation causes a series of possibilities to result in the genome. And then (in line with Darwin's theory of evolution) the possibilities most suited to the environment survive. Piaget viewed behavior and the organism as a whole system, such that any change in a part of the system would result in other changes as behavior balanced the structure of the organism against the characteristics of the environment. Although Piaget's work in biology did not receive much attention during his lifetime from researchers in the field (the exception being Waddington, 1957), a renewed interest has occurred in the work of contemporary scientists as they explore chaos theory and dissipative structures.

Dissipative Structures

For cells to live, evolve, and flourish, there must be an exchange of matter and energy with the environment around them. The flow of matter and energy through complex systems has been described by the Nobel Laureate Ilya Prigogine as a dissipative structure—an open system that maintains itself in a state far from equilibrium. Dissipative structures produce new forms of order—order that arises spontaneously in a complex system when it is far from equilibrium, at "the edge of the chaos." When the flow of energy increases, the increased activity produces instability and a "bifurcation" results. At this bifurcation point, reorganizing occurs—self-organizing that results in the emergence of a new structure for coherence and efficiency. Without dissipative structures, without exchange with the environment, entropy would result. Capra explains the importance of this model:

> This spontaneous emergence of order at critical points of instability is one of the most important concepts of the new understanding of life. It is technically known as self-organization and is often referred to simply as "emergence." It has been recognized as the dynamic origin of development, learning, and evolution. In other words, creativity—the generation of new forms—is a key property of all living systems. And since emergence is an integral part of dynamics of open systems, we reach the important conclusion that open systems develop and evolve. Life constantly reaches out into novelty. (Capra, 2002, p. 14)

Transition Zones

Before self-order and complexity can evolve, they are one with their environment. The time between the emergence of the chaotic environment that leads to bifurcations and novel structures and a preceding time of stasis is a transition zone. This explanation was first introduced by Perry and Kolb (2003, 2004) to bridge time between nonliving chemicals and life (as we know it). The transition zone is a gradual time interspersed with flurries of changes that lead to bifurcations. Self-organization, Darwinian evolution (selection and adaptation), and transitions to life proceed slowly over time. Although the time scale may be long, these transitions are not smooth but rather interspersed with cascades of change or "punctuated evolution" (Eldredge & Gould, 1972, as they applied it to developed life). This "first order coupling" with the environment (Maturana & Varela, 1998), allows for the formation of dissipative structures, in effect miniature Gaia. Just as whirl-winds appear from seemingly quiescent cloudless days, activity in transition zones such as prebiotic systems and in single cell organisms leads to develop-ment and organized structures. In transition zones over time, a myriad of changes and combinations between early pre-biotic molecules evolved and may or may not have led to life (Perry & Kolb, 2003). Only some of the bifurcations produced favorable changes for selection; others were dead ends. But, as "knowledge" (adaptation) improved, fidelity of replication be-came more reliable and chemical systems evolved toward cellular life. Evolu-tion to life was gradual but punctuated with chaotic or quantum events. When the chemical stage was set, life emerged from the transition zone and did not form only a proto-cell, but "googles." Materials from the surround entered (Kauffman, 1993; Margulis, 1982) and left evolving cells (Perry & Kolb, 2004) and formed symbiotic relationships in an interactive dance lead-ing to biological life and developed cognitive systems.

Emergence to Complex Systems: Second Order Coupling

Biological forms and functions are not simply determined by a genetic blueprint, but are emergent properties of an entire epigenetic living network. These networks continually create, or re-create, themselves by transforming or replacing their components. Just as single cell organisms exchange matter and energy via dissipative structures, complex organic systems undergo con-tinual structural changes while preserving their weblike patterns of organiza-tion (Capra, 2002). This autopoetic dynamic of organic systems has been termed "second order coupling" by Maturana and Varela (1998). An inter-play between the surround and the developing system forms whether the system consists of evolving chemicals, biology, or learners and "thus they [organisms] create their environment and in response to their environment they create themselves" (Krumbein & Dyer, 1985, p. 150).

Diversity and Deselection

As order evolves in far from equilibrium nonlinear systems, many paths are deselected and remaining paths are chosen (Prigogine, 1997). Systems before life (as we know it) might be bidirectional, evolving to more or less complexity, but as complexity increases in nonequilibrium systems, new forms of order develop (Gell-Mann, 1994; Prigogine, 1997). Life is the opposite of stasis. Isolation and stasis over time would result in a system running down—entropy, death. Natural selection increases the diversity while at the same time deselecting some of the possibilities. It also thriftily conserves the activity and self-organization accomplished at each stage so that it doesn't have to be done over again (Dennett, 1995). Over eons of time a diversity of species has evolved and less viable organisms have been deselected. Further, structural self-organizing within species also has occurred—that is, *Homo sapiens* have evolved myelination and neuronal networks that allow for language and thought. As we couple with our surround (including others) we evolve ideas and explanatory models that are viable, and deselect those that we deem not viable. Reflection on our activity in the surround, discussed in communities of discourse to generate multiple perspectives (a third-order coupling, Maturana & Varela, 1998) keeps us in a growth-producing, open, evolving state. Recent work in Artificial Intelligence suggests that the generating of diverse possibilities and the subsequent deselection of nonviable activity characterizes learning. Computers programmed to deselect pathways that were deemed not viable after trials, began to self-organize, seemingly learning and constructing new, more efficient pathways, poised in a dynamic state of self-organized criticality (Bak, 1996). This was in stark contrast to computers programmed with positive reinforcement feedback loops, which over time did not self-organize. This position is of course arguable. We continue to make our case by returning to Piaget's work in cognition.

COGNITIVE EVOLUTION

Cognitive Equilibration

Although Piaget's early work was in the field of biology, most of his life was devoted to studying the genesis of cognitive structures. He wrote, "The subject exists because, to put it very briefly, the being of structures consists in their coming to be, that is, their being 'under construction.' . . . There is no structure apart from construction" (Piaget, 1970, p. 140). In essence, he believed that the human was a developing organism, not only in a physical, biological sense, but also in a cognitive sense. Because he viewed the organism as a whole system, a structure (such that emotional, cognitive, and physical development were indissociable), he proposed and demonstrated through much research that the mechanism promoting change in cognition was the same as that in evolution—namely, equilibration. In fact, he proposed that it was the mechanism at play in any transformational growth process. Equilibration was described by Piaget as a dynamic process of self-regulated behavior balancing two intrinsic polar behaviors, assimilation and accommodation. Assimilation (to make similar) is activity, the organization of experience; it is the individual's self-assertive tendency, a tendency to view, understand, and act on the "surround" with one's own activity or ideas in order to preserve one's autonomy as a part within a whole system. Piaget explains how, at times, this process results in a "reach beyond the grasp" as one evolves, searches for new knowledge, and encounters "new territory." In these new situations the organism's activity attempts to reconstitute previous behaviors to conserve its functioning, but every behavior results in an accommodation that is a result of the effects or pressures of the environment. These progressive experiences sometimes foster contradictions to our present understandings, making them insufficient, thus perturbing and disequilibrating the structure and causing accommodations to reconstitute efficient functioning. Accommodation is comprised of reflective, integrative behavior (reflective abstraction) which serves to change one's own self and explicate the object, in order to function with cognitive equilibrium in relation to it. In *The Development of Thought: Equilibration of Cognitive Structures* (1977), Piaget explained that his "earlier model had proved insufficient and that his central new idea is that knowledge proceeds neither solely from the experience of objects nor from an innate programming performed in the subject but from successive constructions" (preface, p. v). He proposed three models of equilibration. The first is between the assimilation of schemes of action and the accommodation of these to the objects; for example, the infant learning to coordinate gazing, reaching, and sucking in order to grasp a rattle and bring it to the mouth for sucking. The second results from the interactions between two logical ideas that the subject finds contradictory. For example, when faced with the conservation of length task where two roads are depicted using matchsticks (see Figure 2.2), a learner may declare that the bottom row is longer because it goes out farther (a preoperational length idea based on visual clues), and then declare that the top road must be longer because it has more sticks (a number idea based on quantity). The contradiction between these ideas engenders disequilibrium, which is resolved with the construction of the idea of conservation of length (Inhelder, Sinclair, & Bovet, 1974).

The third form describes the differentiation and the integration of the whole knowledge structure, relations uniting two systems of thought to the totality that includes them. Consider, for example, two referential systems

FIGURE 2.2. Conservation of length.

that each describes movement, such as a traveler moving on a train and an observer moving alongside the train. To construct an understanding of the displacement involved, one must coordinate each of the systems into a unified system that includes a differentiation of each of the subsystems. In order to understand the concept of equilibration, one must think of it as a dynamic process in an organism functioning at far from equilibrium states, not as a static equilibrium. Piaget was fascinated by the work of Prigogine on dissipative structures, and the idea of self-organizing as a result of activity and bifurcations was key. Equilibration has often been misinterpreted in the literature. It is not a sequential process of assimilation, then conflict, then accommodation; it is not linear. Nor is assimilation a process of "taking in information" as it has sometimes been described. Equilibration is instead a nonlinear, dynamic "dance' of progressive equilibria, adaptation and organization, growth and change. It results from "coupling" with our surround. As we assert ourselves with our logical constructs and "act on" new experiences and information, we exhibit one pole of behavior—the pole of activity on the surround; our reflective, integrative, accommodative nature is the other pole—the pole of self-organization. These two poles provide a dynamic interplay, which by its own intrinsic, dissipative nature serves to keep the system in an open, flexible, growth-producing state. Piaget writes:

> Cognitive equilibriums are quite different from mechanical equilibriums which conserve themselves without modifications or, in the case of "displacement," give rise merely to moderations of the disturbance and not to whole compensations. They differ even more from thermodynamic equilibrium (except when it is reversible), which is a state of rest after destruction of structures. Cognitive equilibriums are closer to those stationary but dynamic states, mentioned by Prigogine, with exchanges capable of "building and maintaining a functional and structural order in an open system," and they resemble above all . . . the biological . . . dynamic equilibriums. (1977, p. 4)

Contradiction

At successive points in this spiraling equilibration, learners construct contradictions to their actions and ideas. These contradictions may be in the form of actions on objects that are not working—for example, an infant who keeps trying to reach for a rattle, but instead keeps bringing only his fist to his mouth. The action of fist to mouth (a primary-circular reaction) becomes insufficient. On the other hand, the contradictions may be in the form of two theories that both seem plausible, and yet are contradictory, or theories that become insufficient given new evidence. Sequences of such contradictions and the subsequent "reequilibria" can be seen in the history of ideas about aspects of the physical world, such as light. Before Newton's time, the notion that light was in the form of rays made it possible for people to explain shadows and "images" from pinholes, but it did not provide a mechanism to explain refraction as light passes through a transparent medium. This was not a big problem until lenses began to be used in Galileo's day. Within one generation the issue was puzzling enough to cause a search for a notion of the nature of light sufficient to handle this inadequacy. Newton suggested that if we thought of light as actual tiny, material particles, spherical in nature, one could explain refraction in terms of a mechanism. He suggested that if you roll actual particles, such as marbles, across a horizontal surface toward a wide ramp sloping down to another horizontal surface you will find that the marbles will approach the ramp traveling in straight lines. At the ramp they will change direction slightly and then change again at the bottom of the ramp, resulting in a change in direction of travel much the same way as light is observed to change direction at the interface between two transparent media. For a while all was well, and light was conceived of as particles by scientists until we could make light sources bright enough and well collimated enough to see detail in the edges of the shadows of objects. Thomas Young resolved the problem this new phenomenon created by convincingly putting forth a wave model of light, in contrast to a particle model. Much later the attempts to interpret the photoelectric effect with a wave model created new problems until Planck, and later Einstein, proved that light was composed of chunks or packets of energy traveling in a similar fashion to billiard balls. When they hit an object they knocked a particle out of the mass of that object, just as a billiard ball hitting another would send it traveling at the same speed as the original ball. This model explained refraction and the photoelectric effect, whereas the wave interpretation had been insufficient, but now a new paradox remained. How could light be packets of energy and yet be waves at the same time? It is important to note here that the paradoxes in the scientists' interpretations existed between the abstractions—for example, light as waves versus light as particles. The experimental results were contradictory only insofar as they fit or contradicted the given abstraction—the currently deemed viable explanation. The notions of light as rays, or waves, or packets of energy are all constructed abstractions as humans evolve, solve problems, and seek coherency. The data by themselves are not contradictory; they are contradictory only in relation to the meaning that the learner (the scientist, in this case) attributes to them. In each of these cases, it is the contradiction (itself a construction on the part of the learner) that causes the imbalance providing the internal motivation for an accommodation. Piaget proposed that three types of compensations, or accommodations, might occur by learners when dealing with such imbalance: (1) they might ignore the contradictions and perseverate with their initial scheme or idea; (2) they might waver, holding both theories simultaneously, dealing with the contradiction by making each theory hold for separate, specific cases; or (3) they might construct a new, more encompassing notion that explains and resolves the prior contradiction. In either case, what is important to note is that all the compensations are a result of the internal, self-organizing behavior of the learner. And Piaget notes that the contradictions are constructed only secondarily after learners first search for similarities between experiences (called affirmations), and attempt to organize each experience with their present schemes. In a sense, the first two levels are like a "transition zone" (Perry & Kolb, 2003) until the organism reaches the edge of chaos from the diversity of explanations (a bifurcation) and begins to deselect and reorganize, thereby evolving a new structure.

Possibilities, Correspondences, and Transformations

So if contradictions are so difficult to construct, and the tendency of all organisms is to preserve themselves, how and why does equilibration ever occur? In two volumes written just before he died (but appearing in English posthumously), Piaget (1987a, 1987b) attempted to address this question. And it is here that one becomes keenly aware of the connection of his cognitive psychology to work in biology. Just as the genome generates new possibilities when disturbed, cognitive structures generate new possibilities when disturbed—possibilities of new actions, or explanations of surprising results. These possibilities are explored and correspondences and/or patterns are constructed because of the human's self-organizing tendency. Subsequent reflection on these correspondences brings about a structural change—an accommodation that transforms the original cognitive structure and one that explains why the pattern occurs, thus enabling generalization beyond the specific experience. Piaget terms this process "reflective abstraction." Possibilities generated by subjects (4 to 8 years of age) as they sought to understand how to balance a series of blocks on a fulcrum are evidence of this process (Fosnot, Forman, Edwards, & Goldhaber, 1988). At first young children tended to plunk blocks randomly on the fulcrum and to push harder or hold them in place if they didn't balance, almost as if they believed that balancing blocks on a fulcrum had to do with stickiness, or the force of their actions. But soon, as they explored this problem further, they began to investigate moving the blocks back and forth across the fulcrum. These procedures resulted at times in balance (with symmetrical blocks), but did not work for asymmetrical blocks; yet children persisted with these actions for some time, even correcting in the wrong direction, seemingly constructing a theory that involved finding the midpoint of their back-and-forth actions! Eventually they began to explore other actions, sometimes correcting in the right direction to restore balance. This successful action generated contradictory data—a negation to their earlier theories. Eventually this contradiction was resolved with the construction of a new theory: find the midpoint of the block, not the midpoint of the back-and-forth actions! This theory eventually met with contradictory data too, though, as learners went on to explore asymmetrically weighted blocks (blocks with more mass on one side, e.g., a ramp-shaped block with lead in the tip). And at first these were even deemed emphatically by children as "impossible" blocks to balance—given their theories! Throughout the sessions exploring the blocks, learners continued to generate possibilities and develop progressively new models to explain balance. Each new perspective resulted in a temporary structural shift in thinking—an example of spiraling equilibration.

Structures

Structures are human constructions—cognitive mental systems with transformational laws that apply to the system as a whole and not only to its elements. Our number system is a good example. When we add two whole numbers together we stay within the system of whole numbers; and the numbers themselves have no meaning except in relation to each other (e.g., 5 has no meaning except as 1 more than 4 or 1 less than 6, etc.). As we watch children exploring quantity, such as various arrangements of 12 apples, for example (1 and 11, 2 and 10, 3 and 9, etc.), we can observe the construction of ideas that describe the transformations of the parts within the system, such as: (1) compensation, 1 and 11 become 2 and 10 because what you gain with one you lose with the other; (2) commutativity, $2 + 10 = 10 + 2$; and (3) reversibility, if $10 + 2 = 12$, then $12 - 2$ must be equal to 10. Structures are characterized by three properties: wholeness, transformation, and self-regulation. Wholeness refers to the fact that the system is a whole that may in fact be larger than the sum of its parts. The parts, interacting and related, are indissociable from each other and the whole and thus have no meaning by themselves. Their meaning is derived only in terms of the whole, and in relation to each other. Transformation explains the relations between the parts, how one part becomes another. It describes the process involved in the changing nature of the parts. Each structure is also self-regulating, meaning that structures inherently seek self-maintenance, organization, and closure. A structural analysis of thought shows the development of such patterns of organization—that is, ordering, classification, setting up correspondences and relations, coordinating contradictions, and explaining transformations by interactions, reversibility, and compensation, et cetera. In fact, the development of structures, according to Piaget and several contemporary biologists, characterizes the growth process. Because of equilibration, the structure expands to include the "reach beyond the grasp," but also seeks organization and closure, keeping the structure always "under construction." Some scholars have argued that Piaget's notion of structure relates more to mathematics and science thinking than to the development of literacy, the arts, or social science. However, structural shifts have been described in reading strategies (Chall, 1983; Ferreiro, 1984), in invented spelling strategies (Henderson, 1985), in writing development (Fosnot, 1989), in the arts (Goodnow, 1977; see also Gardner, 1985), and in the social sciences (Damon, 1977; Furth, 1980; Selman, 1980; see also Edwards, 1986). Although the main body of Piaget's work is centered on illuminating the progressive cognitive structuring of individuals, the effect of social interaction on learning was not overlooked by him. He wrote, "There is no longer any need to choose between the primacy of the social or that of the intellect; the collective intellect is the social equilibrium resulting from the interplay of the operations that enter into all cooperation" (1970, p. 114).

Mind, Consciousness, and Language

It was this dialectic between the individual and society, and thus the effect of social interaction, language, and culture on learning that became the main focus of Vygotsky's work. Like Piaget, he too believed learning to be developmental and constructive, but he differentiated between what he called "spontaneous" and "scientific" concepts. He defined spontaneous concepts as pseudoconcepts, those "emerging from the child's own reflections on everyday experience" (Kozulin, 1986). Vygotsky proposed that scientific concepts, on the other hand, originate in the structured activity of classroom instruction and impose on the child more formal abstractions and more logically defined concepts than those constructed spontaneously. He perceived them as culturally agreed upon, more formalized concepts. Having made this distinction between pseudoconcepts and scientific concepts, one of Vygotsky's main questions became, "What facilitates the learning that moves the child from spontaneous concepts to scientific concepts?" Rephrased from a biological perspective, the question becomes: If learning is a specific case of evolution, how is it that in the short time of a young learner's life, he or she comes to construct ideas that took humans centuries to develop?

Zone of Proximal Development

Vygotsky (1962/1986) argued that scientific concepts do not come to the learner in a ready-made form. They cannot be transmitted simply with language. They undergo substantial development depending on the existing level of the child's ability to comprehend the adult's model. Vygotsky believed that, whereas scientific concepts work their way "down," imposing their logic on the child, spontaneous concepts work their way "up," meeting the scientific concept and allowing the learner to accept its logic. In Vygotsky's words,

> Though scientific and spontaneous concepts develop in reverse directions, the two processes are closely connected. The development of a spontaneous concept must have reached a certain level for the child to be able to absorb a related scientific concept. For example, historical concepts can begin to develop only when the child's everyday concept of the past is sufficiently differentiated— when his own life and the life of those around him can be fitted into the elementary generalization "in the past and now"; his geographic and sociological concepts must grow out of the simple schema "here and elsewhere." In working its slow way upward, an everyday concept clears a path for the scientific concept and its downward development. It creates a series of structures necessary for the evolution of a concept's more primitive, elementary aspects, which give it body and vitality. Scientific concepts, in turn, supply structures for the upward consciousness and deliberate use. Scientific concepts grow downward through spontaneous concepts; spontaneous concepts grow upward through scientific concepts. (1962/1986, p. 194)

Vygotsky used the term "zo-ped," zone of proximal development, to describe the place where a child's spontaneous concepts meet the "systematicity and logic of adult reasoning" (Kozulin, 1986, p. xxxv). This zone varies from child to child and reflects the ability of the learner to understand the logic of the scientific concept. For this reason, Vygotsky viewed tests or school tasks that only looked at the child's individual problem solving as inadequate, and argued instead that the progress in concept formation achieved by the child in cooperation with an adult was a much more viable way to look at the capabilities of learners.

Inner Speech

Early in his career, Piaget had studied the language of preschoolers and concluded that much of their language was egocentric in nature—that they spoke aloud, but to themselves rather than for any social communicative purpose. Vygotsky repeated many of Piaget's early experiments on language and concluded instead that speech was social right from the start. He proposed that "egocentric speech" was actually the beginning of the formation of the inner speech that would be used later as a tool in thinking. For Vygotsky, this was a case of how the outward interpsychological relations become the inner intrapsychological mental functions . . . how culturally prescribed forms of language and reasoning find their individualized realization . . . how culturally sanctioned symbolic systems are remodeled into individual verbal thought (Kozulin, 1986). Inner speech, to Vygotsky, also played a role in the formation of spontaneous concepts. He proposed that spontaneous concepts have two components, a concept-in-itself and the concept-for-others, the former designating the part of the concept dependent on an organization of actions, the latter describing the concept put to speech in order to communicate it to others. These two components provide a dialectical tension right from the start as the child struggles to represent concepts in action with culturally appropriate symbols in order to communicate them to others. This process prepares the way for the zone of proximal development. In Vygotsky's words,

> The double nature of the pseudoconcept predetermines its specific genetic role. The pseudoconcept serves as a connecting link between thinking in complexes and thinking in concepts. It is dual in nature: a complex already carrying the germinating seed of a concept. Verbal communication with adults thus becomes a powerful factor in the development of the child's concepts. The transition from thinking in complexes to thinking in concepts passes unnoticed by the child because his pseudoconcepts already coincide in content with adult concepts. Thus the child begins to operate with concepts, to practice conceptual thinking, before he is clearly aware of the nature of these operations. (1986, p. 124)

Whereas Piaget sought to study and illuminate the role of contradiction and equilibration in learning, Vygotsky sought to study dialogue. He was not only interested in the role of inner speech on the learning of concepts, but on the role of the adult and the learners' peers as they conversed, questioned, explained, and negotiated meaning. He argued that "the most effective learning occurs when the adult draws the child out to the jointly constructed 'potential' level of performance" (Bickmore-Brand & Gawned, 1993, p. 49). Other psychologists (Bruner & Ratner, 1978; Ninio & Bruner, 1978) extended this work on dialogics and proposed the notion of "scaffolding." Studying mother-infant dyads during face-to-face interactions, these researchers focused on and described the communication ritual that occurred in the turn-taking dialogue with the mother at times imitating the baby, but then varying the response slightly to stretch and challenge the child's response. In spite of the difference in language abilities, the two were seen as jointly constructing meaning. Wells (1981) has noted that this scaffolding process continues throughout early language development and the child appears to internalize the adult role and eventually directs herself using the same cues.

Some Considerations

Vygotsky's notion of scientific concepts working downward, while spontaneous concepts work upward—the zone of proximal development—is controversial for some constructivists, as Cobb will further elaborate in Chapter 3. Is the "scientific" concept being viewed as "truth" in the objective sense, and the teacher's role being perceived of as one that facilitates learner's adoption of it? Is an assumption being made that a learner can "absorb" the adult's conceptual understanding if the developmental match is right—that meaning resides in the symbolic representation of the teacher and that it can be "transmitted" to a learner? These assumptions are not based on the new paradigm, but instead are a residue of the old. They are still grounded in an empiricist theory of learning and are based on a belief that we hold identical objective meanings about a world we are discovering, rather than constructing. The same point can be made about the notion of scaffolding in an educational setting. Is there a "truth" that the scaffolding process leads to? Whose truth is it? Some educators have called for a scaffolding process that is grounded in modeling theory and direct instruction, albeit at developmentally appropriate times (Bruner & Ratner, 1978; Cazden, 1983); while others place more emphasis on the child's cognizing and see the scaffolding only as giving the child new possibilities to consider (Graves, 1983). Bruner (1986), for example, arguing for the former approach, suggests that scaffolding should provide "the child with hints and props that allow him to begin a new climb, guiding the child in next steps before the child is capable of appreciating their significance on his own." According to Bruner, "It is the loan of the [adult's] consciousness that gets the child through the zone of proximal development" (p. 132). Cambourne (1988), on the other hand, places less emphasis on modeling and more on the constructive nature of learning. He describes scaffolding as "raising the ante" and he fleshes out what he sees as the most common attributes in a conversation helpful to learning: (1) focusing on a learner's conception; (2) extending or challenging the conception; (3) refocusing by encouraging clarification; and (4) redirecting by offering new possibilities for consideration. For readers interested in the debate on scaffolding, Bickmore-Brand and Gawned (1993) offer a nice overview.

Representation as a Constructive, Evolutionary Act

Although Vygotsky's notions of internalization and appropriation are somewhat problematic to constructivists, his focus on the dialectical interplay between symbol and thought in concept development provided a fertile ground for research. What is the interplay between language and thought?

Is language just a symbolic representation of previously constructed ideas, or does language actually affect thought? Answers to these questions have been controversial, and often even contradictory; thus, many questions still remain. For example, Vygotsky and Luria studied illiterate peasants in rural Soviet Central Asia and found that their speech and reasoning echoed patterns of practical, situational activity, while for people with some formal education the relation was reversed: abstract categories and word meanings dominated situational experience and restructured it (Luria, 1976). This work suggested that symbolic representation actually affected thought. Work by Lave (1988) in mathematics produced opposite results, however— schooling in abstract mathematics showed little connection to approaches used to solve mathematical problems in context. Educated and uneducated alike solved grocery problems in similar ways and these solutions showed no connection to abstractions learned in school. Similarly, Sinclair (1973) found that conservers used comparative language (i.e., taller than, shorter than) to describe the tall-thin and short-fat beakers used in the conservation of liquid task, whereas nonconservers did not; therefore, she taught nonconservers to use the terms to see if the comparative concept embedded in the words would have an effect on the development of conservation. No significant effect was found. Although the effects of language and abstract formalisms do not seem to be direct, there does seem to be an interaction between symbol and thought when one compares representation across media, such as language, dance, music, or drawing. For example, different features of a cup are depicted depending on whether one is representing symbolically in clay, with pencil and paper, or with language. In clay, the most important feature to symbolize appears to be the contour and the volume of the container; with pencil and paper, the handle and side are depicted; with language, subjects described the function of a cup (Olson, 1970). The very act of representing objects, interactions, or meaning embedded in experience, within a medium such as language, paint and canvas, or mathematical model appears to create a dialectical tension beneficial to thought. Each medium has its own attributes and limits and thus produces new constructions, new variations on the contextually embedded meaning (Eisner, 1993; McLuhan, 1964; Olson, 1970). For example, Sherman (1978) demonstrated how the choice of art medium (Styrofoam vs. clay) affects what children represent; with Styrofoam, buildings are more likely to be represented; with clay, people and animals. Golomb's (1974) work shows how the art medium (clay vs. paper and pencil) affects the details that get represented; when using clay to make people, different body parts are included than when paper and pencil are used. And Ives (1980) has argued convincingly that the use of photographs versus language produces different perspective-taking ability. In fact, it was this very point—the beneficial effect of the act of representing on thought—that led the sculptor Henry Moore to write, "I always draw something to learn more about it," and the writer Donald Murray to comment, "I write to surprise myself." Nelson Goodman (1978, 1984) pushes this issue even further, arguing that there is no unique "real world" that preexists independently of human mental activity. Instead, what we call the world is a product of minds whose symbolic procedures construct the world by interpreting, organizing, and transforming prior worldviews, thereby constructing new symbols. For Goodman, the difference between the arts and sciences, for example, is not subjectivity versus objectivity, but the difference in constructional activities and the symbolic systems that result. Howard Gardner (working with Nelson Goodman at Harvard Project Zero) researched the development of early symbolization to characterize the different modes of operation by which intelligence expresses itself. In *Frames of Mind* (1985) he presents evidence for multiple, different "intelligences" that are the result of "minds which become specialized to deal in verbal or mathematical or spatial forms of world making, supported by symbolic means provided by cultures which themselves specialize in their preference for different kinds of worlds" (Bruner, 1986, p. 103). Thus the world a musician builds using a symbolic system that employs rhythm, cadence, and tone is indeed a different world than the one constructed by a visual artist employing space, line, repleteness, and color. Language, too, becomes its own context, for it involves the uses of signs to organize and plan sign-using activity itself. And this building process is developmental because constructions within a medium serve as building blocks to new constructions. Domains of discourse that we generate become part of our existence and constitute the environment with which we couple. Just as single-cell organisms couple with their "surround" symbiotically via activity and self-organization (Kauffman, 1993), humans do so in communities of discourse for identity and adaptation—a natural process of evolution. Maturana and Varela describe it well:

> We humans, as humans, exist in the network of structural couplings that we continually weave through the permanent linguistic trophallaxis of our behavior. Language was never invented by anyone only to take in an outside world. Rather it is by languaging that the act of knowing, in the behavioral coordination which is language, brings forth a world. (Maturana & Varela, 1998, p. 234)

A Synthesis: Knowledge as Construction

The biological landscape characterized by autopoetic systems and dissipative structures, and the cognitive theories of Piaget, Vygotsky, and others provide a basis for a psychological theory of learning called constructivism. Implied is the position that we as human beings have no access to an objective reality since we are constructing our version of it, while at the same time transforming it and ourselves. Widespread interest in constructivism over the last decade led to a debate between those that place more emphasis on the individual cognitive structuring process and those that emphasize the social and cultural effects on learning (Fosnot, 1993; O'Loughlin, 1992; Steffe & Gale, 1995).

Terms like "cognitive constructivism" and "social constructivism" have become common in the literature, and even within these perspectives there is a plethora of definitions, depending on, as Simon (1993) points out, "whether the social or the cognitive is viewed as figure or ground" (p. 4). The important question to be asked is not whether the cognizing individual or the culture should be given priority in an analysis of learning, but instead, What is the interplay between them? When physicists (i.e., Heisenberg, Bohr) studied the particulate nature of the atom, they concluded that sub-atomic particles have no meaning as isolated entities. To the extent that a particle can be studied in terms of its placement in the atom, the momentum becomes ambiguous, and vice versa. Particles are now understood as waves dancing between states of mass and energy. In the words of Neil Bohr, "Isolated material particles are abstractions, their properties being definable and observable only through their interaction with other systems" (cited in Capra, 1982, p. 124). Contemporary biologists once again agree. We quote from a chapter entitled "New Biology versus Old Ideology." The biological and the social are not separable, antithetical, or alternatives, but rather are complementary. All causes of the behavior of organisms, in the temporal sense to which we should restrict the term *cause*, are simultaneously both social and biological, as they are all amenable to analysis at many levels. All human phenomena are not "causes" of those phenomena but merely "descriptions" of them at particular levels, in particular scientific languages (Lewontin, Rose, & Kamin, 1984, p. 282).

So, too, with cognition. We cannot understand an individual's cognitive structure without observing it interacting in a context, within a culture. But neither can we understand culture as an isolated entity affecting the structure, since all knowledge within the culture is only, to use Cobb's terminology, "taken-as-shared" (Cobb, Yackel, & Wood, 1992). Since the process of construction is adaptive in nature and requires self-reorganization, cultural knowledge that is assumed to be held by members of the culture is in reality only a dynamically evolving, negotiated interaction of individual interpretations, transformations, and constructions. At most, cultural knowledge can only be assumed, or "taken-as-shared," by its members. Yet cultural knowledge is a whole larger than the sum of the individual cognitions. It has a structure of its own which interacts with the individuals who are also constructing it. Current biological models help us understand that both the structure of the mind and the knowledge we construct of the world are a part of an open system—in fact, knowledge and mind cannot be separated because one affects the other. Both are being developed as the natural outcomes of the evolution of autopoetic systems characterized by dissipative structures (this includes the social world). Thus, in contrast to the maturationists who believed that development determines what one can "know" and how one "knows" it, to constructivists learning *is* development. Oatley explains this interaction:

> What kind of adaptation to the world is the human one? It is an adaptation that succeeds in transforming the environment. It involves social cultures which shape social selves by their rules; cultures which are themselves shaped by changes in the rules that people create . . . Our constructions of the physical and social world are not static. They continue to change. Part of our mental ontogeny might even be affected by the study we make of it. As an analogy one might imagine a computer program whose function is to rewrite itself in the light of its discovery of how it is working. This recursiveness is, I will argue also, an important aspect of conscious mind. In order to do justice to the brain and its mechanisms we need to have an account of such schemata, which can turn round upon themselves—which consider their own constitution and transform themselves. (1985, pp. 32–33)

We do not act alone; humans are social beings. Throughout our evolution, from the hunter-gatherer days to the technological present, we have sought to establish communities, societies, forms of communication, and thus cultures as an adaptive mechanism. We attempt to survive collectively, rather than individually; we procreate, communicate, and teach our young. Indeed, Harlow's (1950) classical study of chimpanzees demonstrated that attachment was an innate survival need. The infant chimpanzees in his now-famous study preferred the cloth-covered surrogate mothers over the wire mother, regardless of which one supplied food, and to these cloth-covered surrogates they clung and vocalized, especially when frightened. Without the surrogates, some died; others were frightened, irritable, and reluctant to eat or play; and peer contact among infant monkeys at least partially compensated for the deprivation of the mother (Coster 1972, cited in Craig, 1986). Social deprivation in humans has also been found to produce apathy, withdrawal, and general depressed functioning (Bowlby, 1960). Why is social interaction basic? If learning is a case of self-organization and internal restructuring, then what role do language and the community play in its development? Direct transmission, modeling, reinforcement—all principles of learning implied from the old psychology paradigms that have been proposed at one time or another to explain the role of the social environment—become insufficient to explain cognitive restructuring, given our new view of learning. Some evolutionary biologists and neuropsychologists have argued that the encephalization of the brain (and the resulting ability for mental imagery and highly developed language forms) was an adaptation that was viable in that it enabled *Homo sapiens* to make major social changes (Oatley, 1985). According to Maturana and Varela (1998), "Consciousness and mind belong to the realm of 'social coupling' and the domains of discourse that we generate become part of our domain of existence and constitute part of the environment in which we conserve identity and adaptation" (p. 234). The ability to envision and construct tools for cultivation of food led to civilization—the development of fixed communities. Today, mass communication and transportation systems provide the potential for inhabitants of this planet to see themselves as a diverse unity. Representation, cognition, and social change are thus inherently connected. Again to quote Oatley,

> A major function of the human brain is indeed to sustain complex structures of knowledge of the physical world, and also of plans and purposes in the social world. It is the ability to create these structures which I will call schemata, to make inferences within them, and to reuse them symbolically for new purposes in metaphors, that provides the foundation for our peculiar human adaptation. (1985, p. 32)

Vygotsky's emphasis on the sociohistorical aspect of knowledge—how it is that intuitive notions give way to more culturally accepted notions—makes sense from the perspective of this interplay. The culture and collective individuals within it create a "languaging of lived experience" such that the individual is disequilibrated; but reciprocally the culture is disequilibrated by individuals as they construct their environment. Thus, individual thought progresses toward culturally "accepted" ideas, but always in an open dynamic structure capable of creative innovation.

The Role of Representation

All cultures represent the meaning of experience in some way: through symbol, music, myth, storytelling, art, language, film, explanatory "scientific" models, and/or mathematical forms. Abstracting and generalizing experience by representing them with symbols (itself a constructive process) allows the creation of "semiotic spaces" where we can negotiate meaning (Wertsch, 1991). We may not understand in the same way as other humans who have had different experiences, but by using language, stories, and metaphors and models, we can listen to and probe each other's understanding, thereby negotiating and constructing "taken-as-shared" meanings (Blumer, 1969; Mead, 1934). Constructing symbolic representations empowers us to go beyond the immediacy of the concrete, to cross cultural barriers, to encounter multiple perspectives that generate new possibilities, to become conscious of our actions on the world in order to gain new knowledge with which to act. As we attempt to generalize meaning across experiences, "tugs and pulls" may occur—a pull toward categorization, classification, ordering, connecting—the primacy toward correspondences and affirmations that Piaget describes. On the other hand, the construction of this generalization in a symbolic form within a medium creates a tug on the individual experience highlighting the differences between it and the symbolic generalization. This "tug and pull" is the intrinsic motivating force in reflective abstraction. In other words, reflection on these representations—themselves decentered constructions—may bring about new insights, new constructions, new possibilities, when one subsequently returns to reflecting on the experience. The act of representation is what makes us human. The reptilian brain, for example, is reactive and associative in nature; perceptual stimuli cause reflexive action. In humans, myelination of the visual cortex and the development of the cerebral cortex allow us to have mental images of objects and actions on them (Malerstein, 1986; Oakley, 1985) and this ability to represent allows us to reflect on our actions, consider multiple perspectives simultaneously, and to even think about our thinking. Vocal tract structures and the capacity of the brain for language development also have been acquired over time by biological evolution. How does individual representation interface with one's social setting? As ideas are shared within a community, the "surround" (Kauffman, 1993) may intensify individual cognitive activity. Multiple perspectives may offer a new set of correspondences, and at times even contradictions, to individual constructions. Of course, these perspectives shared by others are not "transmitted"; even the shared perspectives are interpreted and transformed by the cognizing individual. But as we seek to organize experience for generalization and communication, we strive to coordinate perspectives, to "get into the head" of others—to attach, thereby constructing further reflective abstractions and developing "taken-as-shared" meanings. From this perspective, learning is a constructive building process of meaning making which results in reflective abstractions producing symbols within a medium. These symbols then become part of the individual's repertoire of assimilatory schemes, which in turn are used when perceiving and further conceiving. For example, a waterfall sparkling in broad daylight and a waterfall at dusk are seen as "waterfalls" even though the light rays hitting the retina are very different. The linguistic symbol "waterfall" represents a reflective abstraction that is the result of a generalization of lived experiences with past waterfalls, but it is then used in perception, selectively, as we isolate stimuli from the environment, transforming and organizing phenomena for coherence and meaning. The medium that is used in the representation as we attempt to communicate our meaning to the community also has an effect on the symbol. A waterfall represented musically may involve cadences, harmonies, and rhythm; represented in dance, turns, twists, and leaps; in the visual arts, form, line, and texture; in the sciences, forces, interactions, continuities, and discontinuities. Meanings, indeed "worldviews," may be unique to the cognizing, self-regulating individual but that is not to say that they are idiosyncratic, nor disconnected to context or the environmental surround: First, because the symbols themselves used in cognizing are the result of previous "taken-as-shared" meanings by a community—and thus are linked to culture right from the start; and secondly, because when the new constructions are justified and communicated to the community they are done so with accepted forms of proof, argument, and justification determined by communities of practice and discourse. What holds up as a good question, a good justification, and a good explanation, and how data are measured, interpreted, and modeled all evolve from interactions in these communities. As they are further reflected upon and discussed, a process that is likely to generate both further possibilities and contradictions, newly constructed, temporary, "taken-as-shared" meanings are consensually agreed upon as viable. This process has been represented by Fosnot [editor's note: in the first edition of this book, 1996, Chapter 2] as a dialectical tripartite model, depicted in Figure 2.3.

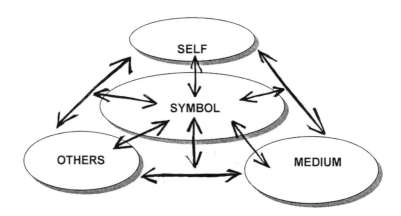

FIGURE 2.3. Constructivist learning model.

The cognizing individual generates possibilities and contradictions when structures are perturbed. In attempting to represent these reflective abstractions in a medium, to make them conscious and to communicate them to others, further tugs occur. But the process is not linear. Indeed, language is almost too linear a medium to use to describe the transactional nature of the interplay. For "others" are other cognizing individuals, therefore a composite of constantly shifting and evolving ideas—not a static entity but a dynamic one. Further, the cognizing individual is operating with cultural symbols that are derived from past negotiated "taken-as-shared" social and cultural meanings. Nor is the medium static: While each medium has limits and features that affect the symbols, as humans create within media they push against these limits and formulate new features. Just as in the vases and the faces in the trick figure–ground pictures, the components are complementary. In fact, they are only perceivable when we organize the picture in one fashion or another. Or as Heisenberg pointed out in relation to particles and their momentum many years ago, the question determines the answer. If we ask a question about the affect of culture on cognition, we get a cultural answer; if we ask about the individual's cognizing we get an answer that reflects that component. In reality, even the components are constructs of human-made worlds. Perhaps the most that can be said is that the striving for symbolic representation and coherent meaning-making with other humans is a spiraling dynamic "dance" of interaction and evolution, a search for equilibrium—a self-organizing criticality (Bak, 1996). From this perspective, living itself is defined as knowing (Deutsch, 1997; Perry & Kolb, 2003). The new paradigm demands, in the words of Bruner (1986, p. 105), that we "abandon the idea that 'the world' is there, once, for all, and immutably, [and that we] substitute for it the idea that what we take as the world is itself no more nor less than a stipulation couched in a symbol system."

APPLICATION OF CONSTRUCTIVISM TO EDUCATION

Constructivism is a theory about learning, not a description of teaching. No "cookbook teaching style" or pat set of instructional techniques can be abstracted from the theory and proposed as a constructivist approach to teaching. Some general principles of learning derived from constructivism may be helpful to keep in mind, however, as we rethink and reform our educational practices.

- Learning is not the result of development; learning *is* development. It requires invention and self-organization on the part of the learner. Thus, teachers need to allow learners to raise their own questions, generate their own hypotheses and models as possibilities, test them out for viability, and defend and discuss them in communities of discourse and practice.

- Disequilibrium facilitates learning. "Errors" need to be perceived as a result of learners' conceptions, and therefore not minimized or avoided. Challenging, open-ended investigations in realistic, meaningful contexts need to be offered which allow learners to explore and generate many possibilities, both affirming and contradictory. Contradictions, in particular, need to be illuminated, explored, and discussed.

- Reflective abstraction is the driving force of learning. As meaning makers, humans seek to organize and generalize across experiences in a representational form. Allowing reflection time through journal writing, representation in multisymbolic form, and/or discussing connections across experiences or strategies may facilitate reflective abstraction.

- Dialogue within a community engenders further thinking. The classroom needs to be seen as a "community of discourse engaged in activity, reflection, and conversation" (Fosnot, 1989). The learners (rather than the teacher) are responsible for defending, proving, justifying, and communicating their ideas to the classroom community. Ideas are accepted as truth only insofar as they make sense to the community and thus they rise to the level of "taken-as-shared."

Learning is the result of activity and self-organization and proceeds toward the development of structures. As learners struggle to make meaning, progressive structural shifts in perspective are constructed—in a sense, "big ideas" (Schifter & Fosnot, 1993). These "big ideas" are learner-constructed, central organizing principles that can be generalized across experiences, and which often require the undoing or reorganizing of earlier conceptions. This process continues throughout development.

CONCLUSION

Constructivism is a poststructuralist psychological theory (Doll, 1993), one that construes learning as an interpretive, recursive, nonlinear building process by active learners interacting with their surround—the physical and social world. It is a psychological theory of learning that describes how structures, language, activity, and meaning-making come about, rather than one that simply characterizes the structures and stages of thought, or one that isolates behaviors learned through reinforcement. It is a theory based on complexity models of evolution and development. The challenge for educators is to determine what this new paradigm brings to the practice of teaching.

REFERENCES

Bak, P. (1996). *How nature works: The science of self-organized criticality*. New York: Springer-Verlag.

Bickmore-Brand, J., & Gawned, S. (1993). Scaffolding for improved understanding. In J. Bickmore-Brand (Ed.), *Language in mathematics* (pp. 43–58). Portsmouth, NH: Heinemann.

Bloom, B. S. (Ed.). (1956). *Taxonomy of educational objectives, Handbook 1: The cognitive domain*. New York: McKay.

Bloom, B. (1976). *Human characteristics and school learning*. New York: McGraw-Hill.

Blumer, H. (1969). *Symbolic interactionism*. Englewood Cliffs, NJ: Prentice-Hall.

Bowlby, J. (1960). Separation anxiety. *International Journal of Psychoanalysis, 41,* 89–113.

Bruner, J. (1986). *Actual minds, possible worlds*. Cambridge, MA: Harvard University Press.

Bruner, J., & Ratner, N. (1978). Games, social exchange and the acquisition of language. *Journal of Child Language, 5*(1), 391–401.

Cambourne, B. (1988). *The whole story: Natural learning and the acquisition of literacy in the classroom*. Gosford, New Zealand: Ashton Scholastic.

Capra, F. (1982). *The turning point*. New York: Simon & Schuster.

Capra, F. (2002). *The hidden connections*. New York: Doubleday.

Cazden, C. (1983). Adult assistance to language development: Scaffolds, models, and direct instruction. In R. Parker & F. A. Davis (Eds.), *Developing literacy: Young children's use of language* (pp. 3–18). Newark, DE: International Reading Association.

Chall, J. (1983). *Stages of reading development*. Boston: Houghton Mifflin.

Cobb, P., Yackel, E., & Wood, T. (1992). Interaction and learning in mathematics classroom situations. *Educational Studies in Mathematics, 23,* 99–122.

Craig, G. (1986). *Human development*. Englewood Cliffs, NJ: Prentice-Hall.

Damon, W. (1977). *The social world of the child*. San Francisco: Jossey-Bass.

Darwin, C. (1859). *On the origin of species by means of natural selection*. Cambridge, MA: Harvard University Press.

Dennett, D. (1995). *Darwin's dangerous idea: Evolution and the meanings of life*. New York: Touchstone.

Deutsch, C. (1997). *The fabric of reality*. New York: Penguin Books.

Doll, W. (1993). *A post-modern perspective on curriculum*. New York: Teachers College Press.

Edwards, C. P. (1986). *Social and moral development in young children*. New York: Teachers College Press.

Eisner, E. (1993). Forms of understanding and the future of educational research. *Educational Researcher, 22*(7), 5–11.

Eldredge, N., & S. J. Gould (1972). Punctuated equilibria: An alternative to phyletic-gradualism. In T.J.M. Schopf (Ed.), *Models of paleobiology* (pp. 82–115). San Francisco: Freeman, Cooper, & Company.

Erikson, E. (1950). *Childhood and society.* New York: Norton.

Ferreiro, E. (1984). The underlying logic of literacy development. In H. Goelman, A. Oberg, & F. Smith (Eds.), *Awakening to literacy* (pp. 154–173). Portsmouth, NH: Heinemann.

Fosnot, C. T. (1989). *Enquiring teachers, enquiring learners.* New York: Teachers College Press.

Fosnot, C. T. (1993). Science education revisited: A defense of Piagetian constructivism. *Journal for Research in Science Education, 39*(9), 1189–1201.

Fosnot, C. T., Forman, G. E., Edwards, C. P., & Goldhaber, J. (1988). The development of an understanding of balance and the effect of training via stop-action video. *Journal of Applied Developmental Psychology, 9,* 1–33.

Furth, H. (1980). *The world of grown-ups.* New York: Elsevier.

Gagne, R. M. (1965). *The conditions of learning.* New York: Holt, Rinehart & Winston.

Gallagher, J., & Reid, D. K. (1982). *The learning theory of Piaget and Inhelder.* Monterey, CA: Books/Cole.

Gardner, H. (1985). *Frames of Mind: The theory of multiple intelligences.* New York: Basic Books.

Gell-Mann, M. (1994). The quark and jaguar—adventures in the simple and complex. New York: W. H. Freeman & Company.

Gesell, A. (1940). *The first five years of life: The preschool years.* New York: Harper & Brothers.

Gesell, A., & Ilg, F. L. (1946). *The child from five to ten.* New York: Harper & Brothers.

Gesell, A., Ilg, F. L., & Ames, L. B. (1956). *Youth: The years from ten to sixteen.* New York: Harper & Row.

Golomb, C. (1974). *Young children's sculpture and drawing.* Cambridge, MA: Harvard University Press.

Goodman, N. (1978). *Ways of worldmaking.* Indianapolis: Hackett.

Goodman, N. (1984). *Of mind and other matters.* Cambridge, MA: Harvard University Press.

Goodnow, J. (1977). *Children drawing.* Cambridge, MA: Harvard University Press.

Graves, D. (1983). *Writing: Teachers and children at work.* Portsmouth, NH: Heinemann.

Harlow, H. (1950, June). Love in infant monkeys. *Scientific American,* 68–74.

Henderson, E. (1985). *Teaching spelling.* Boston: Houghton Mifflin.

Inhelder, B., Sinclair, H., & Bovet, M. (1974). *Learning and the development of cognition.* Cambridge, MA: MIT Press.

Ives, S. W. (1980). Children's ability to coordinate spatial perspectives through language and picture. *Child Development, 51,* 1303–1306.

Kauffman, S. (1993). *The origins of order, self-organization and selection in evolution.* Oxford, United Kingdom: Oxford University Press.

Kozulin, A. (1986). Vygotsky in context. In Vygotsky, L., *Language and thought* (Preface). Cambridge, MA: MIT Press.

Krumbein, W. E., & Dyer, B. D. (1985). Weathering and biology, a multi-faceted problem. In J. I. Drever (Ed.), *The planet is alive* (pp. 143–160). Dordrecht: Reidel Publishing.

Lamarck, J. B. (1809). (R. W. Burkhardt Jr., Trans.). *The spirit of the system: Lamarck and evolutionary biology* Cambridge, MA: Harvard University Press.

Lave, J. (1988). *Cognition in practice.* New York: Cambridge University Press.

Lewontin, R. C., Rose, S., & Kamin, L. (1984). *Not in our genes.* New York: Pantheon.

Luria, A. R. (1976). *Cognitive development: Its cultural and social foundations.* Cambridge, MA: Harvard University Press.

Malerstein, A. J. (1986). *The conscious mind.* New York: Human Sciences Press.

Margulis, L. (1982). *Early life.* Boston: Science Books International.

Maturana, H., & Varela, F. (1998). *The tree of knowledge: The biological roots of human understanding.* Boston: Shambala.

McLuhan, M. (1964). *Understanding media.* New York: McGraw-Hill.

Mead, G. H. (1934). *Mind, self and society* (C. W. Morris, Ed.). Chicago: University of Chicago Press.

National Association for the Education of Young Children (NAEYC) (1988, January). NAEYC position statement on developmentally appropriate practice in the primary grades, serving 5 through 8-year olds. *Young Children,* 64–84.

Ninio, A., & Bruner, J. (1978). The achievement and antecedents of labeling. *Journal of Child Language, 5*(1), 1–15.

Oakley, D. A. (1985). Animal awareness, consciousness, and self-image. In D. A. Oakley (Ed.), *Brain and mind* (pp. 132–151), London: Methuen.

Oatley, K. (1985). Representations of the physical and social world. In D. A. Oakley, (Ed.), *Brain and mind* (pp. 132–151), London: Methuen.

O'Loughlin, M. (1992). Rethinking science education: Beyond Piagetian constructivism toward a sociocultural model of teaching and learning. *Journal of Research in Science Teaching, 29*(8), 791–820.

Olson, D. R. (1970). *Cognitive development: The child's acquisition of diagonality.* New York: Academic Press.

Perry, R. S., & Kolb, V. M. (2003). Darwin to Mars. *Geophysical Research Abstracts, 5,* 07353.

Perry, R. S., & Kolb, V. M. (2004). On the applicability of Darwinian principles to chemical evolution that led to life. *International Journal of Astrobiology, 3*(1), 1–9.

Piaget, J. (1970). *Structuralism.* New York: Basic Books.

Piaget, J. (1977). *The development of thought: Equilibration of cognitive structures.* New York: Viking.

Piaget, J. (1987a). *Possibility and necessity* (Vol. 1). Minneapolis: University of Minnesota Press.

Piaget, J. (1987b). *Possibility and necessity* (Vol. 2). Minneapolis: University of Minnesota Press.

Prigogine, I. (1997). *The end of certainty: Time, chaos, and the new laws of nature.* New York: The Free Press.

Schifter, D., & Fosnot, C. T. (1993). *Reconstructing mathematics education: Stories of teachers meeting the challenge of reform.* New York: Teachers College Press.

Selman, R. (1980). *The growth of interpersonal understanding*. New York: Academic Press.

Sherman, L. (1978). Three dimensional art media and the preschool child. *Presentations in Art Education Research, 1,* 97–107.

Simon, M. (1993, April). *Reconstructing mathematics pedagogy from a constructivist perspective*. Paper presented at the annual meeting of the American Educational Research Association, Atlanta, Georgia.

Sinclair, H. (1973). Language acquisition and cognitive development. In T. E. Moore (Ed.), *Cognitive development and the acquisition of language*. New York: Academic Press.

Skinner, B. F. (1953). *Science and human behavior*. New York: Free Press.

Steffe, L., & Gale, J. (Eds.). (1995). *Constructivism in education*. Hillsdale, NJ: Erlbaum.

Vygotsky, L. (1986). *Language and thought*. Cambridge, MA: MIT Press. (Original work published 1962)

Waddington, C. H. (1957). *The strategy of the genes: A discussion of some aspects of theoretical biology*. New York: Macmillan.

Wells, G. (Ed.). (1981). *Learning through interaction: The study of language development*. New York: Cambridge University Press.

Wertsch, J. V. (1991). *Voices of the mind: A sociocultural approach to mediated action*. Cambridge, MA: Harvard University Press.

CHAPTER 3

Where Is the Mind?
A Coordination of Sociocultural
and Cognitive Constructivist Perspectives

Paul Cobb

Two major trends can be identified in constructivist-based education research during the past decade. The first is the generally accepted cognitive view that students actively construct their ways of knowing as they strive to be effective by restoring coherence to the worlds of their personal experience. The theoretical arguments that underpin this position are primarily epistemological and have been advanced by von Glasersfeld (1984, 1987, 1989a). Empirical support is provided by numerous studies which document that there are significant qualitative differences in the understandings that students develop in instructional situations, and that these understandings are frequently very different from those that the teacher intends (Confrey, 1990; Hiebert & Carpenter, 1992). The acceptance of this brand of constructivism can be contrasted with a second trend that emphasizes the socially and culturally situated nature of activity. At least in the United States, this attempt to go beyond purely cognitive analyses reflects a growing disillusionment with the individualistic focus of mainstream psychology (Brown, Collins, & Duguid, 1989; Greeno, 1991; Schoenfeld, 1987). The theoretical basis for this position is inspired in large measure by the work of Vygotsky and that of activity theorists such as Davydov, Leont'ev, and Galperin (Nunes, 1992). Empirical support comes from paradigmatic studies such as those of Carraher, Carraher, and Schliemann (1985), Lave (1988), Saxe (1991), and Scribner (1984), which demonstrate that an individual's arithmetical activity, for example, is profoundly influenced by his or her participation in encompassing cultural practices such as completing worksheets in school, shopping in a supermarket, selling candy on the street, and packing crates in a dairy.

These cognitive and sociocultural perspectives at times appear to be in direct conflict, with adherents to each claiming hegemony for their view of what it means to know and learn (Steffe, 1995; Voigt, 1992). Thus there is currently a dispute over both whether the mind is located in the head[1] or in the individual-in-social-action, and whether learning is primarily a process of active cognitive reorganization or a process of enculturation into a community of practice (Minick, 1989). Similarly, the issue of whether social and cultural processes have primacy over individual processes, or vice versa, is the subject of intense debate (Fosnot, 1993; O'Loughlin, 1992; van Oers, 1990). Further, adherents to the two positions differ on the role that signs and symbols play in psychological development. Cognitive theorists tend to characterize them as a means by which students express and communicate their thinking, whereas sociocultural theorists typically treat them as carriers of either established meanings or of a practice's intellectual heritage. In general, the attempts of the two groups of theorists to understand the other's position are confounded by their differing usage of a variety of terms including *activity, setting, context, task, problem, goal, negotiation,* and *meaning.*

The central focus of this chapter is on the assumptions that give rise to an apparent forced choice between the two perspectives. In particular the focus will be on mathematical learning and the argument will be that it should be viewed as both a process of active individual construction and a process of enculturation into the mathematical practices of the wider society. The central issue, then, is not to adjudicate a dispute between opposing perspectives. Instead, it is to explore ways of coordinating cognitive constructivist and sociocultural perspectives in mathematics education. The particular perspective that comes to the fore at any point in an empirical analysis can then be seen to be relative to the problems and issues at hand.

It should be noted that the apparent conflict between cognitive and sociocultural perspectives is not merely a matter of theoretical contemplation. Instead, it finds expression in tensions endemic to the act of teaching. For example, Ball (1993) observes that "current proposals for educational improvement are replete with notions of 'understanding' and 'community'—about building bridges between the experiences of the child and the knowledge of the expert" (p. 374). She then inquires:

> How do I create experiences for my students that connect with what they now know and care about but that also transcend the present? How do I value their interests and also connect them to ideas and traditions growing out of centuries of mathematical exploration and invention? (p. 375)

Ball's references to students' experiences and to valuing their interests imply a focus on their qualitatively distinct interpretations and on the personal goals that they pursue in the classroom. This, in my terms, implies a view of mathematical learning as active cognitive construction. In contrast, her reference to students' mathematical heritage suggests a view of mathematical learning as enculturation. Ball goes on to discuss three dilemmas that arise in the course of her practice as a mathematics teacher. She clarifies that these dilemmas of content, discourse, and community "arise reasonably from competing and worthwhile aims and from the uncertainties inherent in striving to attain them" (p. 373). It would therefore seem that the aims of which she speaks, and thus the pedagogical dilemmas, reflect the tension between mathematical learning viewed as enculturation and as individual construction.

COMPARISONS AND CONTRASTS

Sociocultural and cognitive theorists both highlight the crucial role that activity plays in mathematical learning and development. However, sociocultural theorists typically link activity to participation in culturally organized practices, whereas cognitive theorists give priority to individual students' sensory-motor and conceptual activity. Further, sociocultural theorists tend to assume from the outset that cognitive processes are subsumed by social and cultural processes. In doing so, they adhere to Vygotsky's (1979) contention that "the social dimension of consciousness is primary in fact and time. The individual dimension of consciousness is derivative and secondary" (p. 30). From this, it follows that "thought (cognition) must not be reduced to a subjectively psychological process" (Davydov, 1988, p. 16). Instead, thought should be viewed as

> something essentially "on the surface," as something located on the borderline between the organism and the outside world. For thought has a life only in an environment of socially constituted meanings. (Bakhurst, 1988, p. 38)

Consequently, whereas cognitive theorists analyze thought in terms of conceptual processes located in the individual, sociocultural theorists take the individual-in-social-action as their unit of analysis (Minick, 1989). From this latter perspective, the primary issue is that of explaining how participation in social interactions and culturally organized activities influences psychological development.

Sociocultural theorists formulate this issue in a variety of different ways. For example, Vygotsky (1978) emphasized the importance of social interaction with more knowledgeable others in the zone of proximal development and the role of culturally developed sign systems as psychological tools for thinking. In contrast, Leont'ev (1981) argued that thought develops from practical, object-oriented activity or labor. Several American theorists have elaborated constructs developed by Vygotsky and his students, and they speak of cognitive apprenticeship (Brown et al., 1989; Rogoff, 1990), legitimate peripheral participation (Forman, 1992; Lave & Wenger, 1991), or the negotiation of meaning in the construction zone (Newman, Griffin, & Cole, 1989). In contrast to the cognitive theorist's concern with individual students' conceptual reorganizations, each of these contemporary accounts locates learning in co-participation in cultural practices. As a consequence, educational implications usually focus on the kinds of social engagements that increasingly enable students to participate in the activities of the expert rather than on the cognitive processes and conceptual structures involved (Hanks, 1991).

In contrast to sociocultural theorists' frequent references to the works of Vygotsky, Leont'ev, and Luria, cognitive constructivists usually trace their intellectual lineage to Piaget's (1970, 1980) genetic epistemology, to ethnomethodology (Mehan & Wood, 1975), or to symbolic interactionism (Blumer, 1969). As this set of references indicates, it is possible to distinguish between what might be called psychological and interactionist variants of constructivism. Von Glasersfeld's development of the epistemological basis of the psychological variant incorporates both the Piagetian notions of assimilation and accommodation and the cybernetic concept of viability. Thus, he uses the term *knowledge* in "Piaget's adaptational sense to refer to those sensory-motor and conceptual operations that have proved viable in the knower's experience" (von Glasersfeld, 1992, p. 380). Further, traditional correspondence theories of truth are dispensed with in favor of an account that relates truth to the effective or viable organization of activity: "Truths are replaced by viable models—and viability is always relative to a chosen goal" (1992, p. 384). In this model, perturbations that the cognizing subject generates relative to a purpose or goal are posited as the driving force of development. As a consequence, learning is characterized as a process of self-organization in which the subject reorganizes his or her activity in order to eliminate perturbations (von Glasersfeld, 1989b). As von Glasersfeld notes, his instrumentalist approach to knowledge is generally consistent with the views of contemporary neo-pragmatist philosophers such as Bernstein (1983), Putnam (1987), and Rorty (1978).

Although von Glasersfeld defines learning as self-organization, he acknowledges that this constructive activity occurs as the cognizing individual interacts with other members of a community. Thus, he elaborates that "knowledge" refers to "conceptual structures that epistemic agents, given the range of present experience within their tradition of thought and language, consider viable" (1992, p. 381). Further, he contends that "the most frequent source of perturbations for the developing cognitive subject is interaction with others" (1989b, p. 136). Bauersfeld's interactionist version of constructivism complements von Glasersfeld's psychological focus in that both view communication as a process of mutual adaptation wherein individuals negotiate meanings by continually modifying their interpretations (Bauersfeld, 1980; Bauersfeld, Krummheuer, & Voigt, 1988). However, whereas von Glasersfeld tends to focus on individuals' construction of their ways of knowing, Bauersfeld emphasizes that "learning is characterized by the subjective reconstruction of societal means and models through negotiation of meaning in social interaction" (1988, p. 39). In accounting for this process of subjective reconstruction, he focuses on the teacher's and students' interactive constitution of the classroom microculture. Thus, he argues that

> participating in the processes of a mathematics classroom is participating in a culture of mathematizing. The many skills, which an observer can identify and will take as the main performance of the culture, form the procedural surface only. These are the bricks of the building, but the design of the house of mathematizing is processed on another level. As it is with culture, the core of what is learned through participation is when to do what and how to do it. The core part of school mathematics enculturation comes into effect on the meta-level and is "learned" indirectly. (in press)

Bauersfeld's reference to indirect learning clarifies that the occurrence of perturbations is not limited to those occasions when participants in an interaction believe that communication has broken down and explicitly negotiate meanings. Instead, for him, communication is a process of often implicit negotiations in which subtle shifts and slides of meaning occur outside the participants' awareness (cf. Cobb & Yackel, in press). In taking this approach, Bauersfeld uses an interactionist metaphor and characterizes negotiation as a process of mutual adaptation in the course of which the teacher and students establish expectations for others' activity and obligations for their own activity (cf. Cobb & Bauersfeld, in press; Voigt, 1985). By way of contrast, Newman and colleagues (1989), speaking from the sociocultural perspective, define negotiation as a process of mutual appropriation in which the teacher and students continually coopt or use each others' contributions. Here, in line with Leont'ev's (1981) sociohistorical metaphor of appropriation, the teacher's role is characterized as that of mediating between students' personal meanings and culturally established mathematical meanings of the wider society. From this point of view, one of the teacher's primary responsibilities when negotiating mathematical meaning with students is to appropriate their actions into this wider system of mathematical practices. Bauersfeld, however, takes the local classroom microculture rather than the mathematical practices institutionalized by the wider society as his primary point of reference when he speaks of negotiation. This focus reflects his concern with the process by which the teacher and students constitute social norms and mathematical practices in the course of their classroom interactions. Further, whereas sociocultural theorists give priority to social and cultural process, analyses compatible with Bauersfeld's perspective propose that individual students' mathematical activity and the classroom microculture are reflexively related (Cobb, 1989; Voigt, 1992). In this view, individual students are seen as actively contributing to the development of classroom mathematical practices, and these both enable and constrain their individual mathematical activities. Consequently, it is argued that neither an individual student's mathematical activity nor the classroom microculture can be adequately accounted for without considering the other.

It is apparent from this brief summary of the two perspectives that they address different problems and issues. A sociocultural analysis of a classroom episode might both locate it within a broader activity system that takes account of the function of schooling as a social institution and attend to the immediate interactions between the teacher and students (Axel, 1992). This dual focus is explicit in Lave and Wenger's (1991) claim that their "concept of legitimate peripheral participation provides a framework for bringing together theories of situated activity and theories about the production and reproduction of the social order" (p. 47). In general, sociocultural accounts of psychological development use the individual's participation in culturally organized practices and face-to-face interactions as primary explanatory constructs. A basic tenet underpinning this work is that it is inappropriate to single out qualitative differences in individual thinking apart from their sociocultural situation because differences in students' interpretations of school tasks reflect qualitative differences in the communities in which they participate (Bredo & McDermott, 1992).

In contrast, cognitive theorists are typically concerned with the quality of individual interpretive activity, with the development of ways of knowing at more of a microlevel, and with the participants' interactive constitution of classroom social norms and mathematical practices. The burden of explanation in cognitive accounts of development falls on models of individual students' cognitive self-organization and on analyses of the processes by which these actively cognizing individuals constitute the local social situation of their development (Cobb, Wood, & Yackel, 1993). Thus, whereas a sociocultural theorist might view classroom interactions as an instantiation of the culturally organized practices of schooling, a cognitive theorist would see an evolving microculture that does not exist apart from the teacher's and students' attempts to coordinate their individual activities. Further, whereas a sociocultural theorist might see a student appropriating the teacher's contributions, a cognitive theorist would see a student adapting to the actions of others in the course of ongoing negotiations. In making these differing interpretations, sociocultural theorists would tend to invoke sociohistorical metaphors such as appropriation, whereas cognitive theorists would typically employ interactionist metaphors such as accommodation and mutual adaptation. Further, whereas sociocultural theorists typically stress the homogeneity of members of established communities and eschew analyses of qualitative differences in individual thinking, cognitive theorists tend to stress heterogeneity and to eschew analyses that single out pregiven social and cultural practices. From one perspective, the focus is on the social and cultural basis of personal experience. From the other perspective, it is on the constitution of social and cultural processes by actively interpreting individuals.

CONSTRUCTION IN SOCIAL PRACTICE

Against the background of these contrasts between the two perspectives, I now consider possible coordinations between them. In this section, I explore possible complementarities between Rogoff's (1990) analysis of internalization and von Glasersfeld's (1995) discussion of empirical and reflective abstraction. In a subsequent section, I elaborate my argument by focusing on potential relationships between Saxe's (1991) sociocultural analysis and Steffe, Cobb, and von Glasersfeld's (1988) cognitive analysis. My general strategy in both cases is to tease out aspects of one position that are implicit in the other.

One of the central notions in Vygotsky's account of development is that of internalization. For example, in his frequently cited general genetic law of cultural development, Vygotsky argued that

> any higher mental function was external and social before it was internal. It was once a social relationship between two people. We can formulate the general genetic law of cultural development in the following way. Any function appears twice or on two planes. It appears first between people as an intermental category, and then within the child as an intramental category. (1960, pp. 197–198)

From the cognitive constructivist perspective, this account of internalization from the social realm to the internal cognitive realm leads to difficulties because the interpersonal relations that are to be internalized are located outside the child. Researchers can indeed identify patterns of interaction, collective schemes, and so forth when they analyze videorecordings or transcripts. However, a cognitive constructivist might follow Blumer (1969) in arguing that people respond to things in terms of the meaning they have for them rather than to constructs that researchers project into their worlds. From this point of view, the problem of explaining how relations that are real for the detached observer get into the experiential world of the child appears intractable.

Rogoff (1990), who is in many ways a follower of Vygotsky, discusses this difficulty in reference to research on social learning and socialization. She notes that, in this research, children are considered to learn by observing or participating with others. "The underlying assumption is that the external lesson [to be learned] is brought across a barrier into the mind of the child. How this is done is not specified, and remains a deep problem for these approaches" (p. 195). In proposing a solution, Rogoff elaborates Vygotsky's notion of internalization by arguing that children are already engaged in a social activity when they actively observe and participate with others. If children are viewed as being in the social activity in this way

> with the interpersonal aspects of their functioning integral to the individual aspects, then what is practiced in social interaction is never on the outside of a barrier, and there is no need for a separate process of internalization. (p. 195)

Here Rogoff circumvents the need for an internalization process by proposing that the researcher change his or her perspective and focus on what children's interpersonal activity might mean to them. In constructivist terms, this involves a shift in focus to the mathematical meanings and practices that the child considers are shared with others.

Rogoff's point that children are already active participants in the social practice implies that they engage in and contribute to the development of classroom mathematical practices from the outset. Further,

> in the process of participation in social activity, the individual already functions with shared understanding. The individual's use of this shared understanding is not the same as what was constructed jointly; it is an appropriation of the shared understanding by each individual that reflects the individual's understanding of and involvement in the activity. (Rogoff, 1990, p. 195)

Rogoff's distinction between the individual's use of a shared understanding and the shared understanding that is constructed jointly is closely related to the distinction that a cognitive constructivist might make between an individual child's understanding and the taken-as-shared meanings established by the group (Cobb, Perlwitz, & Underwood, in press; Schutz, 1962). It therefore seems reasonable to conclude from Rogoff's treatment of internalization that mathematical learning is a process of active construction that occurs when children engage in classroom mathematical practices, frequently while interacting with others. Significantly, a similar conclusion can be reached when considering von Glasersfeld's (1995) elaboration of Piaget's developmental theory.

Von Glasersfeld develops his view of learning as self-organization by clarifying the distinction that Piaget made between two types of cognitive reorganization—empirical abstraction and reflective abstraction. In doing so, he emphasizes that an empirical abstraction results in the construction of a property of a physical object, whereas the process of constructing mathematical and scientific concepts involves reflective abstraction. He illustrates the notion of empirical abstraction by describing a situation in which someone wants to drive a nail into a wall but does not have a hammer available. After looking around, the person finds a wooden mallet and begins to use this, only to find that the nail goes into the mallet instead of into the wall. Von Glasersfeld argues that, in this scenario, the person assimilates the mallet to her hammering scheme, but then makes an accommodation when things do not go as expected, and a perturbation is experienced. This accommodation involves an empirical abstraction in that it results in the construction of a novel property for the mallet—it is not the sort of thing that can be used to hammer nails into walls.

The interesting feature of this example for my purposes is that hammering is a cultural practice that involves acting with particular cultural artifacts—hammers and nails. The person's hammering scheme can be viewed as the product of active constructions she made in the course of her initiation into this practice. In other words, hammers, nails, and mallets are, for her, cultural tools that she can use for certain purposes. It is against the background of her engagement in this practice of hammering that she makes the empirical abstraction described by von Glasersfeld. This being the case, it seems reasonable to extend the definition of empirical abstraction by emphasizing both that it results in the emergence of novel physical properties and that it occurs as the individual participates in a cultural practice, often while interacting with others. This formulation involves the coordination of perspectives in that the first part, referring as it does to an experienced novelty, is said from the "inside," whereas the second part is said from the "outside" and locates the individual in a cultural practice.

The assumption that individual activity is culturally situated is also implicit in von Glasersfeld's discussion of the construction of mathematical concepts. Here, the notion of reflective abstraction is used to account for the process by which actions are reified and become mental mathematical objects that can themselves be acted upon (cf. Sfard, 1991; Thompson, 1994). For von Glasersfeld, it is by means of reflective abstraction that students reorganize their initially informal mathematical activity. Consider, for example, a situation in which the teacher introduces conventional written fraction symbols to record the results of students' attempts to fairly partition objects such as pizzas. Von Glasersfeld stresses that the students can only interpret the teacher's actions within the context of their ongoing activity. Further, the process by which the symbols come to signify the composition and decomposition of fractional units of some type for at least some of the students is accounted for in terms of the reification of partitioning activity via reflective abstraction. As with the example of the mallet, it can be observed that these conceptual reorganizations occur as the students participate in cultural practices. In this case, these are the mathematical practices that the students help to establish in the classroom. The mathematical concepts they each individually construct are relative to and are constrained by their participation in these practices. It can also be noted that the activities from which the students abstract include their interpretations of others' activity and of joint activities (Voigt, 1992). These considerations suggest that in defining reflective abstraction, we should emphasize both that it involves the reification of sensory-motor and conceptual activity and that it occurs while engaging in cultural practices, frequently while interacting with others. As was the case with the characterization of empirical abstraction, this formulation involves the coordination of perspectives.

In comparing Rogoff's and von Glaserfeld's work, it can be noted that Rogoff's view of learning as acculturation via guided participation implicitly assumes an actively constructing child. Conversely, von Glasersfeld's view of learning as cognitive self-organization implicitly assumes that the child is participating in cultural practices. In effect, active individual construction constitutes the background against which guided participation in cultural practices comes to the fore for Rogoff, and this participation is the background against which self-organization comes to the fore for von Glasersfeld.

COORDINATING PERSPECTIVES

The complementarity between the sociocultural and cognitive constructivist perspectives can be further clarified by considering the analyses of arithmetical activity offered by Saxe (1991) and Steffe and colleagues (1988). In contrast to the majority of sociocultural theorists, Saxe takes an explicitly developmental perspective that focuses on individuals' understandings while simultaneously emphasizing the influence of cultural practices and the use of sign forms and cultural artifacts. He illustrates his theoretical approach by analyzing the body-parts counting system developed by the Oksapmin people of Papua New Guinea.

Saxe explains that "to count as Oksapmin do, one begins with the thumb on one hand, and follows a trajectory around the upper periphery of the body down to the little finger of the opposite hand" (1991, p. 16). With Western contact and the introduction of tradestores, the Oksapmin had to use this indigenous counting system to solve arithmetical problems that did not emerge in traditional life, such as those of adding and subtracting values. In the course of his analysis of the interplay between the Oksapmin's participation in tradestore activities and their construction of mathematical understandings, Saxe identifies four developmental levels in the evolution of the body-parts counting system. At the least sophisticated level, individuals do not recognize the need to keep track of the second addend when they attempt to add, say, seven and nine coins. As a consequence, they frequently produce an incorrect sum. In contrast, the most sophisticated of the four levels involves the use of a "halved-body strategy" that incorporates a base-10 system linked to the currency. Here, in adding seven and nine coins,

> individuals use the shoulder (10) as a privileged value. In their computation, they may represent the 9 on one side of the body as biceps (9) and 7 on the other side of the body as forearm (7). To accomplish the problem, a tradestore owner might simply "remove" the forearm from the second side and transfer it to the first side where it becomes the shoulder (the 10th). He then "reads" the answer as 10 + 6 or 16. (p. 21)

In sociocultural terms, the Oksapmin's increasingly sophisticated computational strategies can be viewed as cultural forms. An account of development made from this perspective might focus on the extent to which individual Oksapmin participate in the new practice of economic exchange. Such an account would stress that typically only tradestore owners, who have the most experience with economic transactions, use the sophisticated halved-body strategy. In contrast to this view that social and cultural practices drive development, a constructivist analysis might treat the Oksapmin's computational strategies as cognitive forms created by self-organizing individuals. An account of this latter type might focus on the processes by which individual Oksapmin reflectively abstract from and thus reorganize their enumerating activity, thereby creating increasingly sophisticated arithmetical units. Interestingly, it is possible to develop such an account by using the cognitive models of American children's arithmetical development proposed by Steffe as a source of analogies (Steffe et al., 1988).

We have seen that Oksapmin at the least sophisticated level do not recognize the need to keep track of counting. In contrast, Oksapmin at the next level consciously attempt to keep track. This suggests that these Oksapmin view their counting acts as entities that can themselves be counted. In Steffe and colleagues' (1988) terms, these acts carry the significance of counting abstract units. This analysis, which is made from the "inside" rather than the "outside," explains why Oksapmin at the initial level do not recognize the need to keep track of counting. They are yet to reify their counting acts, and, as a consequence, body-parts counting as they currently understand it is simply not the kind of activity that can be kept track of.

This analysis can be extended to account for the development of more sophisticated strategies. For example, when the halved-body strategy is used, a body part such as the biceps (9) appears to symbolize not a single unit but the composite of nine abstract units that would be created by counting to the biceps. In Piagetian terminology, counting has been reified via reflective abstraction, and the biceps symbolizes nine experienced as an arithmetical object that can be conceptually manipulated.

Each of the two perspectives, the sociocultural and the cognitive, tells half of a good story, and each can be used to complement the other. For example, consider a situation in which a young Oksapmin works in a trade-store and eventually learns the halved-body strategy used by the store owner. A sociocultural explanation might talk of the novice appropriating or internalizing a cultural form. As we have seen, an account of this type has difficulty in explaining how a cultural form that is external to the novice is brought across the barrier and becomes a cognitive form. The cognitive analysis circumvents this difficulty by stressing that rather than internalizing a cultural form that appears to be pregiven, the novice reorganizes his or her own activity. Thus, to paraphrase Rogoff (1990), there is nothing to bring across the barrier and, consequently, no need to posit a process of internalization from the sociocultural to the cognitive realm.

By the same token, the sociocultural perspective complements the cognitive perspective by emphasizing that the novice trader reorganizes his or her counting activity while attempting to achieve goals that emerge in the course of his or her participation in the practice of economic exchange (Saxe, 1991). From this point of view, it is readily apparent that both what counts as a problem and what counts as a legitimate solution are highly normative. Thus both the process of individual construction and its products, increasingly sophisticated conceptual units, are social through and through. Conversely, it can be argued that the various strategies, viewed as cultural forms, are cognitive through and through in that they result from individual Oksapmin's constructive activities. As was the case with the discussion of Rogoff's and von Glasersfeld's analyses, this coordination of perspectives leads to the view that learning is both a process of self-organization and a process of enculturation that occurs while participating in cultural practices, frequently while interacting with others.

THEORETICAL PRAGMATISM

The discussion of Rogoff's, von Glasersfeld's, Saxe's, and Steffe's work indicates that sociocultural analyses involve implicit cognitive commitments, and vice versa. It is as if one perspective constitutes the background against which the other comes to the fore. This contention concerning the relationship between the perspectives can be contrasted with the claims made by adherents to each perspective that mind is either in the head or in the individual-in-social-action. Claims of this type reflect essentialist assumptions. In effect, adherents of both positions claim that they have got the mind right—this is what the mind really is, always was, and always will be, independent of history and culture. A perusal of Geertz's (1983) discussion of Western, Arabic, and Indic visions of the self and of community might lead proponents of a particular perspective to question whether theirs is the God's-eye view.

Following Fish (1989), it can be argued that theorizing is itself a form of practice rather than an activity that stands in opposition to practice. The discussion thus far suggests that if we want our practice of theorizing to be reflexively consistent with the theories we develop as we engage in that practice, we have to give up essentialist claims and take a more pragmatic approach. In this regard, Rorty (1983), who uses the metaphor of wielding vocabulary rather than taking a perspective, argues that

> the idea that only a certain vocabulary is suited to human beings or human societies, that only that vocabulary permits them to be "understood", is the seventeenth-century myth of "nature's own vocabulary" all over again. (p. 163)

For Rorty, the various vocabularies we use or the particular perspectives we take are instruments for coping with things rather than ways of representing their intrinsic nature. Here Rorty follows Dewey and Kuhn in arguing that we should "give up the notion of science traveling towards an end called 'corresponding with reality' and instead say merely that a given vocabulary works better than another for a given purpose" (p. 157). Thus "to say something is better understood in one vocabulary than another is always an ellipsis for the claim that a description in the preferred vocabulary is most useful for a certain purpose" (p. 162).

The implication of this pragmatic approach for mathematics education, and for education more generally, is to consider what various perspectives might have to offer relative to the problems or issues at hand. In this regard, I suggest that the sociocultural perspective gives rise to theories of the conditions for the possibility of learning (Krummheuer, 1992), whereas theories developed from the cognitive perspective focus on both what students learn and the processes by which they do so. For example, Lave and Wenger (1991), who take a relatively radical position by attempting to avoid any reference to mind in the head, say that "a learning curriculum unfolds in opportunities for engagement in practice" (p. 93). Consistent with this formulation, they note that their analysis of various examples of apprenticeship in terms of legitimate peripheral participation accounts for the occurrence of learning or failure to learn. In contrast, a cognitive analysis would typically focus on the ways in which students reorganize their activity as they participate in a learning curriculum, and on the processes by which the curriculum is interactively constituted in the local situation of development. In my view, both these perspectives are of value in the current era of educational reform that stresses both students' meaningful mathematical learning and the restructuring of the school while simultaneously taking issues of diversity seriously. Cognitive theorists might argue that sociocultural theories do not adequately account for the process of learning, and sociocultural theorists might retort that cognitive theories fail to account for the production and reproduction of the practices of schooling and the social order. The challenge of relating actively constructing students, the local microculture, and the established practices of the broader community requires that adherents to each perspective acknowledge the potential positive contributions of the other perspective. In doing so, cognitive constructivists would accept the relevance of work that addresses the broader sociopolitical setting of reform. Conversely, sociocultural theorists would acknowledge the pedagogical dilemmas articulated by Ball (1993) when she spoke of attending to both students' interests and understandings, and to their mathematical heritage.

In dispensing with essentialist claims, this pragmatic approach to theorizing instead proposes that the adoption of one perspective or another should be justified in terms of its potential to address issues whose resolution might contribute to the improvement of students' education. Voigt (1992) offered a justification of this type when he stated that

> personally the author takes the emphasis on the [individual] subject as the starting-point in order to understand the negotiation of meaning and the learning of mathematics in classrooms. The main reason is that concepts like "socialization", "internalization", "initiation into a social tradition", etc. do not (directly) explain what I think is the most important objective of mathematics education. The prominent objective of mathematics education is not that students produce correct solutions to mathematical problems but that they do it insightfully and

> by reasonable thinking. What on the behavioral level does in fact not make a
> difference should be an important subjective difference. (p. 10)

Justifications of this type are, of course, open to challenge. For example, a
critic might argue that, in certain circumstances, it is more important that
students produce correct answers than that they develop insight. This coun-
terargument does not claim that Voigt's chosen perspective fails to capture
the essence of mathematical development. Instead, it questions assumptions
about educational objectives and, ultimately, about what counts as improvement in students' mathematics education. In general, claims about what
counts as improvement reflect beliefs and values about what it ought to
mean to know and do mathematics (or science, or social studies) in school.
These beliefs and values are themselves open to challenge and criticism, thus
bringing to the fore the moral and ethical aspects of educational research
and theorizing (Nicholls, 1989).

The central claim of this chapter, that the sociocultural and cognitive
constructivist perspectives each constitute the background for the other, implies that justifications should explicitly bring the researcher into the picture
by acknowledging his or her interpretive activity. Essentialist claims involve
a denial of responsibility—it is social reality that dictates the correct theoretical perspective. In contrast, pragmatic justifications reflect the researcher's
awareness that he or she has adopted a particular position for particular reasons. From the sociocultural perspective, a justification of this type would
explain why it is not necessary to focus on the actively cognizing student for
the purposes at hand. Conversely, cognitivists would be obliged to explain
why it is not necessary to go beyond the box of the classroom for their
purposes, while acknowledging that it is appropriate to take a perspective
that locates classroom events within a wider sociopolitical setting for other
purposes.

This pragmatic approach to theorizing also contends that ways of coordinating perspectives should be developed while addressing specific problems and issues. In addition, the suggestion acknowledges that Ball and
other teachers have something interesting to say when they suggest that the
tension in teaching between individual construction and enculturation cannot be resolved once and for all. Teachers instead have to act with wisdom
and judgment by continually developing ways to cope with dilemmas in
particular situations. A similar *modus operandi* would appear to be appropriate for researchers as we engage in our practice. In place of attempts to
subjugate research to a single, overarching theoretical scheme that is posited
a priori, we might follow Ball in reflecting on and documenting our attempts
to coordinate perspectives as we attempt to cope with our specific problems.
In doing so, we would give up the quest for an acontextual, one-size-fits-all

perspective. Instead, we would acknowledge that we, like teachers, cast around for ways of making sense of things as we address the situated problems of our practice.

Acknowledgment. The research reported in this chapter was supported by the Spencer Foundation and by the National Science Foundation under grant No. RED-9353587. The opinions expressed do not necessarily reflect those of the Foundations.

NOTE

1. The phrase "mind in the head" is used as a metonymy to refer to individualistic accounts of cognition. Following Johnson (1987) and Varela, Thompson, and Rosch (1991), the phrase should not be read as implying a mind–body dualism.

REFERENCES

Axel, E. (1992). One developmental line in European activity theories. *Quarterly Newsletter of the Laboratory of Comparative Human Cognition, 14*(1), 8–17.

Bakhurst, D. (1988). Activity, consciousness, and communication. *Quarterly Newsletter of the Laboratory of Comparative Human Cognition, 10*, 31–39.

Ball, D. L. (1993). With an eye on the mathematical horizon: Dilemmas of teaching elementary school mathematics. *Elementary School Journal, 93*, 373–397.

Bauersfeld, H. (1980). Hidden dimensions in the so-called reality of a mathematics classroom. *Educational Studies in Mathematics, 11*, 23–41.

Bauersfeld, H. (1988). Interaction, construction, and knowledge: Alternative perspectives for mathematics education. In T. Cooney & D. Grouws (Eds.), *Effective mathematics teaching* (pp. 27–46). Reston, VA: National Council of Teachers of Mathematics and Lawrence Erlbaum Associates.

Bauersfeld, H. (in press). "Language games" in the mathematics classroom—Their function and their effects. In P. Cobb & H. Bauersfeld (Eds.), *The emergence of mathematical meaning: Interaction in classroom cultures.* Hillsdale, NJ: Erlbaum.

Bauersfeld, H., Krummheuer, G., & Voigt, J. (1988). Interactional theory of learning and teaching mathematics and related microethnographical studies. In H-G. Steiner and A. Vermandel (Eds.), *Foundations and methodology of the discipline of mathematics education* (pp. 174–188). Antwerp: Proceedings of the TME Conference.

Bernstein, R. J. (1983). *Beyond objectivism and relativism: Science, hermeneutics, and praxis.* Philadelphia: University of Pennsylvania Press.

Blumer, H. (1969). *Symbolic interactionism.* Englewood Cliffs, NJ: Prentice-Hall.

Bredo, E., & McDermott, R. P. (1992). Teaching, relating, and learning. *Educational Researcher, 21*(5), 31–35.

Brown, J. S., Collins, A., & Duguid, P. (1989). Situated cognition and the culture of learning. *Educational Researcher, 18*(1), 32–42.

Carraher, T. N., Carraher, D. W., & Schliemann, A. D. (1985). Mathematics in streets and in schools. *British Journal of Developmental Psychology, 3*, 21–29.

Cobb, P. (1989). Experiential, cognitive, and anthropological perspectives in mathematics education. *For the Learning of Mathematics, 9*(2), 32–42.

Cobb, P., & Bauersfeld, H. (in press). The coordination of psychological and sociological perspectives in mathematics education. In P. Cobb & H. Bauersfeld (Eds.), *Emergence of mathematical meaning: Interaction in classroom cultures.* Hillsdale, NJ: Erlbaum.

Cobb, P., Perlwitz, M., & Underwood, D. (in press). Constructivism and activity theory: A consideration of their similarities and differences as they relate to mathematics education. In H. Mansfield, N. Pateman, & N. Bednarz (Eds.), *Mathematics for tomorrow's young children: International perspectives on curriculum.* Dordrecht, Netherlands: Kluwer Academic Press.

Cobb, P., Wood, T., & Yackel, E. (1993). Discourse, mathematical thinking, and classroom practice. In N. Minick, E. Forman, & A. Stone (Eds.), *Education and mind: Institutional, social, and developmental processes* (pp. 91–119). New York: Oxford University Press.

Cobb, P., & Yackel, E. (in press). A constructivist perspective on the culture of the mathematics classroom. In F. Seeger, J. Voigt, & U. Waschescio (Eds.), *The culture of the mathematics classroom: Analyses and changes.* Dordrecht, Netherlands: Kluwer Academic Press.

Confrey, J. (1990). A review of the research on student conceptions in mathematics, science, and programming. In C. B. Cazden (Ed.), *Review of Research in Education* (Vol. 16; pp. 3–55). Washington, DC: American Educational Research Association.

Davydov, V. V. (1988). Problems of developmental teaching (part I). *Soviet Education, 30*(8), 6–97.

Fish, S. (1989). *Doing what comes naturally.* Durham, NC: Duke University Press.

Forman, E. (1992, August). *Forms of participation in classroom practice.* Paper presented at the International Congress on Mathematical Education, Québec City.

Fosnot, C. T. (1993). Science education revisited: A defense of Piagetian constructivism. *Journal of Research in Science Education, 30*(9), 1189–1201.

Geertz, C. (1983). *Local knowledge.* New York: Basic Books.

Greeno, J. G. (1991). Number sense as situated knowing in a conceptual domain. *Journal for Research in Mathematics Education, 22*, 170–218.

Hanks, W. F. (1991). Foreword. In J. Lave & E. Wenger, *Situated learning: Legitimate peripheral participation* (pp. 13–26). Cambridge, England: Cambridge University Press.

Hiebert, J., & Carpenter, T. P. (1992). Learning and teaching with understanding. In D. A. Grouws (Ed.), *Handbook of research on mathematics teaching and learning* (pp. 65–98). New York: Macmillan.

Johnson, M. (1987). *The body in the mind: The bodily basis of reason and imagination.* Chicago: University of Chicago Press.

Krummheuer, G. (1992). *Lernen mit "format": Elemente einer interaktionistischen Lerntheorie.* Weinheim, Germany: Deutscher Studien Verlag.

Lave, J. (1988). *Cognition in practice: Mind, mathematics and culture in everyday life.* Cambridge, England: Cambridge University Press.

Lave, J., & Wenger, E. (1991). *Situated learning: Legitimate peripheral participation.* Cambridge, England: Cambridge University Press.

Leont'ev, A. N. (1981). The problem of activity in psychology. In J. V. Wertsch (Ed.), *The concept of activity in Soviet psychology.* Armonk, NY: Sharpe.

Mehan, H., & Wood, H. (1975). *The reality of ethnomethodology.* New York: Wiley.

Minick, N. (1989). *L. S. Vygotsky and Soviet activity theory: Perspectives on the relationship between mind and society.* Literacies Institute, Special Monograph Series No. 1. Newton, MA: Educational Development Center, Inc.

Newman, D., Griffin, P., & Cole, M. (1989). *The construction zone: Working for cognitive change in school.* Cambridge, England: Cambridge University Press.

Nicholls, J. G. (1989). *The competitive ethos and democratic education.* Cambridge, MA: Harvard University Press.

Nunes, T. (1992). Ethnomathematics and everyday cognition. In D. A. Grouws (Ed.), *Handbook of research on mathematics teaching and learning* (pp. 557–574). New York: Macmillan.

O'Loughlin, M. (1992). Rethinking science education: Beyond Piagetian constructivism toward a sociocultural model of teaching and learning. *Journal of Research in Science Teaching, 29*(8), 791–820.

Piaget, J. (1970). *Genetic epistemology.* New York: Columbia University Press.

Piaget, J. (1980). *Adaptation and intelligence: Organic selection and phenocopy.* Chicago: University of Chicago Press.

Putnam, H. (1987). *The many faces of realism.* LaSalle, IL: Open Court.

Rogoff, B. (1990). *Apprenticeship in thinking: Cognitive development in social context.* Oxford, England: Oxford University Press.

Rorty, R. (1978). *Philosophy and the mirror of nature.* Princeton, NJ: Princeton University Press.

Rorty, R. (1983). Method and morality. In N. Haan, R. N. Bellah, & P. Robinson (Eds.), *Social science as moral inquiry* (pp. 155–176). New York: Columbia University Press.

Saxe, G. B. (1991). *Culture and cognitive development: Studies in mathematical understanding.* Hillsdale, NJ: Erlbaum.

Schoenfeld, A. H. (1987). What's all the fuss about metacognition? In A. H. Schoenfeld (Ed.), *Cognitive science and mathematics education* (pp. 189–216). Hillsdale, NJ: Erlbaum.

Schutz, A. (1962). *The problem of social reality.* The Hague, Netherlands: Martinus Nijhoff.

Scribner, S. (1984). Studying working intelligence. In B. Rogoff & J. Lave (Eds.), *Everyday cognition: Its development in social context* (pp. 9–40). Cambridge, MA: Harvard University Press.

Sfard, A. (1991). On the dual nature of mathematical conceptions: Reflections on processes and objects as different sides of the same coin. *Educational Studies in Mathematics, 22*, 1–36.

Steffe, L. P. (1995). Prospects for alternative epistemologies in education. In L. P. Steffe (Ed.), *Constructivism in education*. Hillsdale, NJ: Erlbaum.

Steffe, L. P., Cobb, P., & von Glasersfeld, E. (1988). *Construction of arithmetical meanings and strategies*. New York: Springer-Verlag.

Thompson, P. W. (1994). Images of rate and operational understanding of the Fundamental Theorem of Calculus. *Educational Studies in Mathematics, 26,* 229–274.

van Oers, B. (1990). The development of mathematical thinking in school: A comparison of the action-psychological and the information-processing approach. *International Journal of Educational Research, 14,* 51–66.

Varela, F. J., Thompson, E., & Rosch, E. (1991). *The embodied mind: Cognitive science and human experience*. Cambridge, MA: MIT Press.

Voigt, J. (1985). Patterns and routines in classroom interaction. *Recherches en Didactique des Mathematiques, 6,* 69–118.

Voigt, J. (1992, August). *Negotiation of mathematical meaning in classroom processes*. Paper presented at the International Congress on Mathematical Education, Québec City.

von Glasersfeld, E. (1984). An introduction to radical constructivism. In P. Watzlawick (Ed.), *The invented reality*. New York: Norton.

von Glasersfeld, E. (1987). Learning as a constructive activity. In C. Janvier (Ed.), *Problems of representation in the teaching and learning of mathematics* (pp. 3–18). Hillsdale, NJ: Erlbaum.

von Glasersfeld, E. (1989a). Constructivism. In T. Husen & T. N. Postlethwaite (Eds.), *The international encyclopedia of education* (1st ed., supplement Vol. 1; pp. 162–163). Oxford, England: Pergamon.

von Glasersfeld, E. (1989b). Cognition, construction of knowledge, and teaching. *Synthese, 80,* 121–140.

von Glasersfeld, E. (1992). Constructivism reconstructed: A reply to Suchting. *Science and Education, 1,* 379–384.

von Glasersfeld, E. (1995). Sensory experience, abstraction, and teaching. In L. P. Steffe (Ed.), *Constructivism in education* (pp. 3–15). Hillsdale, NJ: Erlbaum.

Vygotsky, L. S. (1960). *Razvitie vysshikh psikhicheskikh funktsii* [*The development of the higher mental functions*]. Moscow: Akad. Ped. Nauk. RSFSR.

Vygotsky, L. S. (1978). *Mind and society: The development of higher psychological processes*. Cambridge, MA: Harvard University Press.

Vygotsky, L. S. (1979). Consciousness as a problem in the psychology of behavior. *Soviet Psychology, 17*(4), 3–35.

PART II
Perspectives from the Disciplines

CHAPTER 4

A Constructivist Perspective
on Teaching and Learning Science

Candace Julyan and Eleanor Duckworth

Working with fellow graduate students on a problem related to mirrors, Judy, an experienced biochemist, reconsidered what she knew about science and how to apply that knowledge to her new midlife career switch from science practice to science teaching.

> During our work with mirrors in the classroom, I was feeling as if I "knew a lot" about mirrors. As for the question of where to place the mirror on the wall [so that two people could see one another], I already "knew" how to figure that out because I "know" that "the angle of incidence equals the angle of reflection." Simple, I thought. We worked twice with mirrors. [Both times] I dutifully tried to stand back and listen to the thinking of others in my group as we worked with the little mirrors and string.
>
> After our work, one of the group members commented, "the angle of incidence equals the angle of reflection." These words did not help her at all, although she knew to recite them. That really baffled and intrigued me. [This person], a science teacher of 20 years, confessed to us that she had thought of sharing her "knowledge" of this phrase with us, but she hesitated because it didn't help her to think about the problem. She didn't get the connection, though she knew there must be one. I was quite flabbergasted by this. How can these words that I understood to be a direct and true statement of what we were seeing have no meaning to others who were working with me? What is the message here? (Fallows, 1993, pp. 4–5)

Judy's experience illustrates a common tension for science teachers and learners: that knowing the scientific words used to explain a phenomenon does not necessarily reflect an understanding of what the words describe. As Judy returned to mirrors, this time in another setting, she discovered that once again her magic phrase was not meaningful to someone else.

> [A]fter . . . Melissa said . . . , "If you're at 45 degrees then I have to be at 45 degrees," I shared with her that little phrase and she was still clueless about it. Although it seemed to me she'd stated it perfectly, she still didn't understand the words in my memorizable little litany "angle of incidence is equal to the angle of reflection." It meant nothing to her. I have to shake my head. What a lot more there was to think about with mirrors than I had thought! And that phrase which I thought was such a pure and simple explanation is not so pure or simple. (Fallows, 1993, p. 6)

In the past decades a number of educators have explored Judy's discovery that a "pure and simple explanation is not so pure or simple" (Duckworth, 1986; Hawkins, 1978). As Driver (1983) points out, one difficulty in many science classrooms is that "connections that are apparent to a scientist may be far from obvious to a pupil. It is, after all, the coherence as perceived by the pupil that matters in learning" (p. 2). She goes on to suggest that the pupils' ideas are as important to explore in a science classroom as conventional scientific theories. Driver's suggestion may seem unusual if one assumes that the purpose of a science class is to provide clear, detailed explanations of conventional scientific thought. However, we would argue that the purpose of a science class should be to encourage a fuller understanding of the workings of the physical world, one that requires the articulation and investigation of one's own ideas as well as the ideas of others.

As one of us has written before (Duckworth, Easley, Hawkins, & Henriques, 1990), it is the learner alone who makes the connections in any meaningful way, and it is these connections that should be of interest to the teacher.

> The world may well exist on its own, but knowledge of it, however adequate or inadequate, belongs to each of us. The knowledge that a teacher must be concerned with is that of the student. It is this knowledge that he or she wants to see further developed, and this is the knowledge that the teacher has to work with. Learners construct further knowledge by modifying that which they have already. (p. 24)

These notions that learning must be actively and internally constructed by the learner rather than explained completely by another person are not new. Jean Piaget in his numerous studies detailed examples of the construction of knowledge by children as they acted on objects. His ideas provide an important foundation for all the research in this area, as others have described earlier in this volume.

In fact, the way that a child constructs an understanding of how things work is not significantly different from the way that adults build their understanding. Our beliefs about how the world works are formed around the meanings we construe from the data of our experiences. The work of scientists involves this same process of making meaning. Albert Einstein (1938) viewed science as not just a collection of laws and a catalogue of facts, but rather a creation of the human mind.

As we explore ideas, such as where to put a mirror so that two people can see each other, we must first make sense of the problem before we can consider the usefulness of any related scientific theories or can even see the connection between theories and the problem at hand. The complexity in the development of knowledge is not a new idea in educational literature. John Dewey (1902) stressed the importance of having a student's knowledge grow from experience; and numerous experience-based science curricula do also (e.g., Elementary Science Study [ESS], Science—A Process Approach [SAPA], Science Curriculum Improvement Study [SCIS], Introductory Physical Science [IPS], Biological Science Curriculum Study [BSCS], the Physical Science Study Committee [PSSC], Full Options Science Systems, Science for Life and Living, Insights, and National Geographic Kids Network).

It is important, however, to make a distinction between providing students with experiences and supporting students' developing understanding. Elstgeest (1985) illustrates the difference in his story about "a marvelous science lesson virtually [gone] to ruins." While the teacher may well have believed in student exploration, her actions at the end of the class period impeded, rather than supported, the students' emerging understanding. Some experience-based curricula also embody this contradiction.

> It was a class of young secondary school girls who, for the first time, were let free to handle batteries, bulbs, and wires. They were busy incessantly, and there were cries of surprise and delight. Arguments were settled by "You see?", and problems were solved with, "Let's try!" Hardly a thinkable combination of batteries, bulbs, and wire was left untried. Then, in the midst of the hubbub, the teacher clapped her hands and, chalk poised at the blackboard, announced: "Now, girls, let's summarize what we have learned today. Emmy, what is a battery?" "Joyce, what is a positive terminal?" "Lucy, what is the correct way to lose a circuit?" And the "correct" diagram was deftly sketched and labeled, and the "correct" symbols were added, and Emmy, Joyce, and Lucy and the others deflated audibly into silence and submission, obediantly copying the diagram and the summary. What they had done seemed of no importance. The questions

were in no way related to their work. The rich experience with the batteries and other equipment, which would have given them plenty to talk and think about and to question, was in no way used to bring order and system into the information they actually did gather. (Elstgeest, 1985, pp. 36–37)

Although others may explain the sense that they have made of a specific idea, each individual must construct a personal understanding. For many educators, the significant focus, proposed by Bussis, Chittenden, Amarel, and Klauser (1985), is to determine "*what* a person has learned, not *if* a person has learned" (p. 15).

Constructing an understanding requires that the students have opportunities to articulate their ideas, to test those ideas through experimentation and conversation, and to consider connections between the phenomena that they are examining and other aspects of their lives.

WORKING WITH BALLOONS

The following account of work with helium-filled balloons has a double purpose. On the one hand, we want to show an example of the tortuous development of what can seem to be fairly straightforward ideas. On the other hand, it is an example of the kind of research we think is important, as a basis for developing a science curriculum that respects students' own ways of constructing their understanding. (This kind of research is discussed at greater length in Duckworth, 1987 [pp. 134–140] and 1991 [pp. 12–23].)

The set of ideas in this case concerns the notion of equilibrium—stable and unstable. (Not a wholly random choice for a book on constructivism!) We wanted to learn about high school students' understanding of this set of ideas and to see what is involved in helping those ideas develop. Our original interest had been equilibrium of an ecological system, and we chose to go about it by starting with a simpler problem. We were taken by surprise with the difficulties involved in grasping the workings of the self-regulating system, in this case the string. The distinction between stable and unstable equilibrium never did become explicit in our three sessions, but a basis for it was clearly established.

We conducted the following work with high school students (Duckworth, Julyan, & Rowe, 1985). A "standard" balloon was weighted to a height of some 3 feet from the floor by several lengths of medium twine. The initial question students considered was how to alter a "worker" balloon so that it was level with the "standard" (Figure 4.1). In achieving this, students either could alter the weight the balloon had to lift by adding or cutting string, or could attach a "helper" balloon to the "worker." Which-

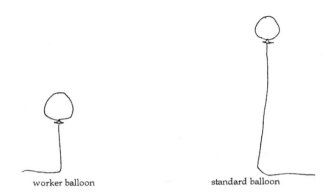

FIGURE 4.1. A "worker" balloon, *left*, and a "standard" balloon, *right*.

ever strategy or combination they adopted, the interviewer tried through questions to get the students to verbalize their thinking, in order to make this thinking clearer both to the interviewer and to the students themselves. For example, the following exchange reveals a ninth-grade student's thinking about why a knot in the string lowered the balloon.

(*Sam ties a knot in the string. The balloon falls noticeably.*)
Interviewer: Why do you reckon it did that?
Sam: Well, because of the weight.
Interviewer: The weight?
Sam: When you put the knot, it has more weight . . .
Interviewer: Some people would say that it's the same weight with or without a knot; it's the same string. Does that make sense to you?
Sam: Mmmm. (*pause*) Maybe it's because the string's more . . . more . . . (*He makes a hand gesture.*) . . . not heavier, but . . . like if you had paper instead of string, and one sheet was flat and the other was all bunched up. The one that was bunched up would come straight down, but the one that was flat would come down like this. (*Sam gestures motion like a feather falling in air.*) Because it has more resistance.

As Sam became able to articulate his ideas of what was happening, the interviewer tried to ask questions that would push Sam to think as clearly as he could about his ideas.

Interviewer: How do you mean "resistance"?
Sam: It has more air pushing against it, so it falls slower than the other one.

pre-knot   post-knot

FIGURE 4.2. At the first session, the students are asked to match the height of a "worker" balloon, *right*, to that of a "standard" balloon, *left*.

Interviewer: So what you're saying is that the knot in the string makes the balloon fall faster?

Sam: Yes.

Interviewer: Would it make it fall *lower* or just faster?

Sam: Mmmm. It *would* make it fall faster; I don't know about lower. We should try it. (*Sam experiments with two balloons, one with a flat sheet of paper attached, one with a crumpled paper of equal size. He makes several attempts, reducing the size of each paper by half each time. Each time the balloon falls to the floor with no noticeable difference in speed.*)

In the following, we have cut out most of the interviewer's interventions, but they played the same role. The description is a detailed account of three sessions with two twelfth-grade students. Their case shows the development of students' thinking over time as they articulate their ideas and create experiments to test those notions. One student, Kim, is constant throughout the three meetings. Ellen is present for the first meeting only; Tina is present for the second and third meetings.

First Meeting

In this session we ask Kim and Ellen if they can bring a yellow "worker" balloon, which rested on its string near floor level, to the height of a green "standard" balloon, which was resting a little higher from the floor (Figure 4.2).

Kim suggests cutting the strings to make the yellow balloon rise. Ellen doubts at first that this would make any difference. If the balloon were to go up, she feels more helium would need to be added. They agree to try Kim's idea, however, and Kim cuts the string about 2 inches above where it touches the floor (Figure 4.3). To the surprise of both, the balloon rises all the way to the ceiling.

FIGURE 4.3. The students then cut the string of the "worker" balloon 2 inches from the floor.

Ellen attaches more string to the balloon to bring it down again, resulting in knots at the top of the original string. As Kim cuts them off, they notice that the balloon rises slightly. Kim wonders if the string "closer to the balloon" is "more important" than the string "at the bottom." After a discussion between the two girls about this possibility, an experiment forms in Kim's mind. Would it be possible to take, say, 5 inches from the tail end of the string on one balloon and 5 inches from the top end of another and compare the effect on each balloon (Figure 4.4)? Although even in working this out mentally it begins to strike her as somewhat absurd, she finds herself almost involuntarily engaged in the experiment.

Before cutting any string, it occurs to her that it might be interesting to redesign the experiment. Instead of cutting the string from the top near the balloon, which would obviously free the balloon to float to the ceiling, she decides to tape 5 inches of string cut from the bottom of the string to the top of the string (Figure 4.5).

She does this and is delighted to see the balloon fall a few inches.

FIGURES 4.4 (*left*) and **4.5** (*right*). The students' other ideas for raising the "worker" balloon: In Figure 4.4, string is cut from opposing ends. In Figure 4.5, 5 inches cut from the end is added near the top.

Hey! All right! So, we've figured something out! We've figured out that the weight near the balloon is more important than the weight . . . you know, far away from the balloon.

Kim then proposes the idea—which will prove to be a sound one—that the balloon can always hold up a particular amount of string; it simply rises or falls until it is holding that amount of string. She decides that if the balloon is holding its maximum quota of string, then its position will be constant as long as that quota is constant, regardless of the arrangement of the string. This much is congruent with her findings so far. But this elegant idea still has many hurdles to overcome, and that is the main story of these three sessions.

Kim decides to explore the idea with a balloon with 5 feet of string. The balloon is floating 3 feet above the floor, and the remaining 2 feet of the string extends along the floor. Kim thought that the balloon should not move if the string that is extended on the floor, and therefore not part of the quota, is cut off (Figure 4.6).

She remembers the first experiment above, though, where the balloon rose when she cut the string. She feels that it is likely to do the same this time, but she repeats the experiment nonetheless: She cuts the string at X, just above floor level, and the balloon rises to the ceiling. This puzzles her greatly. Why should the balloon move when the string, which is apparently not suspended, was cut off?

That doesn't make sense . . . It's really strange . . . (*and then with excitement*) It's sort of like when you cut someone's hair who had long hair and it curls . . . I'm never going to look at a helium balloon the same again!

FIGURE 4.6. A test of the idea that if the string on the floor is cut, the balloon should not move.

The comment about the hair does recapture the basic set of relationships involved with the helium and the string. The equilibrium between the weight of the hair, pulling down, and the tendency to curl, pulling up, determines where the hair will hang. It is not clear how the idea relates to the fact that the balloon rose all the way to the ceiling. Nor does Kim ever go back explicitly to this similarity. Nevertheless, her excitement suggests that she made an assimilation that was important to her and that may well be underlying much of the rest of her thinking about the phenomena.

After another exploration or two, this first session ends. Kim's main idea is that a given balloon can hold up a certain weight of string. But it is still a fragile idea. And, among other things, the position of the weight with regard to the balloon also seems to matter.

Second Meeting

Ellen is not available for subsequent meetings; Tina comes along in her place. After Kim shows Tina some of the things she has done, we ask what will happen to the balloon if they tie a knot in the string. Kim explains that it would "go down because the weight will be closer to the balloon." What effect will tying a knot further down the string have? Kim reports that it would "go down, but not as much." And what if they tie a knot in the string that is lying on the floor? Kim is confident in her response: "Nothing. It doesn't matter. It's just dead weight." Tina, with less experience with the balloons, questions Kim about the reason behind her answers: "But when you tie it further up the string, on the part that's hanging, you're increasing the weight?" "Yes," Kim explains, "you're pulling string off the ground into the air."

Tina thinks about this in her own way and gets half-way there. Because you're taking up . . . the knot. And you're actually taking more in length— you're making it weigh more."

We suggest an experiment. If we take a balloon with a string just touching the floor and mark the point of contact between the floor and the string, then according to Tina's theory, that marker will rise when we tie the knot, thus increasing the length. We tie the knot and no change takes place with the marker, but the balloon moves lower. She saves face, reconstructing for herself what the proposal had been.

Tina: Ah, no. You see, I thought that what you had been doing was picking up the string from the floor and tying a knot and therefore getting more string . . . I didn't realize you were . . . So it *wouldn't* weigh more.

Kim: Hmmm . . . it's [*the balloon*] going down because the length of the string is shorter but it still weighs the same amount. . . . [I]f the length of the string got any shorter by cutting it off, then it would weigh less and go up. But now the string is getting shorter, which is pulling it down, you know. And it can't pull back up because it still weighs the same.

It would appear at this point—especially from the last remark—that Kim has understood the relationship between length/weight of the string and the height of the balloon. But the idea still gets confounded. First, there is this question:

Tina: Is there any way to make a knot up here [*indicating a point near the top of the string*] so that the length of the string between the balloon and the ground is increased?
Kim: Hmm. I just don't know how to do it.

Then another experiment continues the perplexity. They turn their attention to another balloon whose string is just touching the ground. Tina proposes that they tie a knot in the string. Kim and Tina together build a prediction that the balloon will stay at the same height above the ground without the string touching the ground. When asked why this would be true, Tina replies that it is because the string weighs the same with or without the knot. At this point it would seem that they know that the balloon can carry a fixed weight, but they miss the importance of the regulating influence of the string.

They tie a knot in the string, and the balloon falls until the end is once again touching the floor. Both Kim and Tina are surprised at this. When asked, "Why did you think the balloon would be at the same height?" Kim replies: "Because it would have the same amount of weight . . . But now the weight is closer to the balloon . . . That [is] a guess for why it would be low."

So, the idea that the amount of weight the balloon can hold up determines the balloon's height seems central to them. If a knot changes the height, then they have to look for a reason—and the reason they fall back on is the old idea that a weight that is closer to the balloon "counts" more.

They next start exploring what happens where strings of two balloons are tied together. During this exploration, Kim comments, for the first time and with puzzlement, "The string always seems to touch the floor." In the course of tying balloons together, at one point they connect the "dead" end of the string of a green balloon (i.e., the end that is lying along the floor) to the top of the string of a yellow balloon (Figure 4.7).

FIGURES 4.7 (*left*), **4.8** (*middle*), and **4.9** (*right*). An exploration of what occurs when the strings of the two balloons are tied together.

Kim: I think the yellow balloon will go right down to the ground and the green balloon will go back to where it was [*Figure 4.8*].
(*They tie the strings together as planned and release the balloons [Figure 4.9].*) See? The green balloon's about the same height as it was, holding up the same amount of weight, and the yellow balloon's half as high because it's holding up . . . like . . . a double thickness . . .
They're both holding up the same amount of string, right? Same amount they've always held up. This green one is holding up that amount of string, which is about the same as it's always held up—a little bit more than the height of the chair. This yellow one is holding up the same amount as it's always held up because it's about half as high and is holding twice the number of strings. So it kind of seems like they can both hold up the same amount of string, you know . . .
Tina: But why did that other knot a while ago make it go down?
Kim: Because it was holding up more string.
(*This answer does not seem entirely satisfactory to her, as we will see.*)
Tina: But if we take a single balloon with the same amount of string, just touching the ground, and use that string to tie a knot . . .

Kim interrupts and exclaims that they are looking at two different ideas, and she persuades Tina to abandon their knot question and to test the hypothesis—still unconfirmed for her—that the balloon can always hold up the same amount of string. They take a balloon whose string just touches the floor. They fold the string in half and predict that the balloon will fall to half its original height, allowing the string to touch the floor once again. It does just that.

Kim: Hot Dog! I'm good!
Tina: Let's fold the string in half again and see if the balloon goes down by half again. I think it will.

They do this and are pleased to see the balloon fall as predicted. Kim suggests that they attach all the string to the balloon. She tapes all the string to the balloon. When she releases it, the balloon falls to the floor, resting on the pad of string. Kim explains that this experiment shows that the balloon always goes to the end of the string, no matter what the configuration of that string might be.

It is important to note that the observation that puzzled Kim earlier—that the string always touches the floor—no longer seems to be a source of puzzlement. At this point it seems to be a given, but it is not clear whether it is a step forward or a step backward in her understanding.

Tina isn't as sure that it is simply a matter of the amount of string. She seems still to think of knots, or folded string, as having more of an impact: "As long as it has enough weight. Because, I mean, if it was just one string that long it wouldn't go to the end of the string."

This is actually the situation they had just started from—but nobody points this out. Their explorations seem to confirm that the balloon is always able to sustain the same amount of string. But still they appear reluctant—Tina anyway—to give up the idea that the closeness of this weight to the balloon is somehow important.

Third Meeting

At the beginning of the third session Tina is still thinking about doubling the thickness and halving the height. As she works with these ideas, she says:

> I think it's like . . . if you play on a seesaw, if you have the same weight on both sides, it's fun. But if one person is really heavy it's not as much fun because they go all the way down. But if they sit closer in, then they balance it . . . You know what I'm saying? It's the idea of balance . . .
>
> The balance is the helium going up and the string coming down . . . I guess the balance is the point where the balloon stops, where it's no longer moving.

Here, Tina draws on her understanding of another experience—as Kim did earlier with the curly hair—to clarify her thinking. Again, it seems like an apt and helpful assimilation.

After some more work with doubled strings, they start on another tack—attaching two balloons by joining the "dead" end of the string of one balloon to a second balloon (Figure 4.10). They are not sure what the outcome of this might be. They release the balloons and a "V" shape forms (Figure 4.11). Tina says, "That's the same amount of string that they could both hold up, connected in the middle. Each one singly would do the same thing if you cut it here in the middle."

FIGURES 4.10 (*left*) and **4.11** (*right*). The attachment of the two balloons with one string and the results.

So what, we ask, might happen to the "V" if we cut off about two inches of string and then reattach the balloons? Would they still form a "V" shape? And if so, where? At the floor? In midair? At the ceiling? Kim says, "It would make sense if they go all the way to the ceiling. Because they each have less string to hold them to the ground. So if they don't go to the ground they might just go all the way up." They adjust the string, and the balloons rise all the way to the ceiling amid surprise and delight. Tina announces that she is "glad they didn't touch the floor" as that "would have been dumb!"

This is the first suggestion of understanding the instability of the equilibrium when there is not enough string—quite different from their astonishment the first time the balloon rose to the ceiling. Did they think it was possible to get the balloon to hover in midair? Kim doesn't think so because of "the nature of helium. Helium is just going to go up unless you have enough gravity to make it come down." Did the image of the seesaw help here?

Kim: I don't know. You can't hover on a seesaw.
Tina: Yes, you can move right in to a point where you can balance.
Interviewer: Is that possible with balloons?
Tina: Yes. OK. So you have the balance and then after you get out of balance . . . it's just . . . You're never going to stay with one person up and one person down and not touching the ground. Once you've upset your balance—even a little bit—you're going to go down all the way.

As the bell rings and they turn to leave, Kim comments that "this was cool" and she wishes that "it wasn't the last time."

Discussion

Tina's last sentence captures the very essence of unstable equilibrium. It is a fine way to understand what happens to a balloon alone—if we tried to get just the right amount of helium. In these three sessions, though, neither Kim nor Tina ever articulated how having a long string enabled the balloon to remain at approximately a constant height from the ground.

In our experience, we also find very few people who have noticed or been able to articulate the difference between a seesaw—which, in repose, always has one end touching the ground—and a balance—which, in repose, remains horizontal. (And we believe that the parallel with the stability or instability of new ideas is not hard to find.)

The three sessions (which involved a few experiments that we did not include in this account) provided us with a good sense of the issues involved for high school students in coming to understand some form of equilibrium. They showed us some of the difficulties, some of the points of engagement, and some key probing questions. For example, they showed us some of the forces to which the seemingly simple, yet elegant, idea was vulnerable; the length of time needed to take them all into account; and some other experiences, hair and seesaws, that students drew on to help them think about equilibrium. They also showed us that this is potentially a fine field of exploration for high school students.

Inhelder and Piaget (1958) have pointed out the interaction between the degree of adequacy of youngsters' notions about a phenomenon and the degree of adequacy of their means of experimenting to check out their ideas. The indications here are that we hit just about the right level. Kim and Tina were able to keep clear in their minds which aspect they wanted to work on at a given moment and created experiments that would shed light on that particular aspect. They followed through on the implications of each of their ideas. This ability to keep focusing on one thing, one focus at a time, goes hand in hand with an ability to develop an all-encompassing theory about the phenomena. And, significantly, they had a wonderful time doing it.

One concern this type of research raises for some is that students can become frustrated by the considerable time and attention required, and that they prefer to gain their knowledge through transmission rather than construction. As one of the authors has written before (Julyan, 1989), science-as-vocabulary requires less effort on the part of both the teacher and the student, but also provides fewer rewards.

Students are aware of the difference and, we believe, if given the choice, they too would strive for understanding. This point was highlighted by a sophomore, Pam, participating in this same balloon study. This student continued to be surprised and frustrated by the actions of the balloon, and her frustration with her lack of understanding was often visible. The teacher working with us in this study became increasingly concerned with Pam's frustration and began to assert that we "tell the answer" to alleviate the intellectual tension.

The next work session, seemingly on cue, Pam turned to us, demanding to know whether or not we intended to tell her "the answer." What was the question? we asked. At this she seemed momentarily stumped, but then she stated that she wanted to know why helium balloons behaved in the way that they did in all the various experiments that she had conducted. We stated that while we were willing to answer her question, we wanted to make sure that we were clear about what she wanted. Did she want our words to explain the phenomena or did she want to understand them herself? There was a long and poignant pause in the room. Finally she turned and quietly said that the words were *not* what she wanted; she really wanted to understand. We agreed that her understanding was our goal as well and that we would all continue to work toward that end, but that it would take time.

While most students might not articulate the dilemma as clearly as this student, many share her desire to understand, not just to know the correct words. One way to promote this understanding is to give students opportunities to mess about in their science classes, to become participants in constructing their own knowledge. Given the traditional approach to learning, however, those interested in supporting a constructivist approach must be prepared for an initial reluctance and moments of obvious frustration, regardless of the age and inclination of the student.

CONSTRUCTIVISM FOR TEACHERS

During a summer workshop, one of the authors (Julyan) had a revealing example of the ways that teachers, as well as students, can feel both the frustration and the elation of a constructivist experience. The primary purpose of the workshop was to increase the teachers' knowledge of plants and to provide suggestions of ways to incorporate investigations with plants into the elementary curriculum. For most of the two weeks, the workshop activities grew out of the lectures by botanists, collecting samples from the arboretum, and trying out various classroom activities. Our role was to introduce constructivism into the workshop with two three-hour sessions.

In the first session the teachers worked in groups, each group focused on a different part of the plant (roots, leaves, flowers, trunk). The teachers listed what they felt they knew and what was mysterious to them about that plant part and then created a large drawing that showed their beliefs—and in some cases hinted at their mystifications. Later in the morning, each group shared its picture and ideas about the function of the particular plant part. Standing before their large, and often impressionistic, drawings, the teachers, with considerable humor, shared their mysteries. How much of the root can you cut without killing the tree? Do the same species of tree have a different root pattern (close to the surface or deep) in different environmental conditions? How does the bark of the tree accommodate the growing diameter? How does a seed get inside the fruit? While some of the teachers began to speak of their mystifications in self-deprecating ways, their seriousness grew as they realized that the questions were considered legitimate and were also puzzlements for others. Through these conversations we discovered that there were differences of opinion about the functions of various parts. These disagreements were not settled with a "correct" answer, but rather teachers were asked to continue to weigh these different opinions as they continued their studies of trees.

At the end of the session, Julyan suggested that, as they worked with the scientists and spent time during the next week observing trees, the teachers collect some data to support their ideas about the functions and to begin to answer their mysteries. One of the teachers became *very* angry at the suggestion of this task. Why, she wanted to know, were the answers not given right then? Julyan explained that there were many times during the two-week workshop where others were telling them the answers, but the work of this part of the workshop was to look at what questions they had about trees and ways to examine those questions themselves—not a very satisfying answer for this teacher.

In our next session together (almost two weeks later), we repeated the same activity, with each teacher group reviewing the initial and revised ideas about plant parts. Then as one group we talked about what mystifications had been solved and what ideas about functions had changed. The discussion was energetic, full of good spirit, and highly productive. Teachers were eager to share the investigations they had conducted to solve their questions. After reviewing their initial puzzlements, some found that they had collected data that could answer their own or another's question. The conflicting ideas were still in evidence, and, as before, each difference of opinion was explored. In some instances, we found resolution; in other instances, the teachers discovered that they were each unwilling to believe data that conflicted with their newfound beliefs.

Two important discoveries emerged from this day's work. First, teachers were surprised to discover that the most persuasive and most valued evidence came from the observations made by other teachers, not the information from books or the lectures from the scientists. Perhaps the strongest example of this point came when the group was considering how a plant without seeds could reproduce. One teacher described her past success in reproducing banana trees from the root. Her experience clearly persuaded the other teachers. The group began to smile, nod, and through body language indicate that this was persuasive evidence. Julyan asked the group to consider whether they would be as comfortable with this explanation if it had started with, "I read in a book that . . . " or "In his lecture, Peter explained that . . . " The teachers acknowledged, with a fair amount of astonishment, that books and lectures would not have been as credible to them at that moment as this woman's story. In reviewing the work of the past several hours, one teacher remarked that the data that *all* of them had relied on in the discussion had been from their own experiences. This observation generated a lively discussion about learning and the ways in which a teacher can support learning, which led to the second discovery.

In the midst of this discussion about teaching and learning, the teacher who at the end of the first session had expressed deep reservation and frustration about answering her questions herself remarked with amazement that she just then realized how involved she had been in the morning's discussion. She demanded to know what Julyan had done to "make this discussion work," as if the magic of the morning was the result of secrets or tricks. What happened to make her care more about what *she* and her fellow teachers thought, than to care about any correct answer that she thought Julyan could give to her?

CONCLUSION

How *had* Julyan managed to get this woman involved in exploring mysteries of trees, almost against her will? Are there tricks or secrets that transform a classroom into a place where individuals eagerly construct their own understanding or develop their beliefs about a phenomenon? What was the difference between Julyan's approach, in her work with the teachers, and the teacher in the earlier battery and bulb example? Both teachers seemed to be similarly invested in student exploration. What else is required of the teacher? What sorts of teaching techniques are important in supporting a student's construction of his or her understanding?

Perhaps first and foremost, the phenomenon students are asked to think about needs to be interesting, worthy of engaging their time and attention. In addition, it should offer a variety of avenues for exploration, various routes of approach. Once these parameters are established, the teacher needs to listen carefully to students' interpretations of the data, paying particular attention to any individual's conundrums, puzzlements, confusions. And the teacher equally needs to pay attention to differences of opinion within the class, giving equal respect to each one, for as long as any student still takes it seriously. By focusing on puzzlements and contradictions, the teacher establishes the notion that ideas are complicated and worthy of time and consideration and that each student is capable of formulating interesting ideas. Further, the teacher acknowledges that "not knowing" is a state that is important to live with—the state that most of us are in most of the time.

Attending to both the science under study and to the individual's beliefs about the science is an important aspect of constructivist teaching. By encouraging students to express feelings related to their work (their frustrations as well as their interests), the teacher can encourage students to consider the entirety of the learning process. An atmosphere of playfulness also has an important role in this type of exploration, as it is most likely to encourage this expression of feelings and can serve as a healthy and helpful release of the frustration inherent in constructing one's own understanding.

These trademarks of a constructivist classroom may well be inconsistent with the view of science as a static body of facts. However, they are not at all inconsistent with the view of science as an active pursuit. Some teachers, along with practicing scientists, value exploration and believe that exploration will lead one to significant understanding. In both professions, it takes time to make the most of the explorations. It is possible for teachers to get better at all of the principles outlined above as they attend to their students' ideas. They are not tricks or secrets, as the teacher studying trees implied, but rather are principles of teaching which need practice.

REFERENCES

Bussis, A. M., Chittenden, E. A., Amarel, M., & Klauser, E. (1985). *Inquiry into meaning: an investigation of learning to read*. Hillsdale, NJ: Erlbaum.

Dewey, J. (1902). *The child and the curriculum*. Chicago: University of Chicago Press.

Driver, R. (1983). *The pupil as scientist?* Milton Keynes, England: Open University Press.

Duckworth, E. (1986). Teaching as research. *Harvard Educational Review, 57,* 481–495.

Duckworth, E. (1987). *"The having of wonderful ideas" and other essays in teaching and learning*. New York: Teachers College Press.

Duckworth, E. (1991). Twenty-four, forty-two, and I love you: keeping it complex. *Harvard Educational Review, 61*(1), 12–23.

Duckworth, E., Easley, J., Hawkins, D., & Henriques, A. (1990). *Science education: A minds-on approach to the elementary years*. Hillsdale, NJ: Erlbaum.

Duckworth, E., Julyan, C. L., & Rowe, T. (1985). *A study on equilibrium: A final report*. Cambridge, MA: Educational Technology Center.

Einstein, A (1938). *The evolution of physics*. New York: Simon & Schuster.

Elstgeest, J. (1985). The right question at the right time. In W. Harlen (Ed.), *Primary Science: Taking the plunge* (pp. 36–46). London: Heinemann.

Fallows, J. (1993). *Are we having fun yet?* Unpublished manuscript.

Hawkins, D. (1978). Critical barriers to science learning. *Outlook, 29,*

Inhelder, B., & Piaget, J. (1958). *The growth of logical thinking.* New York: Basic Books.

Julyan, C. (1989). Messing about in science: Participation not memorization. In W. Rosen (Ed.), *High school biology: Today and tomorrow* (pp. 184–193). Washington, DC: National Academy Press.

CHAPTER 5

A Constructivist Perspective on Teaching and Learning Mathematics

Deborah Schifter

Anne Hendry, a veteran first-grade teacher in rural western Massachusetts, describes how she began a unit on measurement shortly before Thanksgiving 1990:

> Before school, moving desks and chairs and using masking tape, I outlined the shape of a boat on the classroom floor, 16 by 6 feet. This was to represent the Mayflower. I also prepared a scroll for a child to read to the class and then to post on the bulletin board with our initial problem involving measurement on it. I selected one child, instructing him that at math time he would be a messenger from the King bringing an "Edict" to the Pilgrims.
>
> When math time arrived, Zeb, the child who was appointed to be the messenger, read his "Edict," which said, "This ship cannot sail until you tell me how big it is." The children were puzzled.
>
> "Well, what should we do? Who has an idea?" I asked. Thus our discussion of measurement began . . . or I thought it would begin. But there was a period of silence—a long period of silence.
>
> What do young children know about measurement? Is there anything already present in their life experiences to which they could relate this problem? I watched as they looked from one to another, and I could see that they had no idea where to begin. Surely, I thought, there must be something they could use as a point of reference to expand on. Someone always has an idea. But the silence was long as the children looked again from one to another, to Zeb, and to me. (Hendry, 1996)

To most educators, Hendry's intention to connect her mathematics lesson with the upcoming holiday would appear unexceptionable. They would surely wonder, however, at a veteran teacher choosing to endure a long painful silence from a roomful of confused students. Why had she given her first graders a task without showing them how to complete it? Why ask a question before telling one's students what they need to know in order to answer it? How could so experienced a teacher allow her lesson to falter in this way?

> I was having second thoughts about the enormity of the problem for a first grader when, shyly, Cindy raised her hand. "I think it's three feet long," she said. "Why?" I asked. "Because the letter from the King said so," she responded. "I don't understand," I said. "Can you tell me why you think the ship is three feet?" "Because the King's letter said so. See!" Cindy said. "I'll show you."
>
> Holding the letter up, the light, filtering through the paper, made the capital "E" I had written for the word "Edict" look like a three to some of the children. I clarified this point with her and the others who agreed that they also had seen a three on the King's paper. The King, they thought, already knew the answer.
>
> I felt we were back to square one again with more silence. (Hendry, 1996)

Casting about for a response to their teacher's question, a few children look for a number, any number, connected with the context. But once Cindy's confusion is cleared up, silence again descends, and Hendry's doubts deepen.

Anne Hendry's behavior will likely puzzle readers whose images of teaching derive from the mathematics classrooms in which they themselves once sat as children: The teacher shows the students procedures for getting right answers and then monitors them as they reproduce those procedures. To ask a question without having previously shown how to answer it is actually considered "unfair"!

However, once viewed against the backdrop of an alternative—"constructivist"—perspective on how learning takes place, what "doing" mathematics can mean, and what these imply for mathematics instruction, Hendry's behavior becomes comprehensible. Indeed, in this chapter, her vignette will serve to launch an examination of some aspects, first, of a mathematics instructional practice informed by that perspective, and, second, of one teacher's experience of constructing such a practice. Specifically, we begin by contrasting Hendry's lesson with one taught by second-grade teacher Karen Schweitzer—from the period before Schweitzer began to fundamentally transform her own mathematics instruction. Then we pick up Schweitzer's story, following her through the initial phases of that process of transformation—from the creation of her new vision of mathematics teaching through her inaugural attempts to put that vision into practice. As she articulates her new insights, Schweitzer will reveal additional dimensions of the new mathematics pedagogy.

TWO MATHEMATICS LESSONS

Let us resume with Hendry's account of her measurement unit. Having explained to the class that what they thought was a "3" was actually the "E" in the word "Edict,"

I felt we were back to square one again with more silence, until Tom raised his hand and said, "Mrs. Hendry, I know it can't be three feet because the nurse just measured me last week and said that I was four feet, and this boat is much bigger than me!"

From Tom's initial observation, our discussion on measurement was basically off the ground. Hands immediately went up. The children now realized that they knew a little about measurement, especially in relationship to their own size and how tall they were.

"Let's see how many times Tom can fit in the boat," someone suggested. Tom got down and up several times along the length of the boat: the children decided that the boat was four "Toms" long.

"How can we tell that to the King, since he does not know Tom?" I asked. "Send Tom to the King," was their easy solution, while others protested that they wanted Tom to stay on the boat for the trip. I was really hoping that they would relate to the information Tom had already given us about his size. I thought someone might add four feet, four times, presenting us with a quick solution to the problem. But this was not the route they decided to take.

Mark raised his hand and suggested that we could measure the boat with our hands like they do with horses. His neighbor had a horse that was 15 hands. "Then we could tell the King how many 'hands' long the boat was." The children agreed that this might be a better idea.

"All right," I said. "Since it was Mark's idea, he can measure the length of the boat with his hands." Mark was also the biggest child in the class.

At first, Mark randomly placed his hands on the tape from one end to the other, but when he double-checked, he came out with a different answer. The children were puzzled for a while as to why this happened. It took several more tries and much discussion before they came to an important conclusion. The children decided that it was necessary for Mark to make sure that he began exactly at the beginning of the boat and did not leave any gaps in between his palms and his fingers as he placed them on the tape. Measuring this way, he discovered the boat was 36 hands long.

Great! We decided to tell the King this, but just to be sure, I suggested we have Sue, the smallest child in the class, measure the other side. She did and related to the class that her side was 44 hands long. Now there was confusion.

"Why are they different?" I asked. "Can we use hands to measure?" "No," the children decided, this would not work either, since everyone's hands were not the same size.

Al suggested using feet. We tried this, but once again, when someone else double-checked with their feet, we found two different measurements. The children at this time began to digress a little to compare each other's hands and feet to discover whose were the biggest and smallest.

Finally, our original discussion continued, while the children explored various concepts and ideas. Joan sat holding a ruler, but, for some reason, did not suggest using it. Perhaps, I thought, it might be that her experience with a ruler was limited, and she may not have been quite sure how to use it.

Our dilemma continued into the next day when the children assembled again to discuss the problem with some new insights. One child suggested that since Zeb knew the King, and everyone knew Zeb, that we should use his foot. "Measure it out on a piece of paper and measure everything in 'Zeb's foot.'" Using this form of measurement, the children related to the King that the boat was 24 "Zeb's foot" long and 9 "Zeb's foot" wide.

Curiosity began to get the best of them and the children continued to explore this form of measurement by deciding to measure each other, our classroom, their desks, and the rug using "Zeb's foot." I let them investigate this idea for the remainder of the math period.

On the third day of our exploration, I asked the children why they thought it was important to develop a standard form of measurement (or in words understandable to a first grader, a measurement that would always be the same size) such as using only "Zeb's foot" to measure everything. Through the discussions over the past several days, the children were able to internalize and verbalize the need or importance for everyone to measure using the same instrument. They saw the confusion of using different hands, bodies, or feet because of the inconsistency of size. (Hendry, 1996)

While Hendry's paper goes on to describe how her class arrived at an exploration of the use of rulers and the adoption of conventional units of measurement, some important aspects of her teaching are already available to us.

First, and most strikingly, we do not see Hendry engaged in the commonest of traditional teaching behaviors—giving directions and offering explanations. Instead, we observe her questioning her students, the questions sometimes coming minutes apart. And when they do come, more often than not they appear to elicit, rather than allay or forestall, confusion.

To look more deeply at Hendry's lesson, I will, as promised, contrast it to one described by Karen Schweitzer, a teacher who also works with small groups of children in rural western Massachusetts. While Schweitzer's class was doing a science unit on whales, the children became so fascinated by the fact that blue whales can grow to 100 feet that she decided to have them lay out that length in the hallway. Schweitzer later wrote:

> I told the children exactly how we would go about measuring the whale's length. We would take the yardstick, which we hadn't explored, and we would put it down and keep track of where it ended and then place it there and keep counting till we reached where it ended and then place it there and keep counting till we reached 100 feet. (Schweitzer, 1996)

After they were done, Schweitzer reported, the children ran up and down the hall exclaiming, "Wow!" However, despite the evident pleasure they derived from its results, there was something unsatisfying about the lesson: What, if anything, she wondered, had the children learned?

Similarities between the two lessons are easily identified. Both Hendry and Schweitzer were responsive to what had captured their students' imaginations—Hendry's class had been fascinated by a cutaway of the Mayflower they had made; Schweitzer's, by the length of the blue whale. Both teachers decided to engage the class in measurement activities connected to those topics. And both teachers set up their lessons to involve the children in the actual measuring—their lessons were hands-on.

From the point of view of this discussion, however, the salient difference is that while Schweitzer told her class exactly how to perform the task she had devised, Hendry posed a problem with the expectation that her children would find their own way to a solution. Schweitzer crisply demonstrated the use of a yardstick; Hendry watched her students messily struggle to figure out what the inconsistencies in their results would tell them about the concept of measurement. In addition, while Schweitzer could have demonstrated the procedure to ten, five, or even one student, indifferently, Hendry's lesson depended on her students interacting among themselves.

What can we infer from these two units on measurement about the epistemological assumptions they enact? Hands-on though it may have been, Schweitzer's lesson is nonetheless consistent with beliefs about learning that still order most of our classrooms—that people acquire concepts by receiving information from other people who know more; that if students listen to what their teachers say, they will learn what their teachers know; and that the presence of other students is incidental to learning.

However, although Schweitzer's students might now have been able to picture just how long a blue whale can get, most, as she would come to realize, had probably learned very little about the concept of measurement. For they had not had an opportunity to think through together what a yardstick is, or why they were supposed to lay it down exactly as Schweitzer prescribed.

Implied in Hendry's lesson is an alternative perspective on learning mathematics in the K–12 classroom, a perspective that informs the principles guiding the current movement for mathematics education reform (National Council of Teachers of Mathematics, 1989, 1991, 2000)—that individuals necessarily approach novel situations by interpreting them in the light of their own established structures of understanding; that the construction of new concepts is provoked when those settled understandings do not allow satisfactory accommodation of the novel circumstance; and that this constructive activity is not simply an individual achievement but is embedded in and enabled by contexts of social interaction (Cobb, 1988; Confrey, 1991; Kamii, 1985; Piaget, 1972, 1977; von Glasersfeld, 1983, 1990).

Paralleling this divergence in epistemological assumptions is a fundamental difference in how the nature of mathematics and the "doing" of mathematics are understood: if the math-fact, drill-and-practice approach to instruction has an affinity for a static and timeless conception of mathematical truth—"all the mathematics there is has always already been out there"—constructivists argue that mathematics is a human invention with a long history: Culturally embedded schools of thought compete, fashions change, and some questions may be irresolvable. Until quite recently, it was the apparent certainty of mathematics that raised its status above that of the natural sciences. But today, a keener appreciation of the interplay of imagination and logical necessity, a greater awareness of the roles of convention, philosophical commitment, and technological interest in shaping the development of the discipline favor an emphasis on the similarities between mathematics and the natural sciences. In this view, then, to "do" mathematics is to conjecture—to invent and extend ideas about mathematical objects—and to test, debate, and revise or replace those ideas (Davis & Hersh, 1980; Ernest, 1991; Lakatos, 1976; Lampert, 1988; Latour, 1987; Tymoczko, 1986).

In the 1980s these new perspectives on the learning process and on the nature of mathematics converged to form a drastically revised picture of what should be taking place in the classroom. Teaching mathematics was reconceived as the provision of activities designed to encourage and facilitate the constructive process. The mathematics classroom was to become a community of inquiry, a problem-posing and problem-solving environment in which developing an approach to thinking about mathematical issues would be valued more highly than memorizing algorithms and using them to get right answers. Thus, for example, in the context of explorations of number, operations, data, and space, students would also learn how to construct a mathematical argument and assess its mathematical validity (Ball, 1993a, 1993b; Cobb, 1988; Confrey, 1991; R. B. Davis, Maher, & Noddings, 1990; Duckworth, 1987; Fosnot, 1989; Schifter & Fosnot, 1993).

Returning to Anne Hendry's first graders, we see that their teacher has posed a problem—report to the "King" the size of the "Mayflower"—in order to launch them on an exploration of the basic concepts of measurement. As the children make suggestions about the length of the boat, Hendry does not indicate whether they are right or wrong. Instead, she listens and watches. And only when the children seem satisfied with a solution does she put a further question, leading them to yet another problem, their own problem, which they feel compelled to resolve. As she sees it, her task is to pose questions that will lead *through*—rather than around—puzzlement to the construction of important mathematical concepts. Thus, when the class decides the boat is 4 "Toms" long, she points out that since the King does not know Tom, he cannot know how long the boat is. Again, once they have agreed the boat is 36 hands long, she suggests that a second child measure it, too, knowing that this will reignite their puzzlement and drive them toward a more durable solution to the task and a deeper grasp of the concept of measurement. These children understand that in their mathematics lessons, it is up to them to offer their thoughts about the questions that are posed. And, when faced with contradictions to their own conjectures, it is up to them to find resolution.

During these first days of the measurement project, the children are involved in making meaning out of the activity of measuring the boat. By the third day, Hendry concludes, the children have figured out that in order to say how long something is, they must count the number of times a conventionally agreed-upon unit is laid down, without overlap or gaps, to cover the length of the object; and they must be able to communicate the size of the unit as well as the number of units counted.

CONSTRUCTING A NEW VISION

Karen Schweitzer writes that, having taught kindergarten for a number of years,

> when I first found out that I would be teaching second grade, I became anxious. I was eager to stretch my kindergarten language-arts program to meet the needs of the second graders that I would be facing, but how would I teach math?

Previous in-service work had stimulated her thinking about how children learn:

> [They] need to be invested in what they do, . . . they need to work at their own levels of understanding, and . . . it is important for them to have practice in not

only skill areas, but in identifying the strategies they are using as readers and writers. (Schweitzer, 1996)

But, like so many other thoughtful teachers, her ideas about mathematics and mathematics instruction did not allow her to translate these beliefs about how children learn to use language into her teaching of mathematics. Since she believed that children learn best by doing, her classroom was well stocked with a variety of mathematics manipulatives. But she never encouraged the children to explore for themselves—they used these materials in just the ways she prescribed, in the ways that made sense to her. As she fretted over her new mathematics program, she concluded that

> what I need[ed was] for someone to tell me what activities to do. So I gathered suggestions for activity books that would help me. The books had interesting ideas and some fun games, and between those books, and a few conversations with my colleague, I made it to the spring.

Yet, because she was dissatisfied with the results of her searches, she decided to attend a two-week summer institute for teachers of mathematics.

> I thought, "That's it. This year I really have to do this. But it'll be okay. I'll go to [the institute], they'll tell me what to do, and my worries will be over." I thought that I would . . . get a list of problems for my second graders to solve, or at least a recipe for how to write them, and a list of questions to ask the kids. Then my math program would be all set. (Schweitzer, 1996)

Like most teachers attending in-service programs, Schweitzer expected to be told how to teach. After all, this is what such experiences have traditionally been designed to do. But where the goal is to develop a practice based on ideas about the nature of mathematics and how people learn it, telling teachers what to do simply is not useful.

To see why, let us consider Schweitzer's desire for lists of problems and questions and whether Hendry's lesson offers any clues to how such lists might be created. Hendry did start with a nice problem—to measure the size of a large rectangle representing the *Mayflower*. But, in itself, this exercise is no more promising than Schweitzer's project to measure out the length of the blue whale in the hallway outside her classroom. And what were the questions that drove Hendry's lesson? "What should we do?" "Who has an idea?" "Why?" "I don't understand. Can you tell me why the ship is three feet?" "How can we tell that to the King, since he does not know Tom?" Clearly, what was central to Hendry's lesson was neither the problem she posed nor the specific questions she put, but rather the nature of the discussion her students engaged in—and which she skillfully guided.

A practice like Hendry's cannot be scripted; rather, it depends on one's capacity to respond spontaneously to students' perplexities and discoveries.

A teacher development program that simply provided participants with a repertoire of teaching strategies and techniques would be like Schweitzer's lesson on measurement in which she showed her students how to lay down a yardstick without ever helping them to understand why they should do it in that particular way. In the end, the classroom structures Hendry chose and the questions she asked were all subordinated to the mathematics she wanted her students to learn and to her understanding of how they would best learn it. The subtleties of timing and tone and the appropriateness of her spontaneous responses stem from a coherent conception of what should be happening in her classroom.

One important way to help teachers develop new conceptions of what can happen in their classrooms is to allow them to experience *as students* classrooms that enact the new approach to teaching, classes that provide learning experiences powerful enough to challenge 16 and more years of traditional education. Teachers must be able to recognize for themselves that this is the kind of learning that they would choose to foster in their own classrooms, and they must be given opportunities to critically analyze the process of learning, the nature of mathematics, and the kinds of classroom structures that will promote that goal.

Through mathematics lessons that challenge teachers at their own levels of mathematics competence, they can both increase their mathematical knowledge and experience a depth of learning that is, for many of them, unprecedented. Such activities allow teachers, often for the first time, to encounter mathematics as an activity of construction, of exploration and debate, rather than as a finished body of knowledge to be accepted, accumulated, and reproduced.

The institute Schweitzer attended provided just such experiences. Along with 35 other elementary teachers, she took on the challenge to devise a number system using as symbols 0, A, B, C, and D, in which one can add, subtract, multiply, and divide. In another exercise, she and her colleagues examined the angles of polygons, looked for patterns, made conjectures, argued about why the patterns they found must hold for all polygons; and in the environment of Logo's turtle geometry, she learned to pose her own questions and then to work to find her own answers.

After several days of such active, verbalized problem solving, Schweitzer and her colleagues concentrated on listening. Working with videotapes and in live, one-on-one interviews, they were asked to analyze students' solution processes, assessing the extent of those students' understandings and exploring the significance of the gaps that were exposed.

Throughout, participants were asked to reflect on their experiences. There were frequent small- and whole-group discussions about what had just happened in a lesson or what was seen on videotape; participants kept journals; and they were asked to reflect in writing on such fundamental questions as "How have your ideas about learning changed?" or "What does it mean to understand mathematics?" (For further descriptions of such courses, see Fosnot, 1989; Schifter, 1993, 1998; Schifter & Fosnot, 1993; Schifter, Russell, & Bastable, 1999; Schifter & Simon, 1992; Simon & Schifter, 1991.)

As the summer institute ended, Schweitzer wrote in her final assignment:

I have been greatly influenced by my observations of myself as a learner and the implications that my learning has for my teaching. For example, I have learned that I need to work hard not to shut down when I get the answer to something, but to do the hard work of asking myself more questions after I think I've found the answer. But how does/did the shutting down behavior influence my teaching? Is that what makes it so hard for me to see what the probing questions are? Do I also shut down when a student gets the right answer? I am rediscovering the discipline to make myself wonder. I know that sounds contrary—discipline and wonder—but until it becomes habit again, it will require discipline.

I have looked carefully at the processes that I use to teach. I have usually taught with the methods and materials that make sense to me. I have used manipulatives and other useful aids to show [the children] my way of understanding. My work now is to let them find their way of understanding. A habit of thinking that I have been thinking about is changing who controls the child's exploration processes. It was such a powerful experience for me to be able to pose my own question/investigation in Logo, and to keep myself puzzling over it. . . .

I came to the institute with the goal of learning how to ask questions. What I learned was why I need to ask questions—they help a learner to find words for her/his thinking, they help "get the thinking out," . . . and to help find the questions and explorations. What a big and subtle difference from the past when I think I asked questions after the fact to recap what they had done. The questions sometimes told me what [the children] did, but they didn't help them find a new exploration, and they didn't ask for a change of control. My questions would ask them what they did, but didn't help them ask, "Where can I go?" . . .

I want to remember to affirm the ideas that I came with that have been reinforced here. I feel even more certain than I did before that it needs to be explored that math is part of everything around us, and that it is like a language. I continue to want my students to associate math with playing and puzzles, but now I think it's more. It's the working at wondering and the delight in wondering! (K. Schweitzer, personal communication, 1992)

The institute did not give Schweitzer that recipe for writing word problems or that list of questions she had initially hoped to receive. Instead she was given the opportunity to construct a new vision for her mathematics teaching—a vision grounded in an enlarged sense of mathematics as well as in her own analysis of the kind of learning she wanted for her classroom.

CONSTRUCTING A NEW PRACTICE

Creating a teaching practice guided by constructivist principles requires a qualitative transformation of virtually every aspect of mathematics teaching. The development of a new vision is only the first step. Like many of the participants, Schweitzer left the summer institute with a high level of excitement and anticipation—and some trepidation. The greatest challenges still lay ahead.

We join her now, in early September, just weeks following her participation in the institute:

The first time we had math was during the second day of school. I had intended to start my math program on the very first day with such an exciting and inviting math activity that the children would be captivated and hooked on math for the rest of the year. I wanted to be inspired and to create this magnificent problem by myself—to apply all of the things that I had learned in the institute. But I never quite figured out what that perfect activity was so I just skipped math that day. . . .

On the second afternoon, I announced that it was time for math. One little girl said, almost as if she was asking permission to be excused, "I don't really want to do math." I knew that she was talking about "papers" with counters and endless problems, and so I answered, "I think second-grade math will be quite a bit different from first-grade math, so don't worry yet." She looked momentarily appeased, but her face told me that she wasn't quite ready to believe me. We all sat down on the carpet in the meeting area and several more children voiced their dislike for math. I again said, "Wait. Don't decide yet. See what it's like first." After hearing what they thought of "math," I really felt the pressure to do something that met all my criteria for the perfect math lesson. So I took a deep breath and said, "I noticed that some of the things that you wondered about yesterday sounded like they had to do with math." "Yeah," agreed John and he proceeded to read all of the how-many questions from the chart [where we had listed questions the day before]. "So much for discussion," I thought, "and where is the probing question in here anyway?!" But I figured that I had to go somewhere with it and added, "Why are those math questions?"

John answered, "Because they are counting."

"Is math only counting?" The children slowly began to throw out ideas about what math was.

"It's like putting 3 and 4 together."

"It's when you put unifix [cubes] together to add."

"Could math be patterns?" I asked. "Uh huh," they agreed and they began to make patterns with the unifix cubes that were in the middle of the circle. I made sure to emphasize and affirm all of the different ideas.

I then returned to the question of how many books were in the room. (I chose that item mostly because I thought it couldn't hurt to focus our attention on books.) "How could we answer that question?" I asked. "It's easy, just count them," they told me. I said that we were going to get into groups of three and figure out lots of different ways that we could count the books. . . . Then we would get back together and share all the different ideas, and after that we would count the books.

I really thought that all was going well now. They would go through this process, I would ask lots of great questions, they'd learn a lot, and we'd be off to a great start. Except when I mentioned breaking up into groups, all of a sudden, two children had stomach aches and one child started to sneeze. "But we can't stop here, before we really get started," I thought, and I pushed on.

When the children finally settled down in their groups, they were all quiet and seemed shy about talking to each other in this way. I hadn't expected this task to be as difficult as it was. And when we got back together and they shared their ideas (count by 2's, by 5's, by 10's) I found that the probing question of "How would you do that?" fell flat on its face. We had been working for 35 minutes and I decided to leave the actual counting until the next day, so I re-capped how many different ideas there were and that was our first day of math.

I ended that day frustrated and disappointed. I had wanted to dazzle them, to show them that math is interesting and inviting. Instead we all ended up a little unsure by the end of the lesson. Our nerves were showing, theirs and mine, and none of us were sure what lay ahead this year. (Schweitzer, 1996)

In fact, the session that Schweitzer described might not have been such a bad start to the year. Both she and her students had yet to learn a new way of being in math class, and for now they felt rather unsteady. The children did not yet know how to talk to one another in their small groups, Schweitzer did not yet know how to interpret her students' comments, nor had they—students and teacher—figured out how to have mathematical discussions. But a process had begun—Schweitzer had communicated the expectation that mathematics was something to talk about and that the children were to discuss their own ideas with her and with one another.

At this early stage, though, Schweitzer lacked the perspective that would have allowed her to trust that that process would develop. Two weeks later, she wrote:

I am so frustrated that lately, I've just wanted math to go away! However, I put math in a prominent and unavoidable place in my daily schedule this year so that I couldn't slip past it. So now, there it is. Every day. Waiting to taunt me.

I've tried to create activities that were engaging and meaningful, but the children seem inattentive during discussions and my questions are often answered with silence. I've tried to use resource books to set up activities that are "proven" in order to stimulate thinking and talking, but nothing happens except that I get even more frustrated. So I try to listen to the kids for a direction to go in, but I guess I don't know what I'm hearing yet because that doesn't help me either. (Schweitzer, 1996)

How does one move from the state that Schweitzer has described—frustrated and unsure, unable to identify or assess progress, feeling that things aren't right but not knowing how to make them better—to a coherent practice? Persistence and patience are part of the answer—there is no mystery here. But another key component is the opportunity to reflect on each day's events.

It is widely recognized that, as teachers return to their classrooms from summer institutes or intensive workshops, animated by a fresh sense of possibilities, the provision of continued support is crucial to realizing those possibilities in day-to-day instruction (Cohen et al., 1990; Joyce, 1990; Simon, 1989). Various programs offer different kinds of structures: clinical supervision, biweekly seminars, study groups, full-day retreats. Critical to each is the opportunity to think through events from one's own classroom in the light of new goals, beliefs, and understandings.

Support for Schweitzer came in the form of a writing course (Schifter, 1994, 1996a, 1996b, 1999). Nineteen teachers (with varying levels of experience in a teaching practice based on constructivism) were invited to meet weekly with a program staff member to write about what was happening in their own mathematics classrooms.

The course comprised two major activities: reading assigned materials and writing. The reading materials were authored by teachers writing about their own mathematics instruction—for example, articles by Ball (1993a, 1993b), Heaton (1991), and Lampert (1988, 1989) as well as articles coming out of the current movement to reform the teaching of reading and writing (Atwell, 1985; Hillocks, 1990). In addition to such works, Schweitzer's class read papers written by two groups of teachers who had earlier participated in offerings of the same course (Schifter, 1996a; 1996b). All readings were critically examined for both content and writing style.

The writing component of the course was fashioned after the process-writing model that many of the elementary teachers had already used in their own classes. Consistent with the new mathematics pedagogy, process writers work cooperatively to analyze and edit their projects. For the first several weeks of the course, specific assignments were given so that teachers could explore pedagogical issues and experiment with writing styles (transcribe a classroom dialogue and then write a narrative based on that dialogue about what happened; describe a student who has revealed to you that he or she has learned something that you are trying to teach; write about a student who expresses a mathematical idea that surprises you). Eventually, teachers determined the direction of their own writing and worked on final projects—15- to 40-page reflective narratives on topics of their choosing. Throughout the course, teachers met in both small and large groups to share their efforts and solicit feedback. All work was turned in to the instructor, who responded in writing.

In asking Schweitzer and her colleagues to reflect on their classroom process, the course offered them the opportunity to track the development of their new practice. Schweitzer discovered how, through writing, she could revisit a lesson, "listen" once again to what her students were saying—more closely, perhaps, this time—and consider how what she *now* heard in their words might affect her instruction. She found the requirement that descriptions of classroom events be made understandable to others especially helpful, for it required her to make sense of those events *for herself.* Thus, for example, after an extremely frustrating and confusing lesson, she reported that she had spent hours at her journal, trying to sort out what had happened. However, once she took it upon herself to write a narrative about that lesson, making the sequence of events that had thwarted her comprehensible to an audience:

> The frustration that I felt cleared. Although I ended saying I was frustrated, I wasn't feeling it as passionately as I was when I started. The writing of it cleared things up for me. I saw learning and a continuity that I didn't (and couldn't) see even after writing in my journal. (K. Schweitzer, personal communication, 1993)

Weekly meetings with other teachers and feedback from her instructor allowed Schweitzer further opportunity to reflect on her developing practice. She shared with her colleagues what had been happening in her classroom and entertained their interpretations of those events. As a group, they considered what her students were learning, where they might be confused, and what she might try next. Through similar discussions of her colleagues' stories, Schweitzer could picture other groups of children, working in different classroom structures, and learned about the results of pedagogical decisions she would herself, perhaps, not have made. In addition—and very importantly—she learned from her group that her frustrations and feelings of incompetence were not unique.

> I hoped that I wouldn't feel embarrassed when others read about what was happening in my classroom and how hard a time I was having. When I brought

this to class, I was relieved and encouraged to find out that many other teachers had similar feelings of frustration. (Schweitzer, 1996)

In fact, after several more weeks, Schweitzer began to see progress in the way she worked with her students. Not only that, but she had also become more tolerant of herself when her lesson did not meet her expectations. After one particular lesson that did not go well, she was surprised when:

> I didn't feel that combination of frenzy, frustration, and hopelessness that I felt five or six weeks earlier. By using my journal as a tool, I was able to figure out that if that many children were not on task, there was something wrong with either the structure or the content of the activity and I needed to reexamine both aspects of what we had done before I decided what to do next. . . .
>
> Tonight, I knew that the answers lay in my reflection, not in a book or in a manual. I know now that two of my students, because of their special language needs, and two other students (in addition) have difficulty working in pairs. Maybe it's time to try groups of three to take some of the pressure off of the individual kids. But then how do I keep them involved and accountable? Create an activity that has a task for each child and see how that works out. It sounds good in theory, but the only way I'll know is to try it and to watch how it works. (Schweitzer, 1996)

The previous summer Schweitzer had adopted as a goal for her teaching that her students learn to try out ideas, testing them to see if they worked and modifying them in the light of their analyses. Now she was learning that the same process applied to her own practice. Not every lesson would be dazzling. The children would not always be captivated and engaged in fascinating discussion. As she worked to deepen her new practice, she too would need to try out ideas, test them to see if they worked, analyze results, and develop her plans accordingly. And now she had confidence, not that her practice would always run smoothly, but that she *could* figure out what was going on and come up with new things to try.

Three months into the school year, as Schweitzer looked back on what she had gone through, she wrote:

> One of the most striking things that I have learned about math education is that, at least for the time being, there isn't a source that has the answers neatly prepackaged for me. A year ago I was in search of the perfect resource book to tell me what to do. I looked for answers from someplace else. Now instead, I think, "What are my students thinking about? What interests second graders? What concepts are they ready to explore?" and even "What do these children need to learn in second grade?" Instead of looking for the authorities who "know it all" to tell me the answers, I now look to well-trained, experienced

teachers to help me interpret what is happening and use their experience to offer suggestions.

I have had a few revelations about the direction of my curriculum during this time. It was a big leap to realize that I didn't need to present the curriculum in the order it's always done in second grade. I remember sitting in my writing class one night and saying to my small group, "You mean I don't have to teach adding, *then* subtracting, *then* trading?" At some point, after I decided that the direction of the curriculum had to come from the children, I also realized that it was okay for me to say, "Ah, this is what they are ready to do now. I can present a challenge to them, or introduce a topic, and look for their questions within that area, for there will surely be some."

The . . . Writing Project has played an important role in my course of change. The class gave me a reason to write about what was happening in my classroom, and the writing has had to be clear and understandable because other teachers were going to read it. Part of the way through the class, I realized that writing about my frustrations caused me to reflect on what had happened, and to even reflect on earlier reflections. This was part of what was making me feel different about these frustrations.

Meeting with a group of teachers each week helped me not only by giving me feedback on my writing but on the math that was happening in my class-room as well. It also gave me a chance to read and hear about what was going on in other classrooms. Developing this habit of reflecting and sharing has been a pivotal part of my change. It has struck me several times that these are pieces that are often missing from teacher education programs and from our daily pro-fessional lives, and for me, these were pieces that were essential.

I have also realized that I have a lot of work still ahead of me. If there had been easy answers, I would have gotten them and been done with it, but now every question raises a new question, and often even the answers raise questions. I just hope I've learned enough to figure out how to find the answers, and what to do with them once I've found them. (Schweitzer, 1996)

Several months into the school year Schweitzer recognized that she still had a lot of work ahead of her. In fact, she had started down a road that has no endpoint. Teachers who begin this process expecting to develop a finished repertoire of behaviors that, once achieved, will become routine, will be disappointed. Teaching this way is necessarily disruptive of routine, if for no other reason than that students will continually surprise us with their own discoveries. For many teachers, this implies a change in their rela-tionship to their own profession. Instead of concentrating on technique and strategy—keeping up with the latest trends—the new pedagogy means de-veloping an attitude of inquiry toward classroom process. That is, the ap-proach that Schweitzer has learned—to try out ideas in the classroom and analyze students' learnings—is not merely the means to her new practice, but is its essence. There is no point of arrival, but rather a path that leads on to further growth and change. For those who are willing to face the doubts, frustrations, and uncertainties inherent in a practice based on constructivism, that path is also filled with rewards and satisfactions.

Acknowledgment. This work was supported by the National Science Foundation under grants TPE-9050359 and ESI-9254393. Any opinions, findings, conclusions, or recommendations expressed in this chapter are those of the author and do not necessarily reflect the views of the National Science Foundation.

REFERENCES

Atwell, N. (1985). Writing and reading from the inside out. In J. Hansen, R. Newkirk, & D. Graves (Eds.), *Breaking Ground: Teachers relate reading and writing in the elementary school* (pp. 147–168). Portsmouth, NH: Heinemann.

Ball, D. L. (1993a). Halves, pieces, and twoths: Constructing representational contexts in teaching fractions. In T. P. Carpenter, E. Fennema, & T. Romberg (Eds.), *Rational numbers: An integration of research* (pp. 157–196). Hillsdale, NJ: Erlbaum.

Ball, D. L. (1993b). With an eye on the mathematical horizon: Dilemmas of teaching elementary school mathematics. *Elementary School Journal, 93*(4), 373–397.

Cobb, P. (1988). The tension between theories of learning and instruction in mathematics education. *Educational Psychologist, 23*(2), 97–103.

Cohen, D. K., Peterson, P. L., Wilson, S., Ball, D., Putnam, R., Prawat, R., Heaton, R., Remillard, J., & Wiemers, N. (1990). *Effects of state-level reform of elementary school mathematics curriculum on classroom practice* (Research Report 90-14). East Lansing, MI: The National Center for Research on Teacher Education and The Center for the Learning and Teaching of Elementary Subjects, College of Education, Michigan State University.

Confrey, J. (1991). Learning to listen: A student's understanding of powers of ten. In E. von Glasersfeld (Ed.), *Radical constructivism in mathematics education* (pp. 111–138). Dordrecht, Netherlands: Kluwer Academic Publishers.

Davis, P. J., & Hersh, R. (1980). *The mathematics experience.* Boston: Birkhaüser.

Davis, R. B., Maher, C. A., & Noddings, N. (Eds.). (1990). *Constructivist views of the teaching and learning of mathematics (Journal for Research in Mathematics Education* Monograph No. 4). Reston, VA: National Council of Teachers of Mathematics.

Duckworth, E. (1987). *"The having of wonderful ideas" and other essays on teaching and learning.* New York: Teachers College Press.

Ernest, P. (1991). *The philosophy of mathematics education: Studies in mathematics education.* London: Falmer.

Fosnot, C. T. (1989). *Enquiring teachers, enquiring learners: A constructivist approach for teaching.* New York: Teachers College Press.

Heaton, R. M. (1991, June). *Continuity and connectedness in teaching and research: A self-study of learning to teach mathematics for understanding.* Paper presented to the University of Pennsylvania Ethnography in Education Research Forum, Philadelphia, PA.

Hendry, A. (1996). Math in the social studies curriculum. In D. Schifter (Ed.), *What's happening in math class? Volume 1: Envisioning new practices through teacher narratives* (pp. 9–13). New York: Teachers College Press.

Hillocks, G., Jr. (1990). Teaching, reflecting, researching. In D. Daiker & M. Morenberg (Eds.), *The writing teacher as researcher: Essays in the theory and practice of class-based research* (pp. 15–29). Portsmouth, NH: Boynton/Cook Publishers, Heinemann.

Joyce, B. (Ed.). (1990). *Changing school culture through staff development.* Alexandria, VA: Association for Supervision and Curriculum Development.

Kamii, C. (1985). *Young children reinvent arithmetic: Implications of Piaget's theory.* New York: Teachers College Press.

Lakatos, I. (1976). *Proofs and refutations.* Cambridge, England: Cambridge University Press.

Lampert, M. (1988). The teacher's role in reinventing the meaning of mathematics knowing in the classroom. In M. J. Behr, C. B. Lacampagne, & M. M. Wheeler (Eds.), *Proceedings of the tenth annual meeting of the North American chapter of the International Group for the Psychology of Mathematics Education* (pp. 433–480). DeKalb: Northern Illinois University Press.

Lampert, M. (1989, March). Arithmetic as problem solving. *Arithmetic Teacher,* pp. 34–36.

Latour, B. (1987). *Science in action.* Cambridge, MA: Harvard University Press.

National Council of Teachers of Mathematics. (1989). *Curriculum and evaluation standards for school mathematics.* Reston, VA: Author.

National Council of Teachers of Mathematics. (1991). *Professional standards for teaching mathematics.* Reston, VA: Author.

National Council of Teachers of Mathematics. (2000). *Principles and standards for school mathematics.* Reston, VA: Author.

Piaget, J. (1972). *Psychology and epistemology: Towards a theory of knowledge.* Harmondsworth, England: Penguin.

Piaget, J. (1977). *The principles of genetic epistemology.* London: Routledge & Kegan Paul.

Schifter, D. (1993). Mathematics process as mathematics content: A course for teachers. *Journal of Mathematical Behavior, 12*(3), 271–283.

Schifter, D. (1994). *Voicing the new pedagogy: Teachers write about learning and teaching mathematics.* Center for the Development of Teaching Paper Series. Newton, MA: Education Development Center.

Schifter, D. (Ed.). (1996a). *What's happening in math class? Volume 1: Envisioning new practices through teacher narratives.* New York: Teachers College Press.

Schifter, D. (Ed.). (1996b). *What's happening in math class?. Volume 2: Reconstructing professional identities.* New York: Teachers College Press.

Schifter, D. (1998). Learning mathematics for teaching: From the teachers' seminar to the classroom. *Journal for Mathematics Teacher Education, 1*(1), 55–87.

Schifter, D. (1999). Envisioning new practices through teacher narratives. *New England Mathematics Journal, XXXI*(2), 18–28.

Schifter, D., & Fosnot, C. T. (1993). *Reconstructing mathematics education: Stories of teachers meeting the challenge of reform*. New York: Teachers College Press.

Schifter, D., Russell, S. J., & Bastable, V. (1999). Teaching to the big ideas. In M. Z. Solomon (Ed.), *The diagnostic teacher: Constructing new approaches to professional development* (pp. 22–47). New York: Teachers College Press.

Schifter, D., & Simon, M. A. (1992). Assessing teachers' development of a constructivist view of mathematics learning. *Teaching and Teacher Education, 8*(2), 187–197.

Schweitzer, K. (1996). The search for the perfect resource. In D. Schifter (Ed.). *What's happening in math class? Volume 2: Reconstructing professional identities* (pp. 47–65). New York: Teachers College Press.

Simon, M. A. (1989). The impact of intensive classroom follow-up in a constructivist mathematics teacher education program. Paper presented at the annual meeting of the American Education Research Association, San Francisco. (ERIC Document Reproduction Service No. ED 313 351)

Simon, M. A., & Schifter, D. E. (1991). Towards a constructivist perspective: An intervention study of mathematics teacher development. *Educational Studies in Mathematics, 22*, 309–331.

Tymoczko, T. (1986). *New directions in the philosophy of mathematics*. Boston: Birkhaüser.

von Glasersfeld, E. (1983). Learning as a constructive activity. In J. C. Bergeron & N. Herscovics (Eds.), *Proceedings of the fifth annual meeting of the North American chapter of the International Group for the Psychology of Mathematics Education* (pp. 41–69). Montreal: Université de Montréal, Faculté de Science de l'Éducation.

von Glasersfeld, E. (1990). An exposition on constructivism: Why some like it radical. In R. B. Davis, C. A. Maher, & N. Noddings (Eds.), *Constructivist views on the teaching and learning of mathematics (Journal for Research in Mathematics Education* Monograph No. 4). Reston, VA: National Council of Teachers of Mathematics.

CHAPTER 6

A Constructivist Perspective on Teaching and Learning in the Language Arts

June S.Gould

There are no workbooks or step-by-step guidebooks to a perfect literacy program. To facilitate real learning a teacher must provide a full-immersion approach to the language arts. Classrooms that are moving in this direction provide relevant, literate talk; real literature; spelling taught in context; and writing that grows out of children's interests, experiences, and expertise. Worksheets, canned teacher-proof lessons, assigned topics, and language arts textbooks have no place in these classrooms.

LITERATE ENVIRONMENTS

Constructivist frameworks challenge teachers to create innovative environments in which they and their students are encouraged to think and explore. For conceptual learning to occur, however, it is not enough to organize a classroom with language arts activities in which problems may be encountered. First, learners must play an active role in selecting and defining the activities, which must be both challenging and intrinsically motivating; second, there must be appropriate teacher support as learners build concepts, values, schemata, and problem-solving abilities.

Teaching this way, collaborating with pupils and negotiating the curriculum with them is not easy. It requires a considerable degree of flexibility and an ability and readiness to meet the needs of children by providing information and materials that children will be interested in and wish to pursue. It also demands a constant creative stance with children—receptivity to children's ideas and a willingness to take them seriously, even when, from an adult point of view, they seem naive or immature. At the same time, creating an authentic learning environment requires clear thinking and planning in relation to broad, long-term goals and imagination in finding specific themes, activities, and materials that will spark fresh interests and make connections between those that have already been developed.

Classrooms and schools that encourage the active construction of meaning have several characteristics: They focus on big ideas rather than facts; they encourage and empower students to follow their own interests, to make connections, to reformulate ideas, and to reach unique conclusions. Teachers and students in these classrooms are aware that the world is a complex place in which multiple perspectives exist and truth is often a matter of interpretation, and they acknowledge that learning and the process of assessing learning are intricate and require student and teacher interaction as well as time, documentation, and analyses by both teacher and students.

But does knowing each child and understanding his or her perspective in detail give us all the information we need to provide adequate classroom instruction? The social milieu of the classroom, the relationships between children one to the other and to the group must also be considered when we look at children's learning. The language arts are, in fact, highly social acts, but past instructional practices mistakenly conceived of them as solitary activities. In writing, for example, even if drafting is done alone, most real writing is part of a dialogue, one voice in an ongoing conversation in some larger community. When that conversation is one-sided because students simply write, turn in the paper, and get it back with a grade, we keep them from experiencing a major portion of the available learning experience. Social activities integrated into the language arts processes can actually lead to better writing, reading, and spelling (Graves, 1983), for the talking, sharing, and listening that occur pull down the barriers to communication and enhance the child's literacy growth (Amarel, 1987).

With a population as diverse as our own, we need to become more aware of both the social and cognitive dimensions of classroom activities. To facilitate real learning, we need to look closely at how children with different literacy backgrounds and understandings react to the activities we choose with and for them. Only then will we understand the classroom environment we can revise and reconstruct as we work to create more comfortable and effective classrooms for all students (Freedman, Dyson, Flower, & Chafe, 1985).

COLLABORATION, INTERACTION, AND QUESTIONING

To facilitate real learning, teachers need to organize their classrooms and their curriculum so that students can collaborate, interact, and raise questions of both classmates and the teacher. Crouse and Davey (1989), elementary school teachers, researched what happened in their classroom when they provided for student collaboration. They learned from their children that friendship was much more important to them than they had ever thought because being able to work with someone else made them feel confident and secure and enabled them to make and keep new friends. Children learned a great deal from one another, for together they could plan and organize and help each other with the mechanics of writing. But more significantly, they were able to help one another make "sense" of that writing. Finally, they learned that a certain type of environment fostered collaborative learning. This type of environment provided mobility so that they might be able to interact with their friends when they needed or wanted to. Materials needed to be handy for a variety of purposes. They needed to be free to choose their own topics and to manage their own time.

Teachers who want their students to collaborate and question need to create a safe community like Crouse and Davey's. Safety is brought about by teachers who have made a commitment to providing appropriate boundaries and dependable structures in order to enhance the potential for children both to work together and to ask their own questions. Children's questions are valuable because they help teachers understand where children are developmentally and are yet another window into how they understand literacy tasks and how they operate as learners. Unfortunately, most teachers barely tap into the potential of using children's questions to get a better glimpse of children's inner thoughts. By listening to children's questions over a number of episodes, and waiting for their answers before jumping in with another question or the answer, we can see patterns in children's approaches that help us stretch the child's thinking. The most important step for teachers who want to create a powerful learning environment is to facilitate the children's sense that they can trust that they can ask (Comber, 1988).

Heath (1983), Lindfors (1987), McLure and French (1981), and Wells (1986) point out to us that children ask few questions in a traditional classroom. In fact, the teacher's role is usually to ask the questions and the children's role is to answer them. Teachers who wish to create an atmosphere for questioning need to provide time and a safe haven for children's questions about literature, their own writing, and their classmates' writing. Helping students clarify and formulate their own questions, helping them to be able to state their own questions so they can be pursued on their level, and helping them in interpreting the results in light of their experience and other knowledge they have generated are the central tasks of the teacher.

COLLABORATIVE TALK, DIALOGUE, AND DEVELOPMENT

When we look at lessons as collaborative talk, our emphasis can be on both finding out where the children are and where we can stretch and challenge them to go further. Genishi, McCarrier, and Nussbaum indicate that "Our images of collaborative talk resemble voiceprints, which aren't straight at all but full of complex zigzags that form unique and interesting patterns" (1988, p. 190).

Teachers who talk with children about a piece of literature or writing need to give children a chance to explore half-formed ideas and to expand their understandings of their own writing or literature through hearing others' interpretations. The way a teacher listens and talks to children helps children become learners who think critically and deeply about what they read and write. Writing process workshops have been designed to model and facilitate collaborative talk. Writers are confirmed by the response which tells them that the text fits their intentions. First, the teacher provides an active response by confirming what he or she has heard and by asking a few clarifying questions. Second, the teacher helps the entire class to learn the same procedure during group share time. Each writing period ends with two or three children sharing their pieces with the group while the group follows the discipline of confirming, through pointing to what is in the text and then asking questions to learn more about what the child has written. All of these responses, whether by the teacher or the other children, are geared to help writers learn to listen to their own words, their own ideas, their own texts (Graves, 1983).

A language arts classroom that facilitates a child's development through collaborative talk and dialogue is carefully planned and organized by the teacher, but the curriculum is negotiated and enacted by everyone. "The soul of enactment is the dialogues in which teachers and children inform, err, question, correct, self correct, think aloud, repeat, make sense—in other words, develop together" (Genishi, McCarrier, & Nussbaum, 1988, p. 190).

But in order to create a classroom where curriculum is negotiated, teachers have to give up some old habits. Most teachers are used to informing and asking questions. We need to give children "wait" time (Rowe, 1986). Instead of telling children what to do, we need to react sensitively and intelligently to what the child tells us. But what do teachers need to know so they can intelligently react? A critical part of the give-and-take during conferring consists of the teacher's interpretations of children's actual and potential levels of development, his or her own judgments of where children are and where they might go. Wells and Chang-Wells (1992) call this "leading from behind." It is precisely through frequently engaging in collaborative talk that the teacher is able to increase his or her understanding of children's thinking in general (Duckworth, 1987), and it is only by engaging in such talk with a particular learner while he or she is engaged on a specific task that the teacher can become knowledgeable about that learner's purposes and current state of understanding, and thus be able to make his or her contributions contingently responsive to the learner's needs (Wells, 1986).

SCAFFOLDING: ASSISTING GROWTH

Facilitating a child's development demands new ways to look at and work with children. While we may not be able to explain exactly how learning takes place, we do know that the availability of "scaffolding" in the moment it is needed has an important part to play. Scaffolding is a temporary framework that assists the child's growth. As the child develops, the scaffolding changes.

When I confer with children, I use a scaffolding procedure that I have adapted from Graves (1983). The conference is consistently predictable, that is, the child is able to predict what will happen in the conference. The conference is focused on only one or two features of the child's piece and is designed to help solve the child's problem. The conference is supportive of children's questioning. There is shared responsibility as well as elements of fun, exploration, and adventure.

Calkins (1986) uses mini-lessons as a scaffolding process that is grounded in modeling theory, direct instruction, and developmental theory (Bruner & Ratner, 1978; Cazden, 1988; Graves, 1983). Mini-lessons, which are about five to seven minutes long, are conducted by the teacher at the beginning of writers' and readers' workshops. They give students a strategy they can use often without the expectation that they will integrate the suggested strategy on the day it is given to them (Calkins, 1986). The information or strategies the teacher gives to the children in the mini-lesson contradicts what the child thinks is good enough writing. They perturb the child. They add information that causes the child to experience errors or insufficiencies in his or her own writing. For example, a second-grade teacher may teach the concept of focus over and over again in many different ways and over a period of six months. He or she might discuss how an author focused a story, share a focused story that someone in the class has written, or might show a sample of his or her own unfocused story and its revisions. For second graders who believe everything has equal weight in a story and who find it difficult to focus on the most important points in their stories, these new strategies may foster contradictions to the child's present understandings, making them insufficient, and thus perturbing and disequilibrating structures and facilitating accommodation. Mini-lessons provide for those moments when the teacher takes the child by the hand and participates with him or her in the jointly constructed potential level of performance (Bruner, 1978 and Cambourne, 1988; cited in Bickmore-Brand & Gawned, 1993).

PEER COLLABORATION

In most cases, the participants in collaborative talk are of approximately equal status, each able to take the role of either facilitator or student and to benefit accordingly. Typically, the purposes of the peer interaction are achieved when the task is completed, or at least when the student is able to continue with the next step. However, the benefits of collaborative talk need not be limited to the function of facilitating achievement of the task. Where one of the participants has greater expertise than the other, he or she can engage in interaction with the learner about the task with the deliberate intention of enabling the learner to acquire some procedure, knowledge, or skill that will be useful in other situations beyond that in which he or she is currently engaged.

Equally important is the help collaboration with another child can provide in enabling the learner to marshal and exploit resources he or she already has available, but over which he or she does not yet have explicit and conscious control (Karmiloff-Smith, 1979). What all collaborative talk has in common is that one of the participants has a goal that he or she would like to achieve and the other participant engages in talk that helps the first to achieve that goal (Wells & Chang-Wells, 1992).

Many teachers who are trying to foster collaboration between students have used the following scaffolding for peer conferences in writing:

- The writer reads aloud.
- Listeners respond, or if the piece is confusing, the listeners ask questions, then respond.
- Listeners focus on the content, perhaps asking questions about it. The writer teaches them about the subject.
- The focus shifts to the text. What will the writer do next and how will he or she do it?

Calkins (1986) points out that we must be cautious about emphasizing the skills of peer conferences. She worries that responses can become canned and mechanical; children perform on cue and act a part. We need to keep sight of why we want children to collaborate with one another. Peer conferences need to be about helping children connect with another human being in order to learn from him or her, to empathize, to hear peers' stories and to understand their own stories more fully, to care about another person's interpretation of the world, and to be able to identify and respond to another person's perspective. In Calkins' words, "Perhaps the best way to extend peer conferences is by participating in them: listening, modeling, and gently guiding" (1986, p. 132).

ERRORS: WINDOWS ON DEVELOPMENT

Errors need to be perceived as a result of learners' conceptions and therefore not minimized or avoided. Teachers who listen effectively and gather information regarding children's cognitive and affective functioning help structure the opportunity for children's understandings, but it is the student's own reflective abstractions that create the new understanding in both writing and spelling.

By adult standards, the hypotheses and strategies children form may appear to be mistakes or errors, but Ferreiro and Teberosky (1982) have found that children's development follows a broadly common sequence of development. With the benefit of appropriate experiences, their hypotheses and strategies are ultimately superseded by more conventional ones.

An awareness of spelling, writing, and reading development, as well as the so-called errors children make, can help teachers plan instruction. When teachers observe children's learning, stages of development emerge. Observers, therefore, need to find frameworks in order to organize the information they have gathered. Developmental stages are continuously being examined by scholars and are, therefore, still tentative, but they do offer teachers a way to shape their interactive teaching goals with students. With a schema for children's development in writing, spelling, or reading in mind, a teacher can judge errors as indicators of current functioning level and can determine how to provide the appropriate scaffolding in dialogue over the language arts.

OWNERSHIP, POINTS OF VIEW, AND DECENTERING

Recognition that the construction of knowledge is an active process that each individual learner must carry out has led to a greater emphasis placed on "ownership" of the activities through which learning is intended to take place. This requires that learners be given a share in the responsibility for selecting the tasks in which they engage, for deciding on the means to be employed in carrying them out, and for evaluating the outcomes. Only in this way can they gain an active understanding of the principles involved and of the procedures that may be effective in achieving the desired outcome. Another important reason for encouraging learners to take ownership of learning tasks is that it increases intrinsic motivation to seek and carry through a way of finishing a piece successfully (Wells & Chang-Wells, 1992). Graves (1983) concurs. He states that the data show that writers who learn to choose topics that are most meaningful to them make the most significant growth in both information and skills. By choosing the best topic, children exercise their strongest control, establish ownership, and, with ownership, gain pride in their pieces.

Unfortunately, many teachers view their children's lives as interfering with classroom business-as-usual (Goodlad, 1984). But when children choose to write about their own interests, ideas, experiences, memories, and knowledge, they are expressing their point of view about the world they inhabit and their concepts about that world. I agree with Wells and Chang-Wells when they say:

> Each student's point of view is an instructional entry point that sits at the gateway of personalized education. Teachers who operate without awareness of their students' points of view often doom students to dull, irrelevant experiences, and even failure. (p. 60)

Instruction begins with the child's ideas, hypotheses, strategies, not the product he or she presents to us. We do not want the product—the writing, spelling or reading—to improve without the child's learning something that will help on another day; otherwise, our conversation will have been a waste of everyone's time. Further, a conversation on a product, rather than an idea, may even be quite negative because it tends to make students dependent on our corrections.

There are many ways in which, without meaning to do so, ownership may be taken away from a child in a conversation about his or her work. Sometimes, for example, teachers may stare at the paper the child reads, looking for mistakes rather than listening to what the child is trying to say. Sometimes I find myself reading a student's first line and wanting desperately to have him or her move it to the end of the piece, or I have heard teachers tell children they cannot write about dinosaurs or their sister because they have already written about these topics. Sometimes, before the conference even starts, I know that I want a student to add details. These may seem trivial, but we must become more aware of the kinds of actions we take. They communicate to children that underneath our words, we still want to be in total control.

The teacher's role, both in words and deed, must be to find as many ways as possible for students to express their points of view verbally and in their writing, to reveal themselves and their conceptions, to reflect on their conceptions, but also to enable children to grow intellectually, socially, and emotionally. All of us learn by making choices. We scan our lives and we decide what to write about. Unfortunately, in many American classrooms, the teacher focuses on a unit of study, a textbook, mastery outcomes, the upcoming report card, or what next year's teacher will think about the child. In the meantime, children come to school with their own concerns: a divorce, illness, fear of abandonment or displacement, abuse, misconceptions, superstitions, dreams, and hopes. Unfortunately, the two agendas, the teacher's and the child's, are often emotionally and intellectually a universe apart and this disempowers both the teacher and the child. Greene writes:

> What empowers—what ought to empower—is the recognition that there is no "reality" that is unquestionably given, the same for everyone . . . we can help children realize that reality must be understood as interpreted experience, that there can be multiple perspectives and multiple interpretations . . . a reciprocity of perspectives. (1986, p. 782)

Andy, a third grader, writes about how his bike was stolen and how he cried and cried. His family is too poor to buy him another one this year. He wants his story to be "so good that it will make my Dad feel sorry for me and he'll buy me another bike soon." Doug writes about being kicked out of his mother's car and left in a parking lot because he fought with his sister. He was terrified. He says, "I want to finish my story and make it sound like a real book because I want to get even with my sister." Leah writes about how much she misses her friends in Moscow. She is only 10, but she uses writing as a way to deal with a deeply tragic issue—the loss of her homeland, her first language, and her friends. She revises her writing because she wants to "get my sad feelings out." Mem Fox (1988) says, "Those of us who write best have most power and therefore have most control over our lives" (p. 123).

Decentering from first-hand experience, representing experiences and ideas with words, stories, and pictures about oneself allows the creation of "semiotic spaces" (Wertsch, 1991) where children can negotiate meaning. But there can be no decentering unless the writer first sees a problem, an imbalance; the writer pulls off center because he or she wants another look (Graves, 1983). Decentering implies a moving away from the center but also being aware of where to stand, what to look at. When I write I place myself far enough away to see the problem at a distance. I circle my piece from different vantage points, I take multiple views and perspectives on my work—the view of an audience of peers, of an editor, of my favorite colleagues, of the opposition. I give myself both space and time to help me deal with the problem: I return to my original intention in writing or reread my material one more time with all the other views in mind, but with my own view strengthened. The process is the same for children, too. Writing is a way to make meaning in our lives, and it takes time.

CONCLUSION

Recent research has transformed our definition of literacy and now offers insights into how to create classroom communities of literate thinkers. Literacy develops in response to personal and social needs. It is an extension of speaking, listening, and interacting with one's environment. It is a state of becoming, not a point to be reached. It is functional, real and relevant, and involves an active construing and interpreting of ongoing and changeable texts, not a simple absorption of rules and models.

Teachers informed by the new constructivist theories seek to support learning, not control it. They further inquiry, not orthodoxy. They continuously evaluate themselves, their students, and the system in which they teach. They collaborate with their students and encourage them to collaborate, not to compete, with one another. Rather than waiting for a child to be "ready" or the right age to begin, teachers instead create opportunities for children to participate in joint literacy events with other, more mature members of the literate community. They become planners, models, guides, observers of development, facilitators, and challengers to children's existing personal models of the world. Instead of using a finite list of language arts skills as a curriculum, teachers informed by the new constructivist theories know that learning to write, spell, read, and speak are never-ending processes of meaning-making.

REFERENCES

Amarel, M. (1987). Research currents: The classroom collective—We, them, or it. *Language Arts, 64*(5), 532–538.

Bickmore-Brand, J., & Gawned, S. (1993). Scaffolding for improved understanding. In J. Bickmore-Brand (Ed.), *Language in mathematics* (pp. 43–48). Portsmouth, NH: Heinemann.

Bruner, J. S. (1978). The role of dialogue in language acquisition. In A. Sinclair, R. J. Jarvella, W. J. M. Levelt (Eds.), *The child's conception of language*. New York: Springer-Verlag.

Bruner, J., & Ratner, N. (1978). Games, social exchange and the acquisition of language. *Journal of Child Language, 5*(1), 391–401.

Calkins, L. M. (1986). *The art of teaching writing*. Portsmouth, NH: Heinemann.

Cambourne, B. (1988). *The whole story: Natural learning and the acquisition of literacy in the classroom*. Gosford, New Zealand: Ashton Scholastic.

Cazden, C. B. (1988). *Classroom discourse: The language of teaching and learning*. Portsmouth, NH: Heinemann.

Comber, B. (1988). Any questions? Any problems? Inviting children's questions and requests for help. *Language Arts, 65*(2), 147–153.

Crouse, P., & Davey, M. (1989). Collaborative learning: Insights from our children. *Language Arts, 66*(7), 756–766.

Duckworth, E. (1987). *The having of wonderful ideas and other essays on teaching and learning*. New York: Teachers College Press.

Ferreiro, E., & Teberosky, A. (1982). *Literacy before schooling*. Portsmouth, NH: Heinemann.

Fox, M. (1988). Notes from the battlefield: Toward a theory of why people write. *Language Arts, 65*(7), 111–125.

Freedman, W. A., Dyson, H., Flower, L., & Chafe, W. (1985). Mission statement. A proposal to establish a center for the study of writing. Submitted to National Institute of Education, Washington, DC.

Genishi, C., McCarrier, A., & Nussbaum, R. N. (1988). Research currents: Dialogue as a context for teaching and learning. *Language Arts, 65,* 182–190.

Goodlad, J. I. (1984). *A place called school*. New York: McGraw-Hill.

Graves, D. H. (1983). *Writing: Teachers and children at work*. Portsmouth, NH: Heinemann.

Greene, M. (1986). Landscapes and meanings. *Language Arts, 63*(8), 776–784.

Heath, S. B. (1983). *Ways with words: Language, life, and work in communities and classrooms*. Cambridge, England: Cambridge University Press.

Karmiloff-Smith, A. (1979). Micro- and macro-developmental changes in language acquisition and other representational systems. *Cognitive Science, 3,* 91–118.

Lindfors, J. W. (1987). *Children's language and learning* (2nd ed.). Englewood Cliffs, NJ: Prentice-Hall.

McLure, M., & French, P. (1981). A comparison of talk at home and at school. In G. Wells (Ed.), *Learning through interaction: The study of language development*. Cambridge, England: Cambridge University Press.

Rowe, M. B. (1986, January/February). Wait time: Slowing down may be a way of speeding up! *Journal of Teacher Education, 37*(1), 43–50.

Wells, G. (1986). *The meaning makers: Children learning language and using language to learn*. Portsmouth, NH: Heinemann.

Wells, G., & Chang-Wells, G. L. (1992). *Constructing knowledge together: Classrooms of inquiry and literacy*. Portsmouth, NH: Heinemann.

Wertsch, J. V. (1991). *Voices of the mind: A sociocultural approach to mediated action*. Cambridge, MA: Harvard University Press.

CHAPTER 7

A Constructivist Perspective on
Teaching and Learning in the Arts

Maxine Greene

From the vantage points of our several fields of study, we speak of making meanings today, not of finding or unearthing them. We speak of interpreting texts, not simply of describing or analyzing them; we speak of reading paintings, not simply of detecting in them renderings of what lies outside. We ponder the form-giving and generative powers of consciousness and language; we probe the significance of persons articulating what they think of as their shared "realities." To explore the implications of constructivism, particularly in the domains of the artistic-aesthetic, is to reject the idea that "truth" corresponds to some objective state of things. It is, in fact, to refuse the notion of an objectively meaningful world, as it is to refuse visions of a self-sufficiently and idealized "real." It is to challenge familiar dualisms and either/ors that have haunted cognition over the centuries.

In this chapter, unlike in some of the foregoing, we will take a philosophical approach to constructivism. The explorations undertaken by Jean Piaget, Lev Vygotsky, and others who provided the foundations of constructivism through their work in cognitive psychology cannot but be held in mind in the course of this discussion. For John Dewey, "knowledge, grounded knowledge is science; it represents objects which have been settled, ordered, disposed of rationally" (1916, p. 380). Beginning in hypothetical and deliberative thinking, carried on in collaborative communities, science signified for him intelligence working at its most effective and responsible level. Surely he would have said as much with regard to the psychologists who developed the ideas associated with constructivism. But, for most of his life, he wrote and taught in the field of philosophy of education. "Philosophy," he wrote, "is thinking what the known demands of us—what responsive attitude it exacts. It is an idea of what is possible, not a record of accomplished fact" (1916, p. 381). It is, he went on, an assignment of something to be done; its primary value lies "in defining difficulties and suggesting methods for dealing with them. Philosophy might almost be described as thinking which has become conscious of itself" (1916, p. 381).

In the course of this chapter, with its focus on the arts, notions having to do with the construction of meaning, with contingency, with interpretation, will not be conceived of as inferences to be drawn from constructivist concepts. Nor will they be treated simply as the fruits of constructivist thought. In my view, a whole variety of streams have fed into what is now called constructivism: currents of thought since the days of the great romantics with *their* distinctive concern for the role played by human mind or consciousness or spirit in sense-making by means of transactions with the impinging world. They have clustered into an attack on objectivity, on instrumental rationality, on disembodied abstract ways of defining meaning— against a usually empty sky. Existentialism, phenomenology, interpretivism, experientialism, certain modes of idealism: These have been the sources of constructivist thinking, particularly (to use Richard Rorty's words) since philosophy has gradually receded from its position as the "mirror of nature" (1979) and traditional conceptions of knowledge-getting have given way to hermeneutic conceptions, to efforts to *understand* rather than to know, to acknowledgment that there are many vantage points that may not come together on a common ground.

In the case of teachers in the arts and humanities whose thinking has become "conscious of itself," this demands a special kind of thoughtfulness. No longer expected to present their students with a given heritage or tradition as something self-existent and fully formed, they must ponder the sources of their own understanding in order to grasp what it signifies to move others to engage with *Hamlet*, say, or da Vinci's *The Last Supper*, or George Eliot's *Middlemarch*, or Toni Morrison's *Beloved*. An engagement, a conversation, a quest are required if the student is to make such works objects of her experience, if she is to achieve them as meaningful in some manner that connects with her life. As we shall come to see, encounters with the arts become in some fashion paradigmatic when we recall Piaget's emphasis on assimilation and accommodation in connection with symbolic play and drawing as a semiotic function (Gruber & Vonneche, 1977). The move from a dependence on one's own logical and other structures to a desire to move beyond, to break with the ordinary is characteristic of the aesthetic experience. Lending her life, for example, to Hamlet or Ophelia in bringing their illusioned world into existence, the reader is reshaping her own experience, making connections, opening perspectives, and, by so doing, making meanings by constructing a new "reality" that in time will reconstruct her own. We shall be talking of the focal role of imagination in all this, or the cognitive capacity to constitute "as/if" worlds, to move into provinces of meaning beyond the provinces of "common sense."

Exploring constructivism through examination of various kinds of encounters with the several arts, the writer presumes a certain experience of creativity as new perspectives open for people willing to participate in paintings, dances, musical performances, novels, poems, and the like. This does not, however, exclude from consideration what is sometimes called the "production" aspect of the arts, or art education. There appears to be no question but that, as Goodnow has written, "graphic work" may be regarded as "visible thinking." The features it displays, she went on, "—thrift, conservatism, principles of organization and sequence—are features of all problem-solving, whether by children or adults" (1977, p. 145). Emphasizing the ways in which children tend to create equivalents rather than replicas of what they actually perceive, and the ways in which the medium they use affects what they create, Goodnow clearly took a constructivist approach to the problem of children's drawing. She did not, however, treat the drawings whose sequences and schemata she was describing as works of art. Ellen Winner (1982) takes what is for me a helpful position on the matter of "children's art" when she talks about the development of control over the so-called symptoms of the aesthetic, repleteness and expression, in the following:

> Repleteness refers to the fact that in a work of art, relatively more aspects of the symbol "count" than in a non-art object. And expression refers to the psychological states and sensory qualities metaphorically conveyed by a work of art. While children's drawing appears replete and expressive to adults, it is possible that the children themselves are unaware of these aesthetic symptoms. The quality of the line, for example, may have been produced quite accidentally, perhaps as a result of the pressure they enjoy exerting with their arm. Similarly, a painting that strikes adults as expressing joy, such as a brightly colored picture with yellow daubs of paint, may express this mood unintentionally. (1982, p. 170)

Kindred points can be made with reference to the other arts or symbol systems. Aware though we are that prodigies do appear, we are not going to deal with them or their development in this chapter. Granting the difficulty of defining "art" in any satisfactory way, we are nonetheless going to create some boundaries, one of them having to do with a degree of intentionality on the part of the creator of a work of art, another having to do with the consciousness of the choices he or she makes, still another having to do with the maker's acquaintance with the tradition or with what is called the "art world," stretching back (as it does) in time.

Yes, children do create meanings by using paint brushes, pieces of chalk, triangles, gongs, by making shapes with their bodies in time and space. They construct what are accepted as "unreal" worlds by improvising in theatrical spaces; coming together, they often engage in the construction of distinctive social realities that they can comfortably inhabit, while such realities remain unrecognizable by those "outside." And, obviously, children (like adults) often learn to "see" other people differently because of roles they have played or because of interchanges with people playing different roles. We need only think what it would mean to be playing Tybalt and to listen to Mercutio's dying speech in *Romeo and Juliet*. Or we might recall occasions when young people made street people out of *papier-mâché* and installed them in fabricated doorways or against graffiti-covered walls in the back of the classroom. Or we might summon up the photographs children in *Shooting Back* (Hubbard, 1991) take with their own cameras: pictures of abandonment, of hotel corridors, of drug dealers on city corners, of baby brothers drinking milk on sodden carpets, of friends suddenly leaping from broken chairs into the sun. All these might be viewed as adventures into meaning or into the modes there are of structuring what is sensed in the world around. What is produced is seldom to be called "art" in any serious mode, but they prepare landscapes in this fashion for later engagements with artworks and, perhaps, launching spaces for those who might in fact struggle to make "art."

What children make, what they put on exhibition and account for in their portfolios, must be granted respect and regard (Ernst, 1993). The learning they accomplish in media other than verbal language must be attended to as seriously as learning with basal readers used to be. The journals young people keep, the essays they write in "whole language," and other such classes must be seen as significant, not merely as a means for attaining "outcomes." To assert that, in an average public school or high school class, very few sound like Virginia Woolf, or irradiate their pages as Miro did, or move like an Alvin Ailey dancer, is not in any manner to denigrate what they are doing. To do otherwise—to place their work lower on some invisible scale or hierarchy because it does not rank with Woolf's or Miro's or Ailey's—would be (outside of professional art schools) unconscionable.

Mikel Dufrenne has reminded us of the ways in which traditional art offered an immediate expression of a culture experienced as a whole by a totality of people. Given over to divine worship, it celebrated a sacred element pervading the life of the community. Then, he wrote, this embodiment of art "an art which did not regard itself as such, which is only recognized by us now—finds expression chiefly in archaic society." For Dufrenne, art as we think of it appeared in its autonomy only when the totality of unified culture disintegrated. "Then are the words 'art' and 'artist' invented, and art becomes reflected through the artist and affirms itself as art" (1978, p. 4). It follows that what we conceive of as the realm of the artistic-aesthetic is itself a constructed reality. The way in which we construct it partially accounts for our giving the arts a special *cachet* (despite their frequent neglect in the schools) and thinking of them in relation to particularly gifted individuals with a variety of often inborn talents, strengths, intelligences. Along with this, however, goes the belief in the capacity of such persons to work with materials and symbol systems, as well as their own perceptions of and feelings about the world, in such a fashion as to enable others to see, to feel, to discover, to "unconceal" (Heidegger, 1971), to experience consummations and epiphanies never known before.

Balinese culture and a number of African cultures do not construct their artistic-aesthetic realities in the same fashion; nor, very often, do they view artistic production as something carried out by autonomous individuals whose works, no matter how embedded in traditions, are in some sense singular, unique. We have been reminded by Clifford Geertz about the great range of semiotic systems (made up of signs we call aesthetic) in different cultures. There is always a problem involved in placing art within other modes of social activity,

> how to incorporate it into the texture of a particular pattern of life. And such placing, the giving to art objects a cultural significance, is always a local matter; what art is in classical China or classical Islam, what it is in the pueblo southwest or highland New Guinea, is just not the same thing, no matter how universal the intrinsic qualities that actualize its emotional power . . . may be. The variety that anthropologists have come to expect in the spirit beliefs, the classification systems, or the kinship structures of different peoples, and not just in their immediate shapes but in the way of being-in-the-world they both promote and exemplify, extends as well to their drummings, carvings, chants, and dances. (1983, p. 97)

Made aware in this fashion of cultural diversity where the arts are concerned, we are also made to realize how relevant constructivist theories have come to be. Even if we think in terms of universal or intrinsic qualities (which few do in these times), we are still required to be informed enough about the craft dimension, the symbol systems, the religious and wider cultural significance involved to take them into account as we try to engage with works of art from other cultures from our own vantage points and from the perspective of our locations in the world. To stress the "local" character of the decisions made is to suggest that we, too, must probably begin with the local, the immediate—always with some consciousness that our constructs are not the only ones, that our approaches to aesthetics must always be interpretive and provisional.

Even as this is said, we must reiterate the idea that representations (in painting, sound, the body in motion, prose, film) are always to some degree provisional, no matter what the symbol system involved. Those who take a constructivist position will reject the notion that there exists a representable set of phenomena the same for everyone. In other words, we do not assume that the mountain rising in the Provençal landscape looks precisely the same to any one with normal vision and demands identical renderings from those claiming the skills necessary for representing what they see. Each of us, traveler or professional painter or inhabitant of a Provençal village, constructs that mountain as meaningful (or majestic, or beautiful, or threatening) in the light of present and past transactions between our consciousness and the sun-struck, many-faceted world. We do not expect literary texts to represent "truly" what is objectively the case with respect to the captain of a whaling ship in the nineteenth century, or a young woman caught up in moneyed society and destroyed by her own self-regard as much as by the system or the machine, or a southern African-American seeking "visibility" in an indifferent northern world. We know that, in decoding *Moby Dick* or *The House of Mirth* or *Invisible Man*, we are in some sense reading the texts of our own lived lives. We distinguish now between our attending or our reading and that of the ostensibly "unbiased" or "clear-sighted" or "objective," ordinarily white males. It may be remembered that males were long thought to have a clearer vision of the "truth" because of their capacity to break free of relationships, responsibility, embeddedness. They were thought capable of rising above, of transcending, and (by doing so) contemplating from afar what was "really" there. Theirs was not, quite obviously, a constructivist vision; but it was long defended as *the* vision, the means of attaining objective "truth."

Abandoning such a conception, we are abandoning many of the familiar hierarchies. Not only are we wondering at the arbitrary way in which knowledge has been linked with power. We are driven to questioning more and more intensely the splits between subjects and objects, between consciousness and the appearances of things. We are driven to take renewed issue with such oppositions as the "cognitive" to the "affective," the "male" to the "female," the "black" to the "white." Jacques Derrida (1978), who has made so clear the ways in which our thinking has been structured by means of such oppositions, also helps us see how statements making use of them subordinate one term to the other, usually the right-hand term to the left-hand one. As we reject dualisms, of course, and these kinds of splits and fragmentations, we also treat monologisms as suspect: domination by a single voice, a single belief system that defines the "given" and determines what is "real" with a universalist intent. Along with such rejections goes a questioning of what is presented as canonical in the humanities and the several arts.

The kinds of learning sought, in consequence, are active, reflective, and interpretive. Because of resistance to the one-dimensional and the single perspective, learning is thought to be fundamentally dialogical. Infused by an ongoing conversation surrounding learners in the present and reaching back into the past, learning of this sort involves multiple modes of sense-making. Clifford Geertz (1983), for one, calls multiplicity "the hallmark of modern consciousness" (p. 161). Howard Gardner (1983) offers a psychological warranty when he discusses his theory of "multiple intelligences." When applied to child development and education, it presupposes Lev Vygotsky's (1978) view of "a specific social nature and a process by which children grow into the intellectual life of those around them" (p. 87). In the realm of the arts, as in other realms of meaning, learning goes on most fruitfully in atmospheres of interchange and shared discoveries. There must be those who can point out what is not yet noticed, not yet heard, people who can provoke the young to reach beyond where they are. To reach beyond is to realize that there exist a tradition and a community of knowers, of seekers, none of whom has the final answer to any question, all of whom are engaged in a communal construction of knowledge. It is as much social as it is individual, as much part of a culture as it is personally, privately constructed.

When active learners find themselves reaching beyond to wonder and imagine, they may find themselves deliberately constructing worlds. This does not mean a solipsistic building, something they conduct in some interior place. John Dewey and other philosophers have asserted repeatedly that there is no "inner world" somehow set off against the social and the natural. Again, the constructivist thinker affirms and celebrates the transactional relation, the continuity. It is doubtful that a person can become a poet if she or he does not possess a consciousness of participation in an appearing or a sounding landscape surrounding her or him, entering her or his lived life.

A glance at Elizabeth Bishop's work reminds us of the attention a poet is provoked to pay to "the malignant movies, the taxicabs and injustices at large," to the "rain that beats on the roof of the house . . . foretold by the almanac, but only known to a grandmother," to the "pink Seurat bathers" dipping in and out of the swimming pool (1983, p. 83). She cannot disengage herself from what she perceives, feels, struggles to know. She might well have said with Dewey (1916) that the "self achieves mind in the degree in which knowledge of things is incarnate in the life around . . . ; the self is not a separate mind building up knowledge anew on its own account" (p. 344). For Dewey (1934), mind is a means of transforming, reorganizing, reshaping accepted meanings and values, a means of attending to "the lived situations of life" (p. 263). Mind is active, he kept reminding his readers, a "verb" and not a "noun"; and the poet might have to say the same.

Suspecting that, we find many relevances in Elizabeth Bishop's (1983) "January First." It begins:

> The year's doors open
> like those of language,
> towards the unknown.
> Last night you told me:
> > Tomorrow
> We shall have to think up signs,
> sketch a landscape, fabricate a plan
> on the double page
> of day and paper.
> Tomorrow, we shall have to invent,
> once more,
> the reality of this world (p. 273).

Because this is a selection from a work of literary art and not an essay on poetry, we cannot paraphrase or simply describe what it says in the hope that, by so doing, we will be communicating what the poem "means." Nor can we use or refer to what we think Bishop is saying or use it as an argument with a degree of validity. We cannot, given the way so many think of poetry today, posit an independent, autonomous text replete with immanent meanings, ready to be mined by those who know enough to analyze, to criticize, to decode. We cannot posit a paradigmatic "reader," somehow removed from time and change—or untrammeled by class, gender, or ethnic factors. We realize that there must be a process of interpretation and that interpretation can only be undertaken by a situated person with a particular perspective. Stanley Fish (1980) writes that pure description has become nearly impossible and that interpretation is focal when it comes to engagement with all sorts of texts. This presumes the construction of meanings, not the uncovering of them.

The construction of meanings, or the achievement of the Bishop poem as meaningful, is not wholly arbitrary. There cannot be an infinite variety of meanings, not for those who have learned to attend. Fish, who insists there is no immanent meaning within a text, does admit that there are common interpretative strategies among those who are members of a "community of interpretation" (1980), often emergent from particular departments of literature. We may associate this with what Clifford Geertz says about symbol systems or semiotic systems developing in different cultures. Surely we can see the connection between such communities and the codes used in constructing the social realities we share. Wolfgang Iser (1980), who has developed a "reception theory" with regard to reading, writes about the importance of familiarity with the codes that govern the ways in which works of fiction produce meanings. Very often these codes are in tension with the habits and logical structures a reader brings to her or his reading. We are brought back to Piaget's notion of assimilation when we observe how, in the course of increasingly informed reading, routine beliefs and habits of perception are transformed. Iser describes the ways in which "by gestalt-forming, we actually participate in the text, and this means that we are caught up in the very thing we are producing. This is why we often have the impression, as we read, that we are leading another life" (p. 127). The meanings we discover are those we ourselves produce; and it is this mode of reaction, says Iser, "that, in fact, enables us to experience the text as an actual event" (pp. 128–129). We begin to understand in novel ways; very often, we modify our consciousness of our own identities by means of our readings; and the very construction of our world may be changed.

We impart a resonant reality to Captain Ahab's fated journey in quest of the white whale and at once remake our own lived realities. It may take a deliberate effort to reconcile a shimmering vision of Mrs. Ramsay and her son viewed through a window with the outline of a lighthouse in the clouds (seen by an academic husband and father who thinks in terms of e's, y's, and z's). We may discover there is no reconciliation, that the tension between window and lighthouse persists for us. Still seeking, still making meanings, we may go on a journey to the vivid streets of Harlem in New York, with the sounds of golden horns in the distance, a dead girl in a casket, a memory of a lost mother in the distant South. It may require texts like *Moby Dick* and *To the Lighthouse* and *Jazz*; it may demand the kind of readers willing to lend Ishmael and Mrs. Ramsay and Joe Trace or Violet Trace their lives. Robert Scholes (1989) writes:

> Reading is always, at once, the effort to comprehend and the effort to incorporate. I must invent the author, invent his or her intentions, using the evidence I can find to stimulate my creative process (a stimulation achieved in part by offering restrictions on that process, to be sure). I must also incorporate the text I am reading in my own textual repertory. (p. 9)

Louise Rosenblatt (1978), even earlier, was talking about the significance of reader experience and the transactions that moved readers to make meanings, as it made possible authentically aesthetic encounters.

These points of view—call them "reader response" or "reception theory"—focus on the achievement of meanings through literary experiences.

The more difference there is among interpretations, the more contesting there is among likely meanings, the more conscious will be the construction process. Going back to the Bishop poem for the moment, we can see what this signifies. Most readers will agree that metaphors are deeply important when it comes to the creation of meaning, perhaps especially in a poem. They release unexpected meanings by bringing together very different notions whose difference makes certain things clear that were never clear before. For Northrop Frye (1968), the use of metaphor ("really saying 'this is that'") is a way of showing a world "completely absorbed and possessed by the human mind" (p. 33). (Even to utter words like that is to suggest what the construction of reality can mean.) Metaphor is the enemy of the abstract, writes Cynthia Ozick (1989): "It inhabits language as its most concrete" (p. 282). It has to do with the power of connection; it has a transforming effect; by means of it, writers alter our being and becoming. For Mary Warnock (1978), metaphor has to do with "seeing, hearing, tasting; interpreting what we see, hear, or taste as of a particular kind; interpreting as signifying something beyond itself, perhaps something other than the kind of which it is a member; creating it as symbolic; using symbols to suggest meanings and thought to others" (p. 183).

Looking at the Bishop poem, we may not agree precisely on what is summoned up by "doors." Of course, in our dominant culture, the first day of the New Year is celebrated on January 1; aware of that, we will not find it too hard to associate to such a beginning. If we are not aware of it, if the day is not a holiday, other meanings may be released. When it comes to the comparison between the doors of the year and the doors of language, differences may multiply. For some, the thought that we do not know what we think until we say or write it may surge to the surface. For others, what Toni Morrison calls the generative power of language and voices may seem more suggestive (1994, pp. 20–23). Freeing a diversity of long-silenced voices, Morrison says, paying heed to long-unheard languages, we become aware of multiple meanings in the making. We discover our own reality becoming more and more multifarious, more likely to be transformed. Others may think back to "in the beginning was the Word." After all, may that not be what Bishop had in mind? But then there may be all kinds of responses to "towards the unknown." For Western readers, with memories of frontiers and horizons and untapped possibilities where "America" has been concerned, the "unknown" may beckon as well as threaten, may welcome as well as exclude. But why "think up signs"? Why "sketch a landscape"? Why, after all, "invent . . . the reality of this world"? Whatever "reality" the poem renders visible to the one involved will be a function of the encounters between work and writer, of memories, of past experiences with poetry.

If the work, if any work, becomes an object of a reader's or a perceiver's experience, there will be what Rosenblatt (1978) calls "efferent" as well as aesthetic meanings. It follows that the meanings constructed will go beyond the immediate encounter. They will begin to radiate through dimensions of the reader's or the perceiver's experience, making new connections visible, opening new perspectives on the familiar. This can happen, as we are well aware, with painting, dance performances, drama, film, musical works. Maurice Merleau-Ponty begins one important book with talk about meaning coming into being. "Because we are in the world," he said, "we are *condemned to meaning*" (1967, p. xix, emphasis in original). Writing elsewhere about "Cezanne's Doubt" (1964a), he suggests a connection between this and looking at pictorial art:

> Cezanne did not think he had to choose between feeling and thought, between order and chaos. He did not want to separate the stable things which we see and the shifting way in which they appear; he wanted to depict matter as it takes on form, the birth of order through spontaneous organization. . . . We see things; we agree about them; we are anchored in them; and it is with "nature" as our base that we construct our sciences. (p. 13)

He wanted, Merleau-Ponty said, to paint our "primordial landscape"; he wanted us to look from our "lived perspective." And he made the important point that the painter can only construct an image; it is up to those who come to the painting to bring it to life. When that happens, the work of art will unite a number of separate lives; it will not exist only in one "like a stubborn dream" nor in space as a piece of colored canvas. "It will dwell undivided in several minds, with a claim on every possible mind like a perennial acquisition" (1964a, p. 20). Here, too, there is construction; here, too, art transforms.

In many of those who probe the problem of meaning, the word *seeing* is often used. Joseph Conrad's (1897/1960) words come to mind:

> My task which I am trying to achieve is, by the power of the written word, to make you hear, to make you feel it is, before all, to make you see. That—and no more, and it is everything. If I succeed, you shall find there according to your deserts: encouragement, consolation, fear, charm—all you demand—and, perhaps, also that glimpse of truth for which you have forgotten to ask. (pp. 30–31)

That "glimpse of truth" may be understood to be a shaft of meaning, a view of a resemblance or a connection that may illuminate something never quite clear before. Perhaps it is a sensed connection between a voyage on a whaling ship and a search for identity and community at once, a community of islanders, a coming together of the diverse. Or it may be a vision of the tense relation, even the interdependence between the circle of caring, of mothering, and the sear rationality of the patriarch who is responsible, who in some manner *takes* care. Or, as in the case of *Jazz*, it may be a perception of the links between feelings of loss and familial love, between improvisation and discovering new sounds, new ways of being in the world. Because imagination and cognition are involved in each case, there may well be a feeling of the unexpected when the "glimpse of truth" or the pattern of meaning presents itself. The elements may have been there; they may have been latent in experience. But they were not visible; they were not part of what may have been conceived to be "the order of things."

Language makes this possible, as has been said. So, as has been suggested, does an encounter with a painting or several paintings. There is the generative power of language; there is the sense of that which both artist and perceiver have "forgotten to ask." Where the painter is concerned, there are feelings and perceptions that arise from the act of creation, an act that brings many of them to the surface of consciousness. For Merleau-Ponty, the meaning of what the artist is going to say does not exist anywhere: "It summons one away from the already constituted reason in which 'cultured men' are content to shut themselves, toward a reason which contains its own origins" (1964b, p. 19). Its origins most probably lie in the painter's own life quest, in an expanding vision of life. And, very likely, they may be found in the meanings he constructs in response to the visual questions that arise for every serious artist—questions that have to do with color and line and contour and light. Painting, say, "The House of the Hanged Man," Cezanne would have had to withdraw from "the already constituted reason" in order to resolve unprecedented problems regarding the slanted roof, the tree branches, the geometric shapes of the rocks. As has been said, he was not representing the actual house in its setting. He was interpreting his own perceived "reality," his own world of appearances, and giving it meaning as he "saw" it, as he constructed it by rendering it in paint. And those of us willing to be present to it now, willing to take the time, cannot but find ourselves gazing at a face of the world never accessible before. That, too, expands in our experience, moves beyond the painting and stirs us to construct new meanings, to enlarge what makes sense in the world.

To become conscious of this and reflective about it is to feel ourselves adventuring among realms of meaning. Today, when authority structures and frameworks are becoming so problematic, when dictionaries defining what is meant by "humanities" or "art" or even "science" have become archaic, we have to engage in many language games (Wittgenstein, 1931) to find ways of speaking adequately about what texts, or photographs, or musical pieces, or dance movements are or intend to be. That should make us more than ever aware of the constructed nature of the various realities we inhabit, the fields we study, the discourses in which we engage. Whatever resolutions we can find, we realize, must take shape within complex fabrics of communication, in an always more convoluted conversation. Even the matter of finding standard cases or paradigm instances of portraits, novels, ballet performances, opera performances becomes increasingly difficult. It is as if we were asked continually to construct and reconstruct the "art world" or the domains of the humanities through talk, if not computer networking, across the distances.

When we simply adopt the schemata or patterns of our "predecessors and contemporaries" (Schutz, 1967, p. 10) to structure our social worlds, we may not be conscious of the schemata in use. We simply see *through* those schemata at what becomes a "natural" and coherent world. Berger and Luckmann (writing about the "social construction of reality" [1966]) say that everyday life or commonsense reality is often taken as "given," even though it is presented as a reality "interpreted by men and subjectively meaningful to them as a coherent world" (p. 19). It is presented to each person as a world that is shared with others; but each person organizes that world around the "here and now" of her or his being in it; and each one has a more or less distinctive perspective on the common world (p. 23). There is a correspondence between the meanings achieved by those who share the same commonsense reality; but that does not mean they can be proved to be identical. Traffic lights, movie lines, newspaper stands, emergency rooms, choir stalls, the Oval Office: All take a presumably allotted place in a "normal" universe. So do the institutions and examinations that, according to Foucault (1980), function to "normalize" individuals (p. 107). It can never be claimed, however, that people become mere duplicates of one another, even when the world strikes them as solidified under what Foucault called a "regime of truth" (p. 133).

The point is that the very undecidability involved in aesthetic experiences may enhance awareness of the ways people come together to structure their realities. A century ago, when even romantic and expressive works were ascribed an objective status as works of art, existing in enclaves and distanced from the grasping consciousness of those who came to hear and see, audiences were not challenged to engage with them or to realize them as works of art in their own experience. They may have been impassioned about and possessive of Dickens' novels, say, or court ballet; but it was believed that meanings were immanent in such works—to be sought after and discovered by the few. The public was not consulted even indirectly when it came to the making of traditions; canonical forms were identified by the great and powerful males, who absorbed authority into themselves. Today, perceivers are expected to question, to participate, to engage. They are provoked to be wide awake and aware of the way in which created forms relate to lived social realities. Not only are they asked, however, to play a conscious role in achieving a work as meaningful; they can no longer take it for granted that a given work counts as art, even if it exists in what is called the "art world" of a modern museum. The effort to decide whether a Warhol Brillo Box or a Jenny Holtzer moving strand of neon phrases should be considered art, with all the power and promise traditionally associated with both concept and domain, becomes a phase in the construction of meaning.

Arthur Danto (1981) has said that "only in relation to an interpretation is an object an art work" (p. 113). What are we to say about Cindy Sherman's photographs of herself as a French general dying on a nineteenth-century beach? In what way does it inhabit the same domain as an Edward Weston photograph, an Ansel Adams, a Robert Mapplethorpe? What decision do we make when we approach Borges' "Pierre Menard, Symbolist Poet," half of which is precisely like a fragment of Cervantes' *Don Quixote?* But it is not a copy or a forgery, because Pierre Menard is referring to the scenes of chivalry as having occurred in "the land of Carmen" and from an entirely different point of view from that of Cervantes. Moreover, as Borges tells his readers, Menard is addressing people who are aware that Cervantes' work precedes Menard's and gives Menard's, in consequence, an entirely different location in the tradition of literary art. What sort of attitude, then, should we take to Borges' story? Should it be an aesthetic attitude, or the kind of skeptical or even empirical approach we might make if someone were calling our attention to a fake or a plagiarism?

In this day of copies, overlaps, minglings of "fact" and "fiction"—as, for instance, in Doctorow's novel *Ragtime* or Kushner's play (partly about the actual Roy Cohn) *Angels in America*, or Dichter's painting of the actual terrorist, Ursula Meinhof, strangled on the ground—when are we present in relation to an "unreal" world, a perceived world, demanding a lift of imagination, a pouring out of energy, a bringing to life? What is the difference between taking an aesthetic attitude toward, say, a Crucifixion and taking such an attitude toward an actual torture scene or to police beating a presumed wrongdoer? Again, the perceiver is thought to be active and participant, no longer a passive spectator or receiver. Becoming increasingly aware of the way perception structures what is seen, of the way imagination opens perspectives, of the many modes there are of making meanings, the person—be she or he teacher or learner or artist or speculative thinker—becomes conscious of incompleteness and, yes, of inexhaustibility. There is always more, as we choose the demarcations of our landscapes, as we describe and redescribe, as we move—embodied minds—through the world.

There is always a context, of course—historical, cultural, biographical—in order to provide the perspectives through which to attend to any given work. Ernst Gombrich, the art historian and critic, reminds us that since there is no such thing as an "innocent eye" when it comes to making or perceiving visual art (1965), there is bound to be something equivalent to what we have called "the social construction of reality." In other words, we come to the Miro exhibition with eyes already affected by our having seen Picasso or Cezanne or David or Poussin. We come affected by the expectations we already have of what painting ought to offer us. We come as members of a specific culture; and we are, inevitably, shaped by factors of gender and class and ethnicity. Of course, the meanings we construct in an encounter with Picasso cannot but be affected by our gender, by our familiarity with the great shift to cubism from traditional styles. They may even be conditioned in some manner by the color and climate of our lived landscape, by rural or urban atmospheres, by the ways in which painting is dealt with among those with whom we work and live. But it must be stressed, as Alfred Schutz always did, that aesthetic experiences belong to a "province of meaning" that can only be entered when we move away from the reality of everyday life.

For Schutz (1967), there were multiple provinces of meaning and, in consequence, what he called "multiple realities," since each province makes it possible to structure experience in a distinctive way. Each one has its own cognitive style, wrote Schutz; the experiences within the province are compatible with one other, since they share that style. Attending to the commonsense world through the lenses of, say, natural science is quite different from attending to it by means of the schemata made available by social scientific theories. So it is with the domain of religion or the domain of play. There is a more or less clearly defined province identified with the arts. Entering it, releasing imagination to summon up alternative realities, looking through perspectives that clarify figure and ground, taking symbol systems and perceptual elements into account, we simply attend differently than we do when we enter the realm of chemistry, say, or psychoanalysis, or remembered dreams.

In the province of the arts, which is now our particular concern, the style is much influenced by the role played by imagination in cognition. It is affected, too, by what Schutz (1967) described as the "freedom of discretion of the imagining self" (p. 240). There is little attempt in this realm to distance the self from the appearances of things (or the feel of things, or the beat and the rhythm of things) for the sake of empirical study or measurement or analysis. Certain forms of art (abstract paintings, perhaps, imagist verse, objectivist prose) may demand a kind of neutral or uninvolved attitude. They may appeal to logic alone, let us say; they may require the suppression of feeling or intuition or even free association. But in the realm of the arts, more clearly than in the other realms, the so-called subject has much to do with contributing to the reality and the very existence of the object—be that object Braque's "Bird in Flight," Shakespeare's rendering of a street in Verona, an airplane in *Catch 22*, or the great manor house in *Remains of the Day*. Now it is the case that the role of standpoint and perspective, like the place of constructivism, is being acknowledged in the other provinces of meaning, especially under the influence of feminist thought today (Harding, 1991). But the "reality" that comes into being as a consequence of the perceiver's active construction is at once affected by memories, stored images, half-forgotten stories, as well as the original landscape in which perceiving first began. Aware of this, aware of how much depends on the transaction between perceiver and work, the perceiver cannot but resist both givenness and objectivity.

Setting this beside Dewey's conception of "art as experience" (1934) and his view of the ways in which works of art become objects of experience, we may come to realize how our encounters with art can move us to envisage ways of living and being with others often obscured by the compliances of the everyday. It is not surprising that Denis Donoghue (1983) writes that he cannot regret the arts being so often on the margin because "the margin is the place for those feelings and intuitions which daily life doesn't have a place for and often seems to suppress" (p. 129). Because they provide moments of freedom and presence unattainable in daily living, he believes they can open spaces where we can make choices we cannot make when constrained by convention, routine, and duty. Moving us to interpret differently, to see from unexpected angles, to forge meanings we might never have anticipated or even welcomed, such experiences may well change our lives.

Recalling particular experiences that allowed us to perceive pictorial space differently, to become aware of social textures through reading, say, George Eliot's *Middlemarch*, to attend to new dimensions of the Holocaust because of what we brought to *Schindler's List* on screen, we cannot but become more aware of how lack of attentiveness walled off parts of our world. Habit and convention have so many ways of keeping things inaudible and invisible—as in the case of the negative space made evident by certain painters, as in the case of women's courage and talents, or as in the case of African-American talents and wisdom. Attending with sufficient solicitude, welcoming the moments of defamiliarization, we may be able to construct more and more meanings in the spaces Donoghue speaks of with the arts in mind.

They are not, we must remind ourselves, private spaces. It is not only that the works mentioned exist in shared traditions developing over time. Experiences with them can be and frequently are communicated to other people. Schutz wrote once that there is no reason why experiences that originated in the provinces of dreams or fantasies or created works could not become the contents of communicative acts taking place in the world of working or in the everyday world. Schutz was concerned, as constructivists must be concerned, for the ways in which patterns of meaning constructed within streams of consciousness move in and out of the shared common-sense world. They are not to be considered mere phenomena or phantasms mysteriously becoming present in an interior realm. Originating in diverse encounters with the natural and the multiplex world of culture *as* perceived, *as* felt, *as* imagined, *as* known, they are eventually realized within the currents of dialogue in the social sphere.

This brings us back to the idea of context and, yes, the notion of tradition. Every text or painting or musical composition or dance (at least when available to audiences) has a public presence and is, we are aware, accessible to others. There is a respect in which the awareness of others opens a horizon in addition to the one offered by a particular tradition. For Hugh-George Gadamer (1989), we all move within traditions of various kinds, as if those traditions were streams carried by the medium of language. Oftentimes, they appear transparent; they invisibly affect our viewing of the world around and our own self-understanding. What is crucial is our recognition of the prejudgments to which they give rise, prejudgments that cannot but affect the way we "see" or construct our realities. Reading the Bishop poem with an awareness of a particular lyrical tradition carried by its language, viewing Picasso's *Guernica* within a tradition of historical painting giving way to cubism, hearing Berlioz within a romantic musical tradition, we identify ourselves and our perceiving with relation to what happens in our experience through the encounter with a work of art. The work takes on a reality that is always new; the reality constructed by the engaged person is itself always new, and there is always a tension between the piece being interpreted and the interpreter's lived life. There is a horizon in the tradition as experienced; and there is a horizon with regard to the individual's own situation. For Gadamer (1989), "the horizon is the range of vision that includes everything that can be seen from a particular vantage point" (p. 269). In the search for self-understanding that is so fundamental to education, there is frequently a fusing of horizons. This, for Gadamer, is what makes possible the confrontation of works of art as worlds, not merely objects or texts. We are enabled to view dimensions of our lived worlds through these worlds; and, for Gadamer, art experiences begin to lie at the root of what we are calling construction. Again, it is a matter of being conscious of the process and conscious of connections with others in bringing the "multiple realities" within which we live into being.

It may be noted as well that, for Gadamer, the notion of vantage point may be as important as it is in Merleau-Ponty's writings and the writings of feminist scholars such as Sandra Harding (1991). This makes fundamental the notion of perception and, perhaps, the "primordial landscape" that underlies all cognition (Merleau-Ponty, 1964a). The idea of perception not only carries with it a realization of incompleteness. (Perception, after all, is from a particular location in the world. What are perceived are profiles, aspects, not totalities.) Neisser (1976), writing almost two decades ago, developed a concept of what he called perceptual schemata, which he said might function like plans and anticipations of what might be provided by the environment. Maps and other such constructs clearly derive from the perceptual process because of the very fact that perceived realities are always provisional, open to redescription and change. Richard Prawat (1993) has made the important point that the kinds of ideas thought of as anticipatory educate attention by enabling the perceiver to search out new and significant details as part of the perceptual process itself; and these new details, as Prawat writes, enrich our understanding of ideas, particularly as those ideas change, appear in new contexts, take on more and more suggestive meanings.

Perception and the structuring inherent in perceiving play an important role in all the arts. Engagement with artforms may lead to encouragement and stimulation of perceiving. For Merleau-Ponty (1964a), perception and thought have much in common: "that both of them have a future horizon and a past horizon and that they appear to themselves as temporal." We find here a viewing very close to the notion of anticipatory ideas. "What is given," Merleau-Ponty went on, "is a route, an experience which gradually clarifies itself, which gradually rectifies itself and proceeds by dialogue with itself and with others." What follows is an "openness to *something* . . . and the possibility of a new development" (p. 21).

We might think for a moment of a Cezanne painting of the landscape in Provence or of an Edward Hopper painting of a luncheonette on a city street. Each may be initially grasped by an act of intuition; but paintings like this require attending over a period of time to emerge as works of art. The critic Arnold Isenberg (1973), considering a painting by El Greco, described the way in which a critic

> gives us directions for perceiving and does this *by means* of the idea he imparts to us, which narrows down the field of possible visual organizations and guides us in the discrimination of details, the organization of parts, the grouping of discrete objects into patterns. It is as if we found both an oyster and a pearl when we had been looking for a seashell because we had been told it was valuable. It *is* valuable, but not because it is a seashell. (p. 163)

The critic's meaning is filled in or completed by the act of perception, said Isenberg, in order to *understand* what the critic meant, not to judge its truth. In effect, we take journeys of perception through paintings; and each turn in the road, each new vista multiplies the meanings available, enriches understanding of ideas, moves, as it were, toward possibility.

Mikel Dufrenne (1973) adds further insights to this view of differentiation and expansion, which has so much to do with the construction of ideas. He speaks of the way a work—a painting, perhaps, a dance performance—creates a public "because the meaning of the work is inexhaustible, the aesthetic object profits from a plurality of interpretations. The deciphering of its meaning is never finished, and its public has always to expand in order to begin this deciphering again" (p. 64). This process, this opening of possibilities and pluralities of interpretation, enriches the object, feeds its potentiality. "Everything takes place as if the aesthetic object were metamorphosing, gaining in density or depth, as if something of its being has been transformed by the cult whose object it is" (p. 65). We may find here something analogous to what we have called the "social construction" of reality and a reminder that construction is not simply a private affair taking place in the interior of consciousness or mind.

Much the same can be said about achieving a work of literature as meaningful, with a reminder that the work in many senses is achieved by acts of perception as well as acts of thought. Important roots of what we conceive to be structuralism are to be found in the works of a formalist like Roman Jakobson (1956), an anthropologist like Claude Lévi-Strauss (1966), a structural linguist like Ferdinand de Saussure (1967), Jonathan Culler (1981), and a number of others. There are great differences among them; but what relates them is a concern for the structures of texts and the general laws by which they work. Greatly interested in sign systems, they tend to believe that the individual parts of any system have meaning only in relation to one another; meanings tend almost always to be relational and not substantial. They do not, for instance, refer beyond the networks or the fabrics of the poem or story (or game, or ritual) to be something substantive or objective in the world "out there," although they may well refer to wider systems of meaning, or to other texts or codes in literature or in society as a whole. There are connections with, among others, Gadamer's approach to hermeneutics and the ways in which we are caught up in the streams of tradition; because here, too, there is a certain decentering of the individual subject, no longer regarded as the source of significant meanings. There are those who believe in myths or other great codes that allow for the transmission of messages and become (as traditions do for Gadamer) aspects of collective existence that almost seem to take on a kind of objectivity. The structuralists must be regarded as the ones who made clear that works of literature are constructs, narratives working on many levels, not merely subjective expressions articulating a human "essence" only accessible through high literature. Indeed, one of the emphases of the structuralist thinkers was on the fact that deep structures and sign systems are to be found in detective stories, situation comedies, and romantic novels as well as in the so-called privileged texts long recognized as "high" literature.

Terry Eagleton (1983) has written:

> The structuralist emphasis on the "constructedness" of human meaning represented a major advance. Meaning was neither a private experience nor a divinely ordained occurrence: it was the product of certain shared systems of signification. The confident bourgeois belief that the isolated human subject was the fount and origin of all meaning took a sharp knock: language pre-dated the individual and was much less his or her product than he or she was the product of it. Meaning was not "natural," a question of just looking and seeing, or something eternally settled: the way you interpreted your world was a function of the languages at your disposal. . . . Meaning was not something which all men and women intuitively shared, and then articulated in their various tongues and scripts: what meaning you were able to articulate depended on what script or speech you shared in the first place. There were the seeds here of a social and historical theory of meaning whose implications were to run deep within contemporary thought. (p. 107)

For Eagleton, the seeds never did sprout, in part because of the structuralists' abandonment of how the world actually was. The idea of realities being products of language was difficult to accept, as it still seems to be. He finds, as many of us do, a greater richness and a greater possibility in the work of post-structuralists like Roland Barthes and Michel Foucault and Jacques Derrida, as he does in those who concern themselves with pluralities, difference, and, yes, critical consciousness and emancipation. Having tried to trace connections between what has been called "constructivism" and not "structuralism" and approaches to the arts and aesthetic experiences, this chapter has strained toward something beyond a mechanized systematic approach, even though the theories of meaning linked to structuralism have remained important.

I can only end with an affirmation of the significance of making meaning and of doing so, not through the use of cognition alone, but through the exercise of perception and imagination and an opening to the possibilities in the world. Speaking out for participation, for the growth of a sense of agency through involvement with the several arts, I find in them a model not only for engaged experience but for constructivism as a mode of liberation and expansion. There will be difficulties as we seek out norms on which we can agree. There will be tensions as we create our communities and deal with conflicts between and among such communities. But the end of constructivist thought in the arts and in education is not the attainment of harmony and coherence. It is to open perspectives, untapped perspectives; it is to look out windows never opened; it is to climb stairs never attempted and look for keys to unknown doors.

REFERENCES

Berger, P., & Luckmann, T. (1966). *The social construction of reality.* Garden City, NY: Anchor.

Bishop, E. (1983). "January first," in *Collected Poems.* New York: Farrar, Straus, & Giroux.

Conrad, J. (1960). Preface to *The nigger of the Narcissus.* In J. E. Miller (Ed.), *Myth and method.* Omaha: University of Nebraska Press. (Original work published 1897)

Culler, J. (1981). *The pursuit of signs: Semiotics, literature, deconstruction.* Ithaca, NY: Cornell University Press.

Danto, A. (1981). *The transfiguration of the commonplace.* Cambridge, MA: Harvard University Press.

Derrida, J. (1978). *Writing and difference.* Chicago: University of Chicago Press.

De Saussure, F. (1967). *Cours de linguistique generale.* Paris: Payot.

Dewey, J. (1916). *Democracy and education.* New York: Macmillan.

Dewey, J. (1934). *Art as experience.* New York: Minton, Balch.

Donoghue, M. (1983). *The arts without mystery.* Boston: Little, Brown.

Dufrenne, M. (1973). *Phenomenology of aesthetic experience.* Evanston, IL: Northwestern University Press.

Dufrenne, M. (1978). *Main trends in aesthetics and the sciences of the arts.* New York: Holmes & Meier.

Eagleton, T. (1983). *Literary theory.* Minneapolis: University of Minnesota Press.

Ernst, K. (1993). *Picturing learning.* London: Heinemann.

Fish, S. (1980). *Is there a text in this class?* Cambridge, MA: Harvard University Press.

Foucault, M. (1980). *Power/knowledge.* New York: Pantheon.

Frye, N. (1968). *The educated imagination.* Bloomington: Indiana University Press.

Gadamer, H-C. (1989). *Truth and method.* New York: Crossroads.

Gardner, H. (1983). *Frames of mind.* New York: Basic Books.

Geertz, C. (1983). *Local knowledge.* New York: Basic Books.

Gombrich, E. (1965). *Art and illusion.* New York: Pantheon.

Goodnow, J. (1977). *Children drawing.* Cambridge, MA: Harvard University Press.

Gruber, H. E., & Vonneche, J. J. (Eds.). (1977). *The essential Piaget.* New York: Basic Books.

Harding, S. (1991). *Whose science? Whose knowledge? Thinking from women's lives.* Ithaca, NY: Cornell University Press.

Heidegger, M. (1971). *Poetry, language, thought.* New York: Harper & Row.

Hubbard, J. (Ed.). (1991). *Shooting back: A photographic view of life by homeless children.* San Francisco: Chronicle.

Isenberg, A. (1973). *Aesthetics and the theory of criticism.* Chicago: University of Chicago Press.

Iser, W. (1980). *The act of reading.* Baltimore: Johns Hopkins University Press.

Jakobson, R. (1956). *Fundamentals of language.* The Hague, Netherlands: Mouton.

Lévi-Strauss, C. (1966). *The savage mind.* Chicago: University of Chicago Press.

Merleau-Ponty, M. (1964a). Cezanne's doubt. In *Sense and non-sense* (pp. 9–25). Evanston, IL: Northwestern University Press.

Merleau-Ponty, M. (1964b). The primacy of perception and its philosophical consequences. In *The primacy of perception* (pp. 12–42). Evanston, IL: Northwestern University Press.

Merleau-Ponty, M. (1967). *Phenomenology of perception.* London: Routledge & Kegan Paul.

Morrison, T. (1994). *The Nobel lecture on literature.* New York: Knopf.

Neisser, U. (1976). *Cognition and reality.* San Francisco: Freeman.

Ozick, C. (1989). *Metaphor and memory.* New York: Knopf.

Prawat, R. (1993). The value of ideas: Problems versus possibilities in learning. *Educational Researcher, 22*(6), 9–16.

Rorty, R. (1979). *Philosophy and the mirror of nature.* Princeton, NJ: Princeton University Press.

Rosenblatt, L. (1978). *The reader the text the poem.* Carbondale: Southern Illinois University Press.

Scholes, R. E. (1989). *Protocols of reading.* New Haven, CT: Yale University Press.

Schutz, A. (1964). The dimensions of the social world. In *Collected papers II: Studies in social theory* (pp. 20–63). The Hague, Netherlands: Martinus Nijhoff.

Schutz, A. (1967). On multiple realities. In *Collected papers I: The problem of social reality* (p. 10). The Hague, Netherlands: Martinus Nijhoff.

Vygotsky, L. S. (1978). *Mind in society: The development of higher psychological processes* (M. Cole, V. John-Steiner, S. Scribner, & E. Souberman, Eds.). Cambridge, MA: Harvard University Press.

Warnock, M. (1978). *Imagination.* Berkeley: University of California Press.

Winner, E. (1982). *Invented worlds.* Cambridge, MA: Harvard University Press.

Wittgenstein, L. (1931). *Philosophical investigations.* London: Oxford University Press.

CHAPTER 8

A Constructivist Perspective on the Role of the Sociomoral Atmosphere in Promoting Children's Development

Rheta DeVries and Betty Zan

The preoccupation in most schools with subject-matter content has led to a situation in which sociomoral and affective development are negatively influenced. Ironically, this one-sided preoccupation has created a situation in which intellectual development and understanding of subject-matter content do not thrive, either. Our position is that in order to foster intellectual, sociomoral, and affective development, a certain kind of interpersonal context must be created. For us, the first principle of constructivist education is to establish a sociomoral atmosphere in which mutual respect is continually practiced. By sociomoral atmosphere we refer to the entire network of interpersonal relations that make up the child's experience in school. Interpersonal relations are the context for the child's construction of the self, of others, and of subject-matter knowledge. Depending on the nature of the overall sociomoral atmosphere of a child's life, he or she learns in what ways the world of people is safe or unsafe, loving or hostile, coercive or cooperative, satisfying or unsatisfying. In the context of interpersonal activities, the child learns to think of his or her self as having certain characteristics in relation to others. Within the social context surrounding objects, the child learns in what ways the world of objects is open or closed to exploration and experimentation, discovery and invention. In this chapter, we discuss the nature of the teacher–child relationship in a constructivist classroom and the practical ways in which teachers express respect for children to promote development. We emphasize the sociomoral aspects of a constructivist program but also discuss how the constructivist sociomoral atmosphere creates the necessary context for the child's construction of knowledge of subject matter. In our view, the same conditions that promote sociomoral development are the conditions that promote intellectual development.

In other chapters in this book, constructivist educators insist that the construction of subject-matter knowledge must be embedded in children's interests and personally meaningful activities. This purposeful context is just as necessary for the child's construction of moral knowledge. In our book *Moral Classrooms, Moral Children: Creating a Constructivist Atmosphere in Early Education* (DeVries & Zan, 1994), we describe in detail how teachers use every aspect of the school day to promote children's moral development while they are also promoting intellectual development. In this chapter, we review pertinent research on developmental stages or levels, revealing how children think about social and moral issues, and discuss how the constructivist teacher interacts with children, conducts grouptime, establishes rules, discusses moral issues, responds to conflicts, and deals with misbehavior. (See DeVries & Zan, 1994, for discussion of activity time, clean-up time, lunchtime, nap time/rest time, and academics.) We conclude by discussing the issue of how to integrate sociomoral and cognitive objectives in constructivist education.

HOW CHILDREN THINK ABOUT SOCIAL AND MORAL ISSUES

A large body of research demonstrates that young children think about moral and social issues in ways that differ qualitatively from the ways in which older children and adults think. Here we outline work by Piaget on child thought on social and moral rules and by Selman on interpersonal understanding that is useful to us in thinking about sociomoral aspects of constructivist teaching.

Children's Moral Reasoning

Piaget (1932/1965) described young children as "moral realists" because their judgments about right and wrong, good and bad, are based on what is observable or "real" to them. For example, intentions and feelings of others cannot be directly observed, and their recognition requires the ability to decenter and take the perspective of the other. Therefore, when the adult says not to hit others, the child experiences this instruction as arbitrary. Moral realism also leads children to interpret rules literally because the spirit of the rule is not observable. For example, the rule not to hit is understood narrowly and does not include pinching, kicking, or biting! In addition, moral realism leads children to judge acts in terms of observable consequences rather than in terms of intentions. For example, accidentally knocking down a block structure is considered just as bad as doing it intentionally.

The movement from judging on the basis of observables to judging in terms of intentions is described by Piaget as a developmental progression based on increasing ability to take the perspectives of others. Piaget's research on developmental levels in children's practice of rules in the game of marbles shows that children learn the observable aspects of game rules before they become conscious of opposed intentions and feel the necessity to cooperate in agreeing on the rules, abiding by them, and accepting their consequences. This development has parallels in how children think about moral rules concerning lying, property rights, and fairness. For example, young children believe a lie is any kind of verbal misbehavior (including "naughty" words and mistakes such as $2 + 2 = 5$). Only as they become able to take multiple perspectives into account are children able to understand that a lie is an intentional deceit that leads to a rift in the social bond. Piaget's research suggests that this development is fostered in the context of cooperative relationships characterized by mutual respect. We describe in later sections how teachers can cooperate with children and promote cooperation among children.

How Children Think about Self and Others

Basing his work on Piaget's theory of perspective taking, Robert Selman (1980; Selman & Schultz, 1990) developed a model for assessing interpersonal understanding as reflected in interpersonal behavior. In this model, Selman presents five levels (0–4) of interpersonal understanding. Without going into the technical details, we want to point out that at level 0 (approximately ages 3 to 6 years), the young child does not recognize that others' inner, subjective experiences (feelings, intentions, and ideas) may be different from his or her own. The child simply does not realize that the other has a point of view. Others are viewed as a kind of object. At level 1 (approximately ages 5 to 9 years), the child decenters and knows that each person has a unique subjective experience but usually cannot consider more than one perspective at a time. Others are to command or control. At level 2 (around 7 to 12 years), the child decenters further to reciprocally consider feelings and thoughts of self and other. Others are to persuade or be persuaded by. At level 3 (generally beginning in adolescence), the child decenters still further to simultaneously coordinate these reciprocal perspectives into a mutual perspective. Others are to understand and be understood by.

(We do not discuss level 4 here because it usually emerges only in late adolescence or adulthood, and we are focusing on young children.)

Selman calls these levels rather than stages because each level remains
accessible after the next level is attained. That is, a person capable of level-2
perspective coordination may at times act at level 0 or 1. At times, lower-
level action is even appropriate.

These levels are useful to the classroom teacher who wishes to assess
children's interpersonal understanding in the context of peer interactions
and know how to intervene to promote development. For example, if a child
acts predominantly at level 0, the teacher would not suggest level-3 strategies to the child because these would be beyond his or her understanding.
Instead, the teacher suggests that the child use words instead of fists to tell
another what he or she wants. Likewise, if a child is experiencing the inadequacy of simple commands to others (level-1 strategy), the teacher may suggest trades (level-2 strategy).

Selman's levels are also useful to the teacher in assessing his or her own
level of interpersonal understanding as reflected in interactions with children. They can lead a teacher to become conscious of a preponderance of
commanding and controlling strategies with children and aid movement to
more cooperative strategies with children through taking their views into
account. For example, the constructivist teacher expresses respect for children by consulting them, asking for their opinions, feelings, suggestions,
and ideas. Instead of directing or commanding children, the teacher makes
requests and gives reasons for these. In the next section, we return to Piaget's theory to address the issue of why teachers should cooperate in these
ways with children.

THE TEACHER–CHILD RELATIONSHIP

Adults determine, through daily interactions, the nature of the sociomoral atmosphere in which the young child lives. The child's sociomoral
experience is made up, in large part, of the countless adult actions toward
and reactions to the child that form the adult–child relationship. Peer relations also contribute to the sociomoral atmosphere, but the adult often establishes the framework or limits and possibilities of peer relations. In Piaget's theory we find the most useful guide to thinking about adult–child
relationships. Piaget (1932/1965) described two types of morality corresponding to two types of adult–child relationships, one that promotes children's development and one that retards it.

The first type of morality is a morality of obedience. Piaget called this
"heteronomous" morality. The word *heteronomous* comes from roots mean-

ing "following rules made by others." Therefore the individual who is heteronomously moral follows moral rules given by others out of obedience to an authority who has coercive power. Heteronomous morality is conformity to external rules that are simply accepted and followed without question.

The second type of morality is autonomous. The word *autonomous* comes from roots meaning "self-regulation." By autonomy, Piaget did not mean simple "independence" in doing things for oneself without help. Rather, the individual who is autonomously moral follows moral rules of the self. Such rules are self-constructed, self-regulating principles. These rules have a feeling of personal necessity for the individual. The individual who is autonomously moral follows internal convictions about the necessity of respect for persons in relationships with others.

Most educators would probably agree that they want children to believe with personal conviction in such basic moral values as respect for persons. Without belief that arises from personal conviction, children will not be likely to follow moral rules. Nevertheless, educators generally manage children in ways that promote heteronomous rather than autonomous morality.

The two types of morality have parallels in two types of adult–child relationships, discussed below.

The Coercive or Controlling Relationship

The first type of adult–child relationship is one of coercion or constraint in which the adult prescribes what the child must do by giving ready-made rules and instructions for behavior. In this relation, respect is a one-way affair. That is, the child is expected to respect the adult, and the adult uses authority to socialize and instruct the child. The adult controls the child's behavior. In this sociomoral context, the child's reason for behaving is thus outside his or her own reasoning and system of personal interests and values. Piaget calls this type of relation "heteronomous." In a heteronomous relation, the child follows rules given by others rather than by the self. Heteronomy can range on a continuum from hostile and punitive to sugar-coated control.

In adult–child relations, heteronomy is often appropriate and sometimes unavoidable. That is, for reasons of health and safety, as well as practical and psychological pressures on the adult, parents and teachers must regulate or control children in many ways. However, when children are governed continually by the values, beliefs, and ideas of others, they practice a submission (if not rebellion) that can lead to mindless conformity in both moral and intellectual life. In other words, so long as adults keep children occupied with learning what adults want them to do and with obeying adult rules, they will not be motivated to question, analyze, or examine their own convictions.

In Piaget's view, following the rules of others through a morality of obedience will never lead to the kind of reflection necessary for commitment to internal or autonomous principles of moral judgment. Piaget warned that coercion socializes only the surface of behavior and actually reinforces the child's tendency to rely on regulation by others. By insisting that the child only follow rules, values, and guidelines given ready-made by others, the adult contributes to the development of an individual with a conformist mind, personality, and morality—an individual capable only of following the will of others. Tragically, obedience-based schools simply perpetuate qualities needed for submission.

The Cooperative Relationship

Piaget contrasts the heteronomous adult–child relationship with a second type that is characterized by mutual respect and cooperation. The adult returns children's respect by giving them the possibility to regulate their behavior voluntarily. This type of relation Piaget called "autonomous" and "cooperative." He argued that it is only by refraining from exercising unnecessary authority that the adult opens the way for children to develop minds capable of thinking independently and creatively and to develop moral feelings and convictions that take into account the best interests of all parties.

The method by which the autonomous relationship operates is that of cooperation. Cooperating means striving to attain a common goal while coordinating one's own feelings and perspective with a consciousness of another's feelings and perspective. The constructivist teacher considers the child's point of view and encourages the child to consider others' points of view. The motive for cooperation begins in a feeling of mutual affection and trust that becomes elaborated into feelings of sympathy and consciousness of the intentions of self and others.

Cooperation is a social interaction toward a certain goal by individuals who regard themselves as equals and treat each other as such. Obviously, children and adults are not equals. However, when the adult is able to respect the child as a person with a right to exercise his or her will, one can speak about a certain psychological equality in the relationship. Piaget, of course, was not advocating that children have complete freedom because such freedom is inconsistent with moral relations with others.

The general constructivist principle of teaching is that coercion be minimized to the extent possible and practical. What is most desirable is a mixture increasingly in favor of children's regulation of their own behavior.

When we talk about heteronomy and autonomy, coercion and cooperation, we are talking about processes that are simultaneously cognitive and emotional. Adult coercion produces a constriction of children's minds, personalities, and feelings. Adult cooperation produces a liberation of children's possibilities for construction of their intelligence, their personalities, and their moral and social feelings and convictions.

What does research say about these theoretical hypotheses? While we cannot attempt a review here, we would like to point out research by Deci, Sheinman, Schwartz, and Ryan (1981) in which they studied children taught by adults who were oriented toward control and those oriented toward autonomy. They found that teachers who were more autonomy-oriented had children who were more intrinsically motivated. Teachers with a more controlling orientation had children who were less intrinsically motivated. The children of autonomy-oriented teachers had higher self-esteem. They felt better about themselves and perceived themselves as more competent in the cognitive domain.

GROUPTIME

In grouptime, the constructivist teacher strives to promote a feeling of community in which children care about one another and are truly concerned about issues of fairness and justice. Social and moral reasoning are promoted as children engage in self-governance and in thinking about specific social and moral issues. (See DeVries & Zan, 1994, for discussion of cognitive goals of grouptime.)

Grouptime is a context for encouraging children to take others' perspectives by listening to one another and exchanging ideas. For this reason, the teacher must be careful in his or her exercise of leadership. Young children tend to talk just to the teacher, and grouptime can become a time of competition for the teacher's attention. Sitting in a circle can help children think about communicating with the entire group.

Besides rule making, decision making, and social and moral discussions (discussed below), grouptime activities include singing, performing rituals, listening to and acting out stories, solving group problems, and introducing special activities for activity time.

RULE MAKING AND DECISION MAKING

The overarching objective of involving children in decision making and rule making in their classroom is to contribute to an atmosphere of mutual respect in which teachers and children practice self-regulation and coopera-tion. Three specific objectives are (1) to promote feelings of necessity about rules and fairness, (2) to promote feelings of ownership of and commitment to classroom rules, procedures, and decisions, and (3) to promote feelings of shared responsibility for what goes on in the class and how the group gets along together.

Through reflecting on the problems of classroom life together, children can be led to realize the necessity for rules. By participating in the determi-nation of what happens in the classroom, children can realize that decisions belong to them. They have the chance to understand why they have particu-lar rules and why they do things in particular ways. The sense of ownership resulting from sharing in the decision-making process leads children to de-velop a sense of shared responsibility for what happens in the class, good and bad. This extends even to responsibility for enforcing rules and classroom procedures.

In one class of 4-year-olds at the Human Development Laboratory School at the University of Houston, the teacher (Peige Fuller) was con-cerned because some children had been hurting others. She decides to raise the issue at grouptime and invite children to make some rules. As she begins grouptime, a child points out that Carolyn is crying. It turns out that Zena called Carolyn a "naughty girl." After several children comfort Carolyn, Peige pursues the issue.

Teacher: What do you want to be called?
Carolyn: My name.
Teacher: Your name. So should we have a rule about calling people by their names?
Children: Yeah!
Teacher: How should we write that? Tell me how to write that.
Carolyn: Call them your name.
Teacher (Repeats and writes): Call them your name.
Carolyn: Don't call them naughty girl or naughty boy.
Teacher (Repeats and writes): Don't call them naughty girl or naughty boy. Okay, so that takes care of kids using hurtful words. What about people using hurtful hands and feet?
George: That hurts people, and it's not nice.
Teacher: That hurts them and they don't like it. So what should we tell children to do?
Kate: Use their words.
Teacher: Tell them to use their words? (*Repeats and writes*) Use their words.
Kate: And if the words don't work, go get the teacher.

Teacher (Repeats and writes): And if the words don't work, go get the
teacher. Okay, is there any other guideline that we need to be able to
have friendly people in our class?
Derrick: Friendly hands.
Kate: And friendly words.
Teacher (Repeats and writes): Friendly hands and friendly words. Is that
how everyone wants their friends to treat them? With friendly hands
and friendly words? Okay.

The teacher here focused the rule making on a particular problem in the
class. She promoted children's autonomy by allowing them to dictate the
rules that made sense to them. She respected children by accepting their
ideas, words, and organization. Knowing that children tend to think about
rules in terms of prohibitions, Peige led the children to think about rules in
positive terms by asking children how they wanted to be treated and what
they wanted to have happen in their classroom. She emphasized that the
moral authority of the classroom rests with the children by writing and post-
ing the children's rules and encouraging children to refer to the rules they
made.

Even children as young as 3 or 4 years can be involved in other kinds
of classroom decisions—what they want to learn about, how to share turns
as Special Helper, and what to do when special problems arise. Sometimes
this can be accomplished through consensus, and sometimes it is necessary
to vote to determine the best course of action.

When conducted so that children can follow a clear process, voting experiences provide opportunities for children to construct the idea of equality
as they see that each person's opinion is valued and given equal weight in
the decision-making process (see DeVries & Zan, 1994, for discussion of
how and how not to conduct votes). Children come to feel a sense of cooperative group purposes that transcend the needs and wants of the individual,
coming to terms with the idea of majority rule while being led to show
sensitivity to minority positions. Writing and counting are integral parts of
voting and thus offer children opportunities to construct the meaning of
writing and number.

SOCIAL AND MORAL DISCUSSIONS

Discussions of social and moral dilemmas are excellent opportunities to
promote children's perspective taking and moral reasoning. We want children to think about interpersonal issues in more differentiated ways, becom-

ing better able to think beyond their own perspective to see and consider multiple perspectives and issues.

A social or moral dilemma is a situation in which competing claims, rights, or points of view can be identified. There is no clear right or wrong solution to a dilemma. A dilemma for discussion can take one of two forms—hypothetical or real-life dilemmas from the children's own experience. Both types are useful in helping children think about multiple perspectives. Hypothetical dilemmas are not as emotionally laden as real-life dilemmas, since the children are not personally involved in the issue. There is some emotional distance between the children and the dilemma. No one stands before the class angry or hurt or bleeding. Impersonal issues can often be discussed more rationally, and it is safer to express opinions when no one will react personally, have their feelings hurt, or suffer a real consequence. On the other hand, real-life dilemmas offer certain advantages for discussion as well. Since they occur spontaneously, the situations are intimately familiar to children. The actors involved are themselves and fellow classmates, and the situations usually bear directly on the life of the classroom, so children feel genuine concern about what happens. They also offer the advantage of having consequences children can recognize and evaluate fairly easily.

Some children's literature offers good material for social and moral discussions. For example, in the popular children's book *Doctor DeSoto* (Steig, 1982), we were able to observe several levels in children's moral reasoning. In the story, a fox has a toothache and goes to the only dentist in town, a mouse named Dr. DeSoto. Dr. DeSoto has a policy of not treating cats and other dangerous animals, but Dr. DeSoto's wife is moved by pity for the fox, who is in tremendous pain, and they decide to treat the fox. It becomes clear that the fox plans to eat the mice after they fix his tooth, so Dr. DeSoto comes up with a plan to trick the fox so he will not be able to eat them. They paint his teeth with a "secret formula" that they tell him will prevent toothaches. But the secret formula is really glue, and they glue the fox's teeth together temporarily, making it impossible for him to eat them.

After reading this story many times, the teacher asks a group of 4-year-olds, "Was it okay for Dr. DeSoto to trick the fox?" Most young children first take the perspective of the mice and believe that it was right for them to glue his teeth shut. Progress can be seen when children begin to consider the perspective of the fox and worry that with his teeth glued shut, he will not be able to eat or drink and may starve. We even observed one kindergarten child express concern that the fox will still get toothaches because the glue was not really a secret formula. A still more advanced level was expressed by one 4-year-old girl who stated that it was okay for the mice to trick the fox because if the fox ate Dr. DeSoto, then there would be no one in the town to fix teeth. She takes the perspective of the larger community. This is the teacher's goal, not to teach a right answer, but to lead children to see the situation from multiple perspectives. Therefore, it is important in these discussions for the teacher to ask children why they believe what they believe.

CONFLICT RESOLUTION

It is easy to recognize the practical value of resolving interpersonal conflict. If all adults had this ability, we would have world peace. Practical conflict resolution ability is an important constructivist goal. However, in Piaget's theory, the value of conflict is more complex, and the constructivist rationale also goes beyond the obvious value.

Piaget viewed conflict as critical for development, including both conflict within an individual and conflict between individuals. Conflict within an individual is a key component in the equilibration process by which all knowledge is constructed. Piaget emphasized the important role of interpersonal conflict in facilitating the internal conflict by which an individual begins to take more perspectives into account. For these reasons, conflict and its resolution are part of the constructivist curriculum. Some teachers try to prevent conflicts and suppress them when they do occur. In contrast, the constructivist approach welcomes conflicts as opportunities to promote perspective taking and interpersonal understanding.

The constructivist teacher promotes children's autonomy in conflict situations by recognizing that the conflict belongs to the children and refraining from taking control of the conflict away from the children. For example, a constructivist teacher would not take a disputed toy away from two children and state, "If you can't share it, neither of you can play with it." Believing in children's ability to solve their own conflicts, the constructivist teacher helps children verbalize their feelings and desires to each other and to listen to each other. All children's feelings are accepted, acknowledged, and validated, even when the teacher believes one child is guilty of violating the rights of another. The teacher gives the children the opportunity to suggest solutions and proposes solutions only when children cannot think of solutions on their own. The teacher upholds the value of mutual agreement and gives children the opportunity to reject proposed solutions.

Our research shows that when a teacher creates a cooperative sociomoral atmosphere and promotes children's conflict resolution, children's progress is more advanced than in classrooms where constructivist principles are absent. In a comparison study of children from constructivist, didactic, and eclectic kindergarten classrooms, we found that children from the constructivist classroom resolved significantly more of their conflicts (twice as many) than children from the other two classrooms (DeVries, Reese-Learned, & Morgan, 1991). Children from the didactic classroom tended to end their conflicts by overwhelming the other physically or emotionally. Children from the eclectic classroom tended to ignore their playmates' grievances. Children from the constructivist classroom tried to work out their differences and used significantly more of Selman's level-2 strategies.

THE CONSTRUCTIVIST ALTERNATIVE TO DISCIPLINE

A common misperception of constructivist education is that since constructivists do not believe in rewards and punishments, children are allowed to run wild. While constructivist classrooms do tend to be noisier and more active than traditional classrooms, constructivist classrooms are not out of control, and constructivist teachers are not passive about classroom management. They are highly active in their efforts to facilitate children's self-regulation. Their activity, however, does not take unilateral forms of training, drilling, or punishing. Rather, it takes cooperative forms to enable children to construct convictions and follow their own social and moral rules that are independent of adult coercion.

The constructivist alternatives to discipline focus on strategies to foster children's construction of convictions about relating to others in cooperative ways. Piaget's distinction between two kinds of sanctions provides the basis for planning general responses to misdeeds. The criterion of reciprocity leads constructivist teachers away from arbitrary sanctions and toward sanctions that emphasize the social bonds broken by children's misdeeds. These sanctions include allowing natural consequences to occur and leading children to such logical consequences as making restitution for causing material or physical harm to another.

For example, in a class of 4-year-olds, one child, Ralph, was always a problem on field trips, running away from the group and violating the field trip rules. As a class, the children discussed the field trip rules and decided that any child who could not listen to the teacher and follow the rules would not be allowed to go on the next field trip. On the next field trip, Ralph violated the rules, and the teacher invoked the logical consequence by telling him that he could not go on the next field trip. However, she did not want him to miss the planned trip to the zoo. So she planned two small field trips before the zoo trip. On the first, Ralph was not allowed to go on a walk across campus to play on some favorite trees. The teacher emphasized that this was the consequence on which the group had agreed. Before the second trip, the teacher talked with Ralph about his behavior, explaining why he would not be allowed to go on the zoo trip if he did not follow the rules. She asked him if he could demonstrate to the group that he could be trusted on field trips now. He said that he could. The teacher gave him the opportunity to regain the group's trust on the second small trip so that he would not experience the disappointment of missing the trip to the zoo. By helping Ralph understand that the reason for not being allowed to go on the field trip was his safety and the safety of the group, the teacher also helped him see the logical connection between the misbehavior and the consequence. The teacher hoped to foster Ralph's increased self-regulating ability by inspiring him to construct the feeling of necessity about safety or, at least, to construct the desire to adapt to the rule in order to be with the group. Logical consequences are not punishments when the child understands the reason for the consequences.

INTEGRATING SOCIOMORAL AND COGNITIVE OBJECTIVES

While our emphasis in this chapter is on sociomoral objectives in constructivist education, we do not want to leave the impression that cognitive objectives are absent in our approach. On the contrary! First of all, the perspective taking so central to sociomoral activities is a cognitive process of decentering. Second, the sociomoral atmosphere of respect for children is the intellectual atmosphere that supports the child's construction of knowledge and intelligence. Respect for children's reasoning includes reasoning both about the world of people and about the world of objects. By refusing to be all-knowing or all-powerful, the constructivist teacher opens the way for children to struggle with issues and not rely on adults for truths and values. Teachers who take an "expert" attitude lead children to look to adults to define both truth and moral values. When ready-made truths and values are "pasted on" the child's egocentric understanding, these are empty verbalisms that do not transform the child's reasoning. In contrast, adult cooperation liberates the child's mind to construct personal beliefs about truth and value. Only self-constructed truths are really understood, and only self-constructed values are real convictions that will guide behavior in the absence of adult constraint.

To shift the focus to the cognitive aspects of constructivist education, let us consider the activity time and the specific teaching of academics.

Activity Time

Children in constructivist classrooms spend a significant portion of each day freely choosing individual or small-group activities. For an hour to an hour and a half each morning and afternoon, they freely move among centers and engage in group games (Kamii & DeVries, 1980), physical-knowledge activities (Kamii & DeVries, 1978/1993), pretend play, literacy activities, blockbuilding, computers, and art. The general objective of activity time is that children will be intellectually, socially, and morally active, and more and more self-regulating. The atmosphere of activity time is both sociomoral and intellectual because the teacher's cooperative attitude communicates that children are free to be intellectually and morally active. For example, constructivist teachers ask children in a physical-knowledge activity to reflect on why some objects sink and some float, encourage children to consider contradictory opinions, and support the search for truth through acting on objects and discussing results. The constructivist teacher also asks children to reflect on how to take turns with the sink/float activity, helps them become conscious that many want this privilege at the same time, and suggests that they try to figure out a way to agree and satisfy everyone.

Recognizing that the child's construction of knowledge and morality depends on an active, motivated mind, the constructivist teacher plans activity time so as to appeal to children's interests, purposes, and reasoning. The general categories of activities mentioned above have proven to appeal to children's interests. Constructivist teachers ask children what they want to know about and plan activities based on their suggestions, communicating to children that they can find out what they want to know in school. Careful observation of children's spontaneous activities can be a source of new ideas for activities that appeal to children's interests. Children bring a special energy to activities derived from their own expressed interests. The importance of interest in education was stressed both by Dewey (1913/1975) and Piaget (1954/1981, 1971).

Some educators feel that young children must learn to do things in which they are not interested. Adults and older children are often capable of constructive effort even when interest is at a low level and they feel the pressure of some kind of coercion. Even for adults, however, the absence of interest can prevent effective effort. When our interest is thoroughly engaged, our efforts are most productive. This condition is even more necessary for young children, whose interests are yet relatively undifferentiated. According to Piaget, interest is central to the actions by which the child constructs knowledge, intelligence, and morality. Without interest, the child would never make the constructive effort to make sense out of experience. Without interest in what is new to him or her, the child would never modify reasoning or values. Interest is a kind of regulator that frees up or stops the investment of energy in an object, person, or event. It is fuel for the intellectual motor. Thus methods aimed at promoting the constructive process must arouse the child's spontaneous interest that is inherent in constructivist activity. Insisting that children do something in which they have no interest leads to low-level reasoning and to heteronomous submission to adult dominance.

Interest is the springboard for purpose. We feel strongly that we must help children find *their* purposes in activities. We mean that children must find in the activities something that they are motivated to do out of their own interest, not because they are being asked to do them by the teacher. This principle, however, does not mean that the teacher should never suggest purposes. The teacher can suggest a purpose that inspires children's genuine enthusiasm.

After appealing to children's interests and purposes, reasoning is close behind. The constructivist teacher plans in terms of possible interesting purposes that will engage reasoning. Stephanie Clark, the Investigators' (3½ to 4½ years) teacher at the University of Houston Human Development Laboratory School, wrote the following plan.

> Physical-knowledge activities will focus on sprinklers. Monday, I will put containers without holes in the water table. Tuesday, I will ask the children if they have any ideas about making sprinklers out of these containers. We will use a variety of tools to make these changes. Where do I need to make the holes? How many holes do we need? Can we use these sprinklers for something useful like watering plants? Thursday, I will put out a variety of tin cans perforated to facilitate the flow of water. Which can will pour the most water? I expect the children to guess the largest can (with only one small hole). Then I will show the children the perforations (some just around the edge of one can, some in a straight line across the middle of one, and many all over the bottom of a small can).

Children did take up these suggestions as ideas they personally wanted to pursue. Had they not responded with interest, making the suggested purpose their own, Stephanie would have abandoned the activity.

A Word About Academics

One misconception about constructivist education is that because it includes play, it does not include academics. However, constructivist educators are serious-minded about children's engagement with literacy, number and arithmetic, science, social studies, and fine arts. This can be seen in the state of Missouri, where the State Department of Elementary and Secondary Education adopted constructivist education (which they call "Project Construct") for grades prekindergarten through first grade, to be implemented on a voluntary basis. We recently observed an excellent Project Construct second-grade class in which children pursued independent journal writing, reading literature, reading and writing reports on crystals (and making them and studying them under a microscope to discover their different geometric structures), figuring out math puzzles, and exchanging ideas on different ways to do mental math. What impressed us was the intensity of the children's investment in their activities. It was clear that their engagement was not derived from the teacher's direction but from their own interests and purposes. The sociomoral atmosphere of respect and cooperation inspired children's academic studies in a way that coercion could never accomplish.

While we consider academics of critical importance in children's schooling, we see a danger in making academics the only or highest priority. With academics as the priority and with learning considered a matter of direct transmission, teachers easily fall into a heteronomous relation to children. With development as the priority and with learning considered a matter of the child's construction, a heteronomous relation is not possible. Our research indicates that when a strong authoritarian approach is combined with a strong emphasis on academics, children are less advanced in their sociomoral development (DeVries, Haney, & Zan, 1991; DeVries, Reese-Learned, & Morgan, 1991). We therefore maintain that the ethical position in planning and implementing the teaching of academics is to "do no harm." When the teaching of academics results in harm to children's sociomoral development, it cannot be defended as ethical.

We remind the reader of Piaget's (1932/1965) view that adults' heteronomous regulation of children can result in mindless conformity in both moral and intellectual aspects of the child's life. Emphasis on obedience fosters self-doubt and other qualities needed for submission. Educational experience preoccupied with giving back correct information destroys curiosity and leads to intellectual dullness and knowledge full of egocentric misunderstanding—"school varnish." Authoritarian regulation of academic lessons reinforces moral as well as intellectual heteronomy. The intellectual heteronomy that accompanies moral heteronomy is reflected in a passive orientation to the ideas of others, an unquestioning and uncritical attitude, and low motivation to reason.

Piaget's view is that adults' cooperative relations with children result in active reflection in both moral and intellectual aspects of the child's life. Emphasis on the child's self-regulation fosters self-confidence, an attitude of questioning and critical evaluation, and motivation to think about causes, implications, and explanations of physical and logical as well as social and moral phenomena. When the adult respects the child's reasoning and provides extensive opportunities for exploration and experimentation, intellectual sharpness results.

Our effort to define constructivist conditions for teaching academics is prompted not just by the aim to "do no harm" but also by the more positive aim of optimal construction of knowledge, including academics. While life in a moral classroom creates general conditions for intellectual development, it is possible to establish a cooperative atmosphere with inadequate attention to academics. The challenge for constructivist teachers is to incorporate academics into classroom life and to integrate developmental and academic objectives. In fact, we argue that the best teaching of academics is rooted in knowledge of developmental transformations in children's conceptions of academic content.

CONCLUSION

We emphasize the cooperative sociomoral atmosphere as essential to constructivist education. We know that teachers trying to base teaching on the principle that children construct knowledge often approach children in coercive ways, deciding what children should be interested in, telling them how they should "explore" or "experiment" with materials, deciding in advance what children should know and think, and ignoring the important role of children's constructive errors. In our view, failure to create a cooperative sociomoral atmosphere for learning academics not only undermines children's sociomoral development, but it also undermines children's construction of knowledge related to academics. We urge constructivist educators to consider the cooperative sociomoral atmosphere as a necessary context for promoting all aspects of children's development and learning.

REFERENCES

Deci, E., Sheinman, L., Schwartz, A., & Ryan, R. (1981). An instrument to assess adults' orientations toward control versus autonomy with children: Reflections on intrinsic motivation and perceived competence. *Journal of Educational Psychology, 73*(5), 642–650.

DeVries, R., Haney, J., & Zan, B. (1991). Sociomoral atmosphere in direct-instruction, eclectic, and constructivist kindergartens: A study of teachers' enacted interpersonal understanding. *Early Childhood Research Quarterly, 6,* 449–471.

DeVries, R., Reese-Learned, H., & Morgan, P. (1991). Sociomoral development in direct-instruction, eclectic, and constructivist kindergartens: A study of children's enacted interpersonal understanding. *Early Childhood Research Quarterly, 6,* 473–517.

DeVries, R., & Zan, B. (1994). *Moral classrooms, moral children: Creating a constructivist atmosphere in early education.* New York: Teachers College Press.

Dewey, J. (1975). *Interest and effort in education.* Edwardsville, IL: Southern Illinois Press. (Original work published 1913)

Kamii, C., & DeVries, R. (1980). *Group games in early education: Implications of Piaget's theory.* Washington, DC: National Association for the Education of Young Children.

Kamii, C., & DeVries, R. (1993). *Physical knowledge in preschool education: Implications of Piaget's theory.* New York: Teachers College Press. (Original work published 1978)

Piaget, J. (1965). *The moral judgment of the child.* London: Free Press. (Original work published 1932)

Piaget, J. (1971). *Science of education and the psychology of the child.* New York: Viking Compass.

Piaget, J. (1981). *Intelligence and affectivity.* Palo Alto, CA: Annual Reviews. (Original work published 1954)

Selman, R. (1980). *The growth of interpersonal understanding.* New York: Academic Press.

Selman, R., & Schultz, L. (1990). *Making a friend in youth.* Chicago: University of Chicago Press.

Steig, W. (1982). *Doctor DeSoto.* New York: Farrar, Straus, & Giroux.

CHAPTER 9

A Constructivist Perspective from the Emerging Field of Disability Studies

D. Kim Reid and Jan Weatherly Valle

In today's schools, disability constitutes a dilemma. Medicalized, deficit, and therefore largely negative (and sometimes equally detrimentally romanticized) images of disabled students lead to their exclusion from classrooms for all or part of the school day. The research literature demonstrates that many general-education teachers believe that they do not know how to teach such students and both general and special educators often believe that disabled students somehow learn differently from others. Consequently, teachers interacting with these students in accordance with their beliefs and expectations typically use the teacher-directed, fragmented, drill-and-practice instructional methods that they believe these students need. There is a widespread assumption that disabled students cannot learn from constructivist approaches to instruction: constructivist approaches are reserved for the "normal," and particularly the gifted—the students who are perceived as self-directed and who can think creatively for themselves. The *disability dilemma,* then, lies in the fact that it is their categorization as disabled that positions students as incompetent learners. People often assume that even wheelchair users are cognitively impaired! Once labeled, identified students are taught in ways that confirm their failure to learn: in segregated settings with other like-labeled students; at a slower pace; using a watered-down curriculum composed of repetitive, low-level tasks; and without the opportunity for group work and stimulating, holistic instruction.

In this chapter we argue that disabled students are naturally active learners who learn in the way that all humans do: through the life-sustaining processes described so ably in the first three chapters of this book. We share selections from transcripts from our own and others' research to demonstrate how teachers instruct disabled students in ways that obstruct, discourage, or at least fail to recognize and build on disabled students' spontaneous activity. We also use transcript selections to reveal their self-initiated, self-regulated activity. We end by examining how we might provide better instructional opportunities for disabled students. Before we begin our discussion of typical classroom activity, we would like to suggest, in keeping with the tenets of the emerging field of Disability Studies, that disability itself is socially constructed through the beliefs and expectations that circulate in the wider out-of-school, as well as in-school, culture.

DISABILITY STUDIES IN EDUCATION

In the last several decades, scholars have paid increasing attention to the sociopolitical, sociocultural analysis of special education. Rather than explain disabilities as solely cognitive, emotional, sensory, and/or physical deficits, many have begun to examine the relations among differences, impairments, and disability—that is, to examine and problematize the "conventions that structure the meanings assigned to disability and the patterns of response to disability that emanate from, or are attendant upon, those meanings" (Linton, 1998, p. 8).

Scholars in the field of Disability Studies use the term *difference* to refer to human variation that is ideologically neutral because it is ordinary and pervasive. Many such variations, however, depending on the historical moment (Franklin, 1987; Stiker, 1987) and the demands of a given culture (Kalyanpur & Harry, 1999), become labeled as *impairments*. Learning disability is a case in point. This diagnostic category to label bright students who seem unable to keep up with their peers in school did not exist until school standards were raised in response to the Cold War arms race (Franklin, 1987; Sleeter, 1995). *Disability,* on the other hand, is a term reserved for describing the product of social, political, economic, and cultural practices (Corker & Shakespeare, 2002): Oppression is a key factor in self-identifying as disabled. Highlighting these distinctions brings taken-for-granted assumptions to the fore. For example, although we do not often think of it this way, impairment too is, as Vygotsky (1987) noted over 100 years ago, socially determined. A difference is just a difference until cultural consensus makes it a problem. We can think of impairment, then, as a culturally constructed category materially shaped by the interactions of social and biological factors and processes and existing in particular times and places (Thomas, 1999). Disability, then, is a term reserved to describe social oppression and the resultant minority-group status.

To confront their ongoing oppression, large numbers of disabled people banded together in the Disability Rights movement (see Fleischer & Zames, 2001). One major outcome was passage of the Americans with Disabilities Act, just as the activism of parents and educators led to passage of the Individuals with Disabilities Education Act (which in its requirement for the specification of long- and short-term objectives in Individual Educational Programs instantiated a behavioral instructional approach to disability). Through such movements, disabled people and their advocates bring to national attention the injustice of having medical, government, and educational "experts" (including teachers and researchers) label them and make decisions about their lives. For disabled people, the personal is clearly political. As people battling for the right to self-determination and equal access, they make clear that categorization, because it puts people in a hierarchy, leads to discrimination: It positions disabled people as "objects" and marginalizes their voices. These movements, therefore, instruct us in the power of the disciplines (e.g., medicine, law, education) to define truth, to determine what constitutes knowledge, and to authorize some people, but not others, to speak.

When we regard education as one of those truth-defining disciplines, we begin to ask ourselves: If students were to be in charge of schools, would they choose to divide into groups of disabled and nondisabled? Would they separate themselves by choice into various classrooms according to test results or ease of teaching? Would they choose to engage in drill-and-practice exercises? How might their research questions differ from those that are now being addressed? Do teachers who identify as disabled teach differently? How would they reorganize schools if they were given the liberty to do so? Would they choose to be labeled? These are not trivial questions, because they reflect a difference in perspective and positioning that disabled people, their advocates, and Disability Studies scholars use in an effort to modify what counts as current knowledge.

Although there has been a long history of dissent in special education, only recently have scholars formed a new special interest group within the American Educational Research Association (AERA): Disability Studies in Education (DSE). These scholars stand apart from and, in many ways, in opposition to the AERA Special Education special interest group. Because it is engendering a new community of scholars, this is a reframing of the field that is significant. The burgeoning discipline of Disability Studies, closely linked to the Disability Rights movement through its emphasis on the social and political dimensions of disability, offers a different set of truths about disability.

DSE has in common with Disability Studies more broadly an interdisciplinary focus informed by the knowledge base and methodologies of the traditional liberal arts. It is grounded, as is constructivism itself, in postpositivist perspectives (as opposed to the positivist science of medicine, rehabilitation, and special education (see Danforth, 1999; Gallagher, 2001). One aim of DSE is to promote understanding of disability as a function of both (1) ordinary, pervasive human variation (as opposed to pathology and deficit) and (2) the meanings attributed to those variations (i.e., impairment and disability [Linton, 1998]). By examining the social meanings we give to variations that exist in human behavior and appearance, DSE challenges the implicit or explicit differential valuing of people that enables us to construct "taken-as-shared" exclusionary categorical binaries, such as normal versus abnormal, abled versus disabled, and so forth. DSE recognizes them as mutually constitutive and mutable: We can change the nature of disability by revising our conceptions of ability and abnormality, by revising our definitions of normal. As mentioned earlier, such changes do, in fact, occur both over time and across cultures.

The second aim of DSE is to examine the role that disability has played, is playing, and can potentially play in the arts, humanities, sciences (for examples, see such works as Adams, 2001; Garland Thomson, 1996, 1997; Longmore & Umansky, 2001; Mitchell & Snyder, 2000; Stiker, 1987) and education (e.g., Dudley-Marling & Dippo, 1995; Reid & Valle, in press; Sleeter, 1995). Within this new framework, the external conditions—social, political, and cultural—that contribute significantly to the disability experience share center stage with, or even eclipse, human variation (labeled as *impairment*). Scholars and advocates alike shift their focus of attention from the individual to the interaction between the individual and society, a clearly constructivist orientation, and to the constraints imposed by the structures of society itself.

In contrast to an understanding of disability solely in terms of deficits located within the individual (i.e., variations labeled as impairments), this new discourse acknowledges that disability may be experienced differently depending upon an individual's race, class, and gender as well as other aspects of positionality (Bordieu, 1986) and identity (Artiles, 2003; Ferri, in press). Typically, studies dominating special education, however, are situated in the medical and science discourse. They randomize away or otherwise ignore (Reid, 2001) personal identity factors, unless such factors are specifically selected as the focus of the study. Given the impact of such varying combinations of identity dimensions on the material consequences of disability, however, it follows that there can be no single experience of disability and that attention to raced, classed, and gendered perspectives (both those of the researcher and of the researched) are necessary.

If we reconceptualize disability as socially constructed and examine the societal systems designed to deal with it, including special education, we can document how it has been constructed by science (Carrier, 1986), the structure of schools (Skrtic, 1995), public policy (Bogdan & Knoll, 1995), historical events (Franklin, 1987; Sleeter, 1995), and popular and scientific discourses (Dudley-Marling & Dippo, 1995; Reid & Valle, in press). Recognizing that disabilities are a set of socially constructed categories also enables us to observe that segregating students into category or disability-defined classrooms is also a social decision, one that may serve better the interests of school order than the students and their families (Thomas & Loxley, 2001). In addition, it silences the debate about whether all children should receive a free and appropriate education in the least restrictive environment—that is, in inclusive educational settings.

Aligning ourselves with the DSE perspective, we find the sociopolitical repositioning of disability troublesome for many of the foundational assumptions underlying the practices of special education. The taken-as-shared assumptions that encourage drill-and-practice exercises and skills-based, fragmented, teacher-dominated instruction position disabled students as passive and in need of expert direction—from government officials, healthcare workers, parents, and teachers. Examining disability from the outside as "experts" and focusing on human variation as necessarily problematic and individual are clearly incompatible with the view that there is no impairment until society constructs one. Unfortunately, the widespread belief that disabled students are impaired plays an important role in perpetuating oppressive instructional practices (i.e., in disabling them), even if only by denying disabled students the opportunity to engage with their peers in learning environments, such as constructivist classrooms that support their natural, spontaneous human activity and creativity.

In sum, education is always construed according to someone's vision and someone's system of values (Barton & Armstrong, 2001). Educators and the public seldom acknowledge that we are making choices in the ways that we design and implement education, and that with those choices comes ethical responsibility. We can continue to sort and segregate students according to the current special education discourses despite the lack of evidence that these practices are helpful to them and despite the serious overrepresentation of students of color in special education and particularly in segregated educational settings (Losen & Orfield, 2002). Or we can work in solidarity with and for disabled students to foster a set of different assumptions: public school classrooms are for all America's children; ordinary human diversity is mutually enhancing, not restricting; all humans actively and spontaneously struggle to make meaning, even those we have labeled and often segregated; students learn better through cooperation than through competition; problem-solving dialogue is more powerful than exercises; and students need not be protected from making errors but need instead an opportunity to reflect on the errors they make.

Finally, it is not our intention to minimize the extent or seriousness of the problems that students labeled as "disabled" experience in school. Our argument is that many of those problems result from attitudes about what is acceptable and "normal" as well as the ways in which both lessons and schools are structured (rather than the impairment itself).

CONSTRUCTING DISABILITY IN THE CLASSROOM

In recent years, the taken-as-shared assumptions that undergird special education (e.g., disabled students *require* teacher-directed, fragmented, skills-based instruction), have come under increasing criticism (Brantlinger, 1997; Heshusius, 1989; Poplin, 1988a, 1988b; Varenne & McDermott, 1998). Moreover, a growing number of special education scholars, most of whom ground their work in Piagetian and Vygotskian theories of learning (Dudley-Marling, in press; Englert, 1992; Gallagher & Reid, 2002; Mariage, Paxton-Buursma, & Bouck, in press; Poplin, 1988a, 1988b; Reid, 1998; Reid & Stone, 1991; Stone & Reid, 1994) document how behavioral approaches to instruction, predominant in special education practice, operate to *construct* "disabled" students as passive and dependent learners. In the discussion below, we present examples from the literature as well as our own research to illustrate the process by which "disabled" students become positioned by language and practice in the classroom.

In this first example, Englert (1992), a scholar in early literacy practices, critiques the following transcript of a lesson in paragraph writing that takes place in a special-education classroom for elementary students labeled as "learning disabled."

T: I'll give you the topic and topic sentence. All you'll have to come up with is your own . . .
S: Paragraph.
S: Supporting details.
T: Supporting details . . .
S: Closing sentence.

[Teacher turns on the overhead. On the overhead is a picture of a girl sitting down to resume painting a picture; however, the chair is falling over, and the paint is about to spill on the girl.]

T: Put your hands down. You'll all get a chance to write what you think happened to Sally (*the girl in the picture*). You'll all indent, write complete sentences, and use proper punctuation. Michael, how many times will you indent?

M: (*no response*)

T: One, five, ten, twenty?

M: One time.

T: One time. Only one with Sally . . . Keep looking at the picture as much as you need to and decide what happened. You need to think in your mind, "What happened to Sally?" Think of emotion words to say how Sally felt. Think of describing words.

S: Can we draw a picture?

T: No. I need you to tell me what happened with words. Decide what happened after what you see in the picture. (*T begins to walk around . . .*) "Where is your cursive? Left it at home? Why are you printing? Let's write cursive, and get off to a fine start." [To second student] "We're not going to write Sally with a small letter, and we're not going to start at the margin . . ." (*To class*) Come on guys, we have to at least copy the first sentence properly. We should be able to copy correctly. (Englert, 1992, p. 154)

The underlying assumption that students labeled as learning disabled *need* teacher-directed, skills-based instruction is unmistakable in this classroom scenario. In response to what she perceives as the children's state of "disabledness," the teacher offers a highly decontextualized and mechanistic approach to paragraph writing. The act of writing, *inherently* a meaning-making activity, is reduced to a set of discrete skills (e.g., topic, topic sentence, supporting details, closing sentence, indentation, complete sentences, cursive, capitalization rules) to be practiced and applied to a formulaic process. In this highly teacher-driven lesson, the children are afforded no opportunities to think aloud or collaborate with peers, effectively eliminating all use of language as "a tool for thought" (Wertsch, 1991). In fact, the only opportunity the children have to speak is in response to the teacher's fill-in-the-blank questions that require them to supply a word (or words) that the teacher is thinking of. Positioned as passive learners and astrategic thinkers, the children are dehumanized further in the requirement to write about a topic chosen *for* them, as if to imply that they have no legitimate experiences upon which to draw or the capability to do so.

Given that school professionals routinely describe children labeled as learning disabled in terms of language deficits, we might presume that the teacher chooses this strategy in her attempt to target "the needs" of her students. In other words, she operates under the taken-as-agreed assumption that *these* children learn in ways that are somehow altogether different from the ways that "ordinary" children learn. Thus, the children in this classroom, deemed in need of education that is "special," become positioned, on the basis of their disability, as incapable of benefiting from instruction that supports natural, spontaneous, human activity.

Dudley-Marling (in press) supplies us with another example. He reveals how an 8-year-old boy's "LD identity" is both constructed and sustained within a verbal exchange with his special education teacher. Mrs. Stroh, the teacher, is speaking with Regis, a student in her self-contained class for students labeled LD (learning disabled), about his reading worksheet.

Mrs. Stroh: Show me all of the pictures that begin with "mmm." Does this begin with "mmm" Regis? (*pointing to a picture of a car*)

Regis: Nope.

Mrs. Stroh: I want you to go through the page. Show me the pictures that begin with "m."

Regis: (*Points to the pictures on the page that begin with "m."*)

Mrs. Stroh: Alright. You missed one. See if you can find the one you missed . . .

Regis: No. Yeah.

Mrs. Stroh: Where is it? Where is the one you missed?

Regis: Right here . . .

Mrs. Stroh: No, you showed me that one before. What's this? (*Pointing to a picture of a match*)

Regis: I don't know. What it is?

Mrs. Stroh: We talked about that yesterday, Regis. What is it that you use to start a fire? (*pause*) Do you have a fireplace . . .? When you want to build a fire in the fireplace what do you have to have?

Regis: This thing? (*points to the picture of the match*)

Mrs Stroh: Yes, I know you have to have that thing, but what's it called? Who starts the fires in your house?

Regis: My grandpa gets the fire to—

Mrs. Stroh: (*Interrupts*) Does he ever say, "Bring me a _____?

Regis: Wood.

Mrs. Stroh: Well, probably, yes. Does he ever say, "Bring me a match, please"?

Regis: No, he doesn't say that.

Mrs. Stroh: Oh, he doesn't say *that*. What is *that*?

Regis: He sometimes, when he goes down in the basement, sometimes I
    help him carry up the wood, get the wood and bring it upstairs to the
    fire.
Mrs. Stroh: Good. Get that _____
Regis: Wood.
Mrs. Stroh: What did I just say?
Regis: I don't know. . . . I couldn't hear you.
Mrs. Stroh: Oh yes. You could hear me. What did I say? Does grandpa
    ever ask you to bring him a _____?
Regis: Wood.
Mrs. Stroh: Match [clearly exasperated]
Regis: A match. (Dudley-Marling, in press)

Dudley-Marling (in press) offers two perspectives from which to interpret this exchange. We can view this scenario using a traditional deficit lens
and understand Regis as displaying "word finding" difficulty, a characteristic
commonly identified among children labeled as learning disabled. Or we can
view this same scenario using a social constructivist lens and understand
Regis as an individual-in-social-action. As Dudley-Marling suggests, the task,
the setting, and the interaction between the teacher and Regis "are all instrumental in producing (or, in this case, re-producing) Mrs. Stroh's identity as
'teacher' and Regis's identity as 'learning disabled' . . . [providing] the right
task, at the right time, in the right place to make visible Regis's *learning
disability.*"

Mrs. Stroh, operating under the assumption that Regis is experiencing
word-finding difficulty, persists in her attempts to elicit the answer she
deems correct (i.e., "match"). She appears to believe that getting Regis to
produce the word that *she* is thinking will provide her with evidence that
learning has taken place. Mrs. Stroh's instructional approach reflects what
Fosnot (1996) refers to as "the belief that we hold identical objective meanings" which, in turn, undergirds the assumption that "a learner can 'absorb'
the adult's conceptual understanding if the developmental match is right—
that meaning resides in the symbolic representation of the teacher and that
it can be 'transmitted' to the learner" (p. 21). Special education practice is
rife with such "transmission-infused" instruction reflecting the taken-as-
agreed assumption that children with disabilities not only *can* absorb meaning in this way but they actually *need* this type of instruction in order to
learn.

In contrast to the preceding examples that take place in segregated special education sites, Kliewer (1998) documents the positioning of Down
syndrome children within inclusive educational settings. In his 2-year ethnographic study, Kliewer observes that diagnostic/prescriptive instruction,

common to segregated special education classrooms, actually *follows* disabled children into their general education environments. As Kliewer notes, "This shift in locale acknowledges the alienation from the community inevitably constructed by segregation but maintains a consistent separation of learners within the shared environment" (p. 59). In other words, despite the children's *access* to general education, teachers position them within the classroom in ways that minimize their actual engagement.

Kliewer describes specific incidences of how such positioning operates. For example, in response to faculty concerns about including Down syndrome children in a preschool program, nondisabled 4-year-olds attend school 3 days a week while their disabled counterparts attend 5 days a week. On the days that only disabled children attend, teachers provide direct instruction in "attending skills."

> While the students with disabilities were in school receiving direct instruction in *attending*, their nondisabled classmates participate in neighborhood activities . . . the image of the nondisabled learner benefiting from the community outside the school stood in contrast to the perception that the disabled learners required professional intervention in order that they might someday participate in the community. (Kliewer, 1998, p. 60)

Once again, we see teachers operating under the taken-as-agreed assumption that disabled children not only require teacher-directed, skills-based instruction, but that they must *master* these skills in order to participate with nondisabled peers. Kliewer offers the following comments regarding his observations of the disabled children on segregated and integrated school days:

> It appeared that the *paying attention curriculum*, implemented on segregated days, had less impact on students' developing attending skills than did the act of increasing the complexity of the activities themselves. The level of attention demonstrated by students with disabilities reflected their level of interest in the topic at hand: On days when the nondisabled students joined the class, adult-established functional skills and operant instruction were de-emphasized and largely replaced by child-initiated and cooperative activities focused on what teachers described as *developmentally appropriate* learning goals. (Kliewer, 1998, p. 61)

Thus, Kliewer provides compelling evidence for both the ineffectiveness of decontextualized, direct instruction for disabled children as well as their enhanced response upon being included in the kind of cooperative, child-initiated activities routinely offered to their nondisabled peers.

Unlike each of the preceding examples that represents a researcher's *interpretation* of observed classroom events, Nanette Hutchinson, a hearing-impaired woman attending the graduate teacher education program at the City College of New York (CUNY), writes in a reflective journal assignment about her *lived* experience of being positioned as incapable by her third-grade teacher.

> I felt very lonely in the classroom because I was always seated in a corner in the back of the classroom away from the other children. I was never part of a group discussion or group activities or even able to work in the learning center. All the children seemed to have been learning something new each day and having fun while I worked on math or reading worksheets by myself in the corner. I was not getting the attention I needed and expected from my teacher. Her attention was too focused on her "normal" children. I then realized that I was of the least importance to her and not part of the "whole" class. Why? Was it because of my disability? Or was it that she did not have the patience to deal with me? I assumed that because I wore a hearing aid, I was not considered a normal person. I was a person who was incapable of performing class work, a person not allowed to work with other children as if I had a disease that was contagious. This was a terrible experience for me.

Nanette's narrative supports Kliewer's (1998) observation that including students with disabilities in the general classroom does not guarantee integration into a shared environment. Although she is physically present in a general education classroom, Nanette remains positioned as *needing* something different than her nondisabled peers in order to learn—specifically, drill and practice. Perhaps more significantly, Nanette reveals how, as an 8-year-old child, she understood the *ideology* that justified her exclusion—namely, that there are two types of children, normal and abnormal, that normal children, by virtue of their normality, are considered to be more valuable, and that a hearing impairment signifies not only incapability to learn but also the potential to interfere with the learning of normal children who *deserve* to learn.

Nanette comments upon her awareness, as a child, that she was seen as someone different in school than at home.

> As for my family, they treated me no different; I was their "normal" little sister which I think is why I succeeded very well at speaking fluently, especially for a person whose hearing loss is considered severe.

Thus, Nanette makes explicit how disability is constructed by the social meaning people attribute to it. In one context, she is seen and treated as "normal"; in another, she is seen and treated as "abnormal." She illustrates this point again in her recollection of fourth grade, a context in which the teacher *sees* her as a capable student.

> [In] social studies, I had the opportunity to understand the complex world in which I lived, enabling me to be productive and happy within a social framework. I learned that each person is a unique individual and I learned about self-awareness . . . I developed a basic understanding about the world around me and that was what stood out about that year. It all started as a surprise class trip in which we were to study our school community. Provided with a sketch pad, and in groups having their own particular part of the community to study, we walked slowly and observed our community carefully. I remember how we had to describe the community around our school by drawing what we saw such as streets, businesses, churches, houses, apartment buildings, parks, police stations, traffic lights, vacant lots, etc. Not knowing the results, with everyone's sketches and drawings, we as a class developed one big map. I do recall how much fun and excitement there was when this project was being put together. There was so much engagement/interaction, laughter, expression of positive thoughts, questions and answers from the teammates, and sharing of ideas as a group. In all, it was [a] "sense of belonging" to me, regardless of my disability. I did not feel like an outsider.

Nanette's disability seems to disappear entirely within the context of this inclusive classroom. Here, she is constructed as an active, valuable, and contributing member of a vibrant classroom community. She clearly benefits from this learning environment in the *same* way that her nondisabled peers do. In this case, Nanette again understands the ideology that justifies, this time, her *inclusion*—namely, that all children are valuable, regardless of ability or disability, that she belongs in the classroom by virtue of her humanity, and that all children contribute to each other's meaning-making in the world.

CONSTRUCTING ABILITY IN THE CLASSROOM

As Nanette's narrative so powerfully illustrates, the beliefs and expectations that teachers hold regarding disability impact the ways in which disabled students are positioned in the classroom. Given that the dominant ideology circulating in schools constructs disabled students as passive and dependent, teachers who act upon a different set of beliefs and expectations about disability may meet with resistance from colleagues invested in traditional special education practice.

In a 2-year ethnographic study, Kasa-Hendrickson (in press) studied how teachers come to know, interpret, and act upon the ability of nonverbal students with autism. In the following excerpt, Kasa-Hendrickson relates an example of resistance to new ways of thinking about and responding to disability. This general education classroom scene opens as first graders, including Sam, a student labeled as autistic and mentally retarded, scurry to the rug for Read Aloud. The teacher, Lisa, reads to the highly engaged group of children.

> About halfway through the chapter, the principal entered and asked in a loud voice, "What are you doing?" "Reading," Lisa replied. "Why is he a part of this?" In an effort to stop the principal from going any further, Lisa asked if she could talk with the principal about this later. "Oh yes we will talk about this. You can be sure of that." She left and Lisa continued reading and then engaged in her routine activities of discussing the events in the book, charting them on a time line, comparing characters, and looking up and recording new vocabulary. Curious about the teacher's concern, I stayed longer that day. After the lesson, Lisa shared, "She wrote me up last week for 'teaching inappropriate curriculum for a student with mental retardation.'" (Kasa-Hendrickson, in press)

The power of ideology is unmistakable in this scenario. Much like the teachers in Kliewer's (1998) study who persist in providing direct instruction to their disabled students despite evidence that it is ineffective, the principal appears "unable" to see what is happening because it does not "fit" with her conceptions of "how things ought to be."

Despite such incidents, the teachers in Kasa-Hendrickson's (in press) study continue to operate out of an ideological framework that constructs disabled students as competent. In the following example, Kasa-Henrickson relates how David, a 5-year-old boy labeled with both autism and mental retardation, is assumed by his general education kindergarten teacher to be a competent learner who is capable of possessing and pursuing interests. Margo, his teacher, notices that David seems particularly drawn to a small poster about presidents. She acknowledges his interest and suggests that he might check out a book about presidents from the school library. She further observes David *appearing* to read and reread a *New York Times* article about presidential candidates. In a subsequent interview with Kasa-Hendrickson, Margo explains:

> You know how at the end of an article it says continued on B3? I was sitting there the first day watching him and I thought, "He will not be able to find B3." Well he proved me wrong . . . That really blew me away. And later his

mom told me that he got very mad last week when she tried to turn the presidential debates off. I think he has a new interest here and is learning more about it because of all of the coverage in the news. (Kasa-Hendrickson, in press)

Drawing upon Dudley-Marling's (in press) perspective of the individual-in-social-action, we can see how the task, setting, and interaction between teacher and student function, in this case, to construct a disabled student as an *able* learner. Significantly, Kasa-Hendrickson (in press) observes that Margo recognizes and appreciates David's initiation, believing that he has the capacity to engage with an abstract concept such as presidency. In encouraging his moves toward literacy and learning, Margot validates David as a person who engages in spontaneous human activity like anyone else.

Our own research in an inclusive fourth-grade classroom (2002–2003) reveals similar outcomes for disabled students when teachers view them as competent learners. Much like Kasa-Henrickson's (in press) research, we studied *how* a collaborative team (a general education teacher and a special education teacher) work together in an integrated environment to include *all* students, regardless of disability. Although the school had practiced inclusion for over ten years, our observations indicated that, in practice, they had merely replaced "pull out" with "pull aside," reflecting the type of re-creation of separation *within* the classroom reported by Kliewer (1998). In seeking to disrupt such practices, the collaborative team met with resistance (and, at times, ridicule) from some colleagues. In particular, the speech/language therapist openly denigrated their choice to include students labeled as "language impaired" in class Read Alouds and book discussions, flatly stating that these children were not capable of benefiting from such instruction.

The following transcript illustrates the active participation of disabled students and nondisabled students in a lesson on interpreting poetry. Although we strenuously object to labels because they tend to create a unidimensional lens through which teachers read students, we do note in this transcript the designated labels of the students in order to clarify for the reader the power and creativity of thinking that the students so labeled demonstrate. In this classroom scenario, the teacher begins by modeling a "think aloud" strategy for the class.

Teacher: The poem is *The Blue Between.* I am going to model reading this poem. Then you will talk to a partner about what I am doing in my brain.

"The Blue Between."
In poetry, titles are super important.

"Everyone watches the clouds."
A lot of people watch clouds.
"naming creatures they've seen"
People lay on their backs in the park and see clouds that look like a
   car, a giraffe—not like a car in the sky, but people *see* things in the
   clouds.
"I see the blue between."
Instead of looking at the clouds, she is looking at the sky in between.
   It is different than what other people are doing.

Turn to a partner. What did you notice me doing?

[*As the children engage in discussion, the teacher circulates, listens in, and
facilitates conversations as needed.*]

Teacher: I listened to a couple of people talking. Jamal noticed that I took
   notes. Raymond noticed that I stopped to talk to myself. Let's go back
   to the first four lines.
Serena (LD): She sees animals in the clouds.
Teacher: Anyone want to add on to what Serena said?
Gary: She is looking at the cloudless part. The blue surrounded by the
   clouds.
Harriet:(LD): I agree.
Teacher: Does she actually see a blue woman in the sky?
Children: Nooooo!

By this point in the lesson, the teacher has made a number of moves that
reflect her belief that *all* children are active meaning-makers. She consciously
chooses a "think-aloud" strategy to introduce the class to poetry interpretation (as opposed to direct instruction), reflecting trust in the children to
draw their own conclusions about what they hear and see. She regards each
child as a valuable, contributing member to the knowledge they construct
as a classroom community. Serena, a student labeled as LD, enters the dialogue by offering a valid, yet concrete, idea about the poem. Her contribution is embraced in the community conversation and acknowledged by the
teacher as a point worth adding on to. Harriet, another student labeled LD,
participates by noting her agreement with a peer's contribution. This is significant in that Harriet, who typically needs time to formulate verbal expression,
easily enters the discussion by listening to a peer's well-crafted response and
evaluating whether or not it fits with her own not-yet-verbalized understanding of the poem.

Teacher: Read the next few lines with your partners.

[*The teacher moves from the front and listens among the children. She cues for one remaining minute, then "regroups" the children.*]

Teacher: I saw people sketching a picture. Zachary was helping Howie [Asperger's] by drawing out what it might look like. That is a good way to help your partner.
Frank: There is a lot of distance between the clouds because of the giraffe. It is stretched.
Andy: It is not a stormy day. It had to be a sunny day to see the blue.
Jamie: The dolphins need a big space because it is a pod. A lot of them!
Andy: There are lots of cloud.
Jamal: The cargo ships are like clouds full of rain.
Teacher: Everybody listen. He just said something really smart.
Jamal: I looked at the word "cargo." I know cargo ships hold something and the clouds hold something.
Susan: A boy twirling his clouds around and then blue fingertips. Since it is thin, the clouds are closer together.

In this section of transcript, the teacher clearly supports children working together to construct meaning. It is particularly noteworthy that she acknowledges the spontaneously generated drawing strategy used by Zachary and Howie, not to highlight how a nondisabled student "helps" a disabled student, but rather as an example of an effective way that *all* partners might work together to help one another.

Teacher: The last stanza, I will read it to you and then I want you to talk to your partner about what you think it means.

[*The teacher reads the last stanza. The children engage with one another in discussion. The teacher moves among the children to listen to their conversations.*]

Serena (LD): Because she was looking at spaces in between, she sees something different than people looking at the clouds.
Jamie: We noticed that the first and third stanzas are similar. They repeat.
Sharon: It's kind of like Jabberwocky. It ends with what it started with.
Iris (CP/LD): We imagined the clouds separating.
Teacher: This is something you can do with any kind of text. With poems, it is easy to do this. Look at each word and infer from the clues the writers give you. It is like being a detective.

Here, Serena offers a second and more sophisticated idea than her first response. Although she does not contribute verbally to the previous discussion (transcript 2), she is listening, constructing ideas, and benefiting in a way that enables her later to contribute an important thought that reflects a higher level of abstraction. Her level of participation is particularly noteworthy in that, after having been positioned as less capable by years of traditional special education practice, Serena began the school year with little understanding of *how* to engage in a group and hardly any confidence in her ability to do so. Her growth in this constructivist environment is staggering.

In another example of group dialogue that takes place in this classroom, the teacher engages the class in a reading workshop in which they read and interpret *Fly Away Home* by Eve Bunting, a story about a homeless father and daughter who manage to "live" in an airport. Each student has a copy of the story to read silently. They read the story in short sections, then stop to engage in conversation about the story. The teacher rereads parts aloud from a copy on the overhead to ensure that all students have access to the story. The transcript begins midway through the reading workshop.

Teacher: How does "Dad and I sleep sitting up" fit into what we just read?

Talk to a partner.

[*The children engage with one another. Colleen notices that Jon (LD) is not talking to anyone. She encourages him to join a conversation.*]

Teacher: Raise your hand if you have an idea.

Angie: So it *seems* like they are about to get on a plane. They don't want to get caught.

Teacher: How many people agree or want to add on?

Jamal: They want to look like they are napping, waiting for a plane.

Randy (LD): (*referring to a homeless woman in the airport who pushes a cart of belongings*) They don't want to look like *her.*

Jamie: (*referring to the notebook the father carries*) It might be a map of the airport.

Sharon: Or a schedule. To keep track.

[*Colleen asks the children to read the next section.*]

Teacher: If you have an idea, jot it in the margin or underline an idea.

[*The children read to themselves.*]

Teacher: Turn to your neighbor. How does this fit in?

[*The children engage in conversation. The teacher directs their attention to a particular section.*]

Teacher: What does this part mean?
Lisa: Everything's moving. Even the escalator, but *they* stay.
Teacher: Can anyone repeat what Lisa said?

[*Students continue to build upon one another's thoughts about the story.*]

Randy (LD): [referring to statements just made by his peers]: I agree with Lisa and Kenny.

[*Using text evidence to support his opinion, Randy spontaneously reads from the text, "Sitting together will get you noticed."*]

Randy (LD): I'm thinking that they [all of the homeless people who inhabit the airport] don't sit together because they don't want to get caught.

[*The teacher emphasizes that Randy has connected back to the earlier idea of not getting caught.*]

In this section of transcript, we see Randy, a student labeled as LD, actively contributing to the discussion. Randy, a struggling reader who has been constructed by previous special education teachers as benefiting *only* from drill and practice, demonstrates his capacity to engage intelligently with a text considered to be significantly "above his reading level." Like Serena, Randy began the school year without having learned the language for engaging in conversation about a text—a result of having been relegated to worksheet instruction in previous years. In this transcript, he tracks the conversation and adds appropriate remarks, uses conversational turn-taking strategies (such as "I agree with . . ."), and offers text evidence to support his own interpretation. Given the *opportunity* to participate, Randy demonstrates just how capable he *is* in engaging in meaningful discussion with his peers.

In the last section of the transcript, the teacher has generated conversation around a part in the story in which a bird becomes trapped in the airport.

Teacher: Why is *that* there? Turn to a neighbor and discuss.

[*The children talk with one another. The teacher engages Jon (LD) in conversation.*]

Teacher: Okay, we have one minute to see if we can figure this out. Why is there a bird here?
Sharon: I think the bird is like a symbol. *Fly Away Home* is the name of the story, so I think it is a symbol.

Teacher: So, you are saying something similar to what Jon (LD) was saying.

Jon (LD): They want to go free like the bird.

Lisa: She knew what it was like, so even if she couldn't be free, she wanted the bird to be free.

Teacher: How many people felt like they were doing some good digging?

Throughout the reading workshop, Jon (LD), a struggling reader, appears reluctant to engage in conversation. In a previous section of the transcript, the teacher facilitates Jon's entry into a peer conversation. Here, she decides to engage in conversation with him to get a better feel for his engagement with the text. When the group discussion ensues, the teacher opens a space for reluctant Jon to choose whether or not to contribute. He does so confidently, stating that "They want to go free like the bird." Sharon and Lisa's verbalizations about the meaning of the bird might be considered more developed and textured; nonetheless, Jon's more simply expressed interpretation reveals that he, too, grasps the meaning of symbolism, demonstrating his capability for thinking abstractly.

CONCLUSION

Together, these excerpts from real classrooms suggest that we promote academic achievement in a reflective environment in which educators (1) actively consider the meanings we give difference (to recap: a physical or cognitive difference is only an occasion for social framing as an impairment) and (2) focus on the context as the site of the realization, or actualizing, of the impairment or disability.

We cannot make judgments about "types" of students because they share a label. Every student is different. Disabilities, then, are social constructions that refer to heterogeneous groups of students—all of whom, despite a shared label, have distinct personalities, histories, abilities, and interests. When given an opportunity to consider ideas beyond the minutia of reductionist exercises, they demonstrate time after time that they are not only capable of participating, but also of contributing.

Neither is curriculum static and easily defined. It is enacted in each classroom with each teacher and each group of students during each minute of the day. The least restrictive environment, so often touted as the solution for placing students in appropriate educational settings, is in fact no more a place than is special education itself (See Rueda, Gallego, & Moll, 2000).

Our hope is that we learn to "do education" in new ways. First, every classroom would become a place where both teachers and students would welcome all students and enable them to work collaboratively on appropriately engaging tasks. Second, both parents and teachers would maintain high expectations, recognizing that all students are self-regulating (i.e., able to engage in the processes of assimilation, accommodation, and equilibration) without step-by-step guidance from teachers. All students would be respected as competent, active learners regardless of their "level" of activity. Some might need more time and/or support, progress more slowly than others, or ultimately not advance as far as their peers, but most will in fact conform to typical patterns of learning (Gallagher & Reid, 2002; Reid, 1978).

We challenge ourselves and fellow educators to recognize that the *disability dilemma* is an ethical matter to which we act and respond in particular ways. We must acknowledge that the ways in which we *choose* to respond to disability have material consequences for children and their families. It is time that we abandon practices that unnecessarily limit disabled children and begin operating out of the belief that *all* children, regardless of disability, actively engage with the world as meaning-makers and thrive in environments that support their natural, spontaneous, human activity and creativity.

REFERENCES

Adams, R. (2001). *Sideshow U. S. A.* Chicago: University of Chicago Press.

Artiles, A. J. (2003). Special education's changing identity: Paradoxes and dilemmas in views of culture and space. *Harvard Educational Review, 75*(2), 164–202.

Barton, L., & Armstrong, F. (2001). Disability, education, and inclusion: Cross-cultural issues and dilemmas. In G. L. Albrecht, K. D. Seelman, & M. Bury (Eds.), *Handbook of disability studies* (pp. 693–710). Thousand Oaks, CA: Sage.

Bogdan, R., & Knoll, J. (1995). The sociology of disability. In E. L. Meyen & T. M. Skrtic (Eds.), *Special education and student disability: An introduction.* Denver: Love Publishing.

Bourdieu, P. (1986). Forms of capital. In J. Richardsson (Ed.), *Handbook of theory and research for the sociology of education.* New York: Greenwood Press.

Brantlinger, E. A. (1997). Using ideology: Cases of non-recognition of the politics of research and practice in special education. *Review of Educational Research, 74*(4), 425–459.

Carrier, G. (1986). *Learning disability: Social class and the construction of inequality in American education.* New York: Greenwood Press.

Corker, M., & Shakespeare, T. (2002). *Disability/postmodernity: Embodying disability theory.* New York: Continuum.

Danforth, S. (1999). Pragmatism and the scientific validation of professional practices in American special education. *Disability & Society, 14*(4), 733–751.

Dudley-Marling, C. (in press). The social construction of learning disabilities. *Journal of Learning Disabilities.*

Dudley-Marling, C., & Dippo, D. (1995). What learning disability does: Sustaining the ideology of schooling. *Journal of Learning Disabilities, 28,* 406–414.

Englert, C. S. (1992). Writing instruction from a sociocultural perspective: The holistic, dialogic, and social enterprise of writing. *Journal of Learning Disabilities,* 28(3), 153–172.

Ferri, B. A. (in press). Interrupting the discourse: A response to Reid and Valle. *Journal of Learning Disabilities.*

Fleischer, D. Z., & Zames, F. (2001). *The disability rights movement: From charity to confrontation.* Philadelphia: Temple University Press.

Fosnot, C. T. (1996). *Constructivism: Theory, perspectives, and practice.* New York: Teachers College Press.

Franklin, B. M. (1987). The first crusade for learning disabilities: The movement for the education of backward children. In T. Popkewitz (Ed.), *The foundations of the school subjects* (pp. 190–209). London: Falmer Press.

Gallagher, D. J. (2001). Neutrality as a moral standpoint, conceptual confusion and the full inclusion debate. *Disability and Society,* 16, 637–654.

Gallagher, J. M., & Reid, D. K. (2002). *The learning theory of Piaget and Inhelder.* Austin, TX: Pro-Ed.

Garland Thomson, R. (Ed.). (1996). *Freakery: Cultural spectacles of the extraordinary body.* New York: New York University Press.

Garland Thomson, R. (1997). *Extraordinary bodies: Figuring physical disability in American culture and literature.* New York: Columbia University Press.

Heshusius, L. (1989). The Newtonian mechanistic paradigm, special education, and contours of alternatives: An overview. *Journal of Learning Disabilities,* 22(7), 403–415.

Kalyanpur, M., & Harry, B. (1999). *Culture in special education.* Baltimore, MD: Paul H. Brookes Publishing Company.

Kasa-Hendrickson, C. (in press). "There's no way this kid is retarded": Teachers' optimistic constructions of students' ability. *International Journal of Inclusive Education.*

Kliewer, C. (1998). *Schooling children with Down syndrome.* New York: Teachers College Press.

Linton, S. (1998). *Claiming disability.* New York: New York University Press.

Longmore, P. K., & Umansky, L. (2001). *The new disability history: American Perspectives.* New York: New York University Press.

Losen, D. J., & Orfield, G. (2002). *Racial inequity in special education.* Cambridge, MA: Harvard Educational Press.

Mariage, T. A., Paxton-Buursma, D. J., & Bouck, E. C. (in press). Interanimation: Re-positioning possibilities in educational contexts. *Journal of Learning Disabilities.*

Mitchell, D. T., & Snyder, S. L. (2000). *Narrative prosthesis: Disability and the dependencies of discourse.* Ann Arbor: University of Michigan Press.

Poplin, M. S. (1988a). Holistic/constructivist principles of the teaching/learning process: Implications for the field of learning disabilities. *Journal of Learning Disabilities,* 21, 401–416.

Poplin, M. S. (1988b). The reductionist fallacy in learning disabilities: Replicating the past by reducing the present. *Journal of Learning Disabilities,* 21, 389–400.

Reid, D. K. (1978). Equilibration and learning. *Journal of Learning Disabilities,* 16, 51–71.

Reid, D. K. (1998). Scaffolding: A broader view. *Journal of Learning Disabilities, 31*(4), 386–396.

Reid, D. K. (2001). Montague and Rinaldi and Meltzer, Katzir-Cohn, Miller and Roditi: A critical commentary. *Learning Disability Quarterly, 24,* 99–106.

Reid, D. K., & Stone, C. A. (1991). Why is cognitive instruction effective? Underlying learning mechanisms. *Remedial and Special Education, 12,* 9–19.

Reid, D. K., & Valle, J. W. (in press). The discursive construction of learning disabilities: Implications for instruction and parent-school relations. *Journal of Learning Disabilities.*

Rueda, R., Gallego, M. A., & Moll, L. C. (2000). The least restrictive environment: A place or a context. *Journal of Learning Disabilities, 21,* 70–78.

Skrtic, T. M. (1995). *Disability and democracy: Reconstructing (special) education for postmodernity.* New York: Teachers College Press.

Sleeter, C. E. (1995). Radical structuralist perspectives on the creation and use of learning disabilities. In T. M. Skirtic (Ed.), *Disability and democracy: Reconstructing (special) education for postmodernity* (pp. 153–165). New York: Teachers College Press.

Stiker, H. J. (1987). *A history of disability.* Ann Arbor: University of Michigan Press.

Stone, C. A., & Reid, D. K. (1994). Social and individual forces in learning: Implications for the instruction of children with learning difficulties. *Learning Disability Quarterly, 17,* 72–86.

Thomas, C. (1999). *Female forms: Experiencing and understanding disability.* Philadelphia: Open University Press.

Thomas, G., & Loxley, T. (2001). *Deconstructing special education and constructing inclusion.* Buckingham, U.K.: Open University Press.

Varenne, H., & McDermott, R. (1998). *Successful failure.* Boulder, CO: Westview Press.

Vygotsky, L. S. (1987). *The collected works of L. S. Vygotsky.* New York: Plenum Press.

Wertsch, J. V. (1991). *Voices of the mind.* Cambridge, MA: Harvard University Press.

PART III
Classroom Practice

CHAPTER 10

"Mathematics" or "Mathematizing"?

Catherine Twomey Fosnot and Maarten Dolk

It is a truism that the purpose of teaching is to help students learn. Yet in the past teaching and learning were most often seen as two separate, even polar, processes. Teaching was what teachers did. They were supposed to know their subject matter and be able to explain it well. Students were supposed to do the learning. They were expected to work hard, practice, and listen to understand. If they didn't learn, it was their fault; they had a learning disability, they needed remediation, they were preoccupied, or they were lazy. Even when we spoke of development, it was usually in connection with assessing learners to see whether they were developmentally ready for the teacher's instruction.

Interestingly, in some languages, *learning* and *teaching* are the same word. In Dutch, for example, the distinction between learning and teaching is made only by the preposition. The verb is the same. *Leren aan* means teaching; *leren van* means learning. When learning and teaching are so closely related, they will be integrated in learning/teaching frameworks: teaching will be seen as closely related to learning, not only in language and thought but also in action. If learning doesn't happen, there has been no teaching. The actions of learning and teaching are inseparable.

Of course, different teachers have different styles of helping children learn. But behind these styles are frameworks based on teachers' beliefs about the learning/teaching process. These frameworks, in turn, affect how teachers interact with children, what questions they ask, what ideas they pursue, and even what activities they design or select. Teachers make many important decisions—some of them in a split second in the nitty-gritty of the classroom. In making these decisions, some teachers are led by the structure of mathematics or the textbook, others by the development of the children.

LEARNING AND TEACHING IN THE CLASSROOM

Join us in Carol Mosesson's fourth/fifth-grade classroom in New Rochelle, New York. She is telling her students about a dilemma that occurred in her class the previous year and how she wants to be sure it doesn't happen again.[1]

"Last year," Carol explains, "I took my students on field trips related to the projects we were working on. At one point, we went to several places in New York City to gather research. I got some parents to help me, and we scheduled four field trips in one day. Four students went to the Museum of Natural History, five went to the Museum of Modern Art, eight went with me to Ellis Island and the Statue of Liberty, and the five remaining students went to the Planetarium. The problem we ran into was that the school cafeteria staff had made seventeen submarine sandwiches for the kids for lunch. They gave three sandwiches to the four kids going to the Museum of Natural History. The five kids in the second group got four subs. The eight kids going to Ellis Island got seven subs, and that left three for the five kids going to the Planetarium." As she talks, she draws a picture on chart paper of the context she is developing. "Now we didn't eat together, obviously, because we were all in different parts of the city. The next day after talking about our trips, several of the kids complained that it hadn't been fair, that some kids got more to eat. What do you think about this? Were they right? Because if they were, I would really like to work out a fair system—one where I would know how many subs to give each group when we go on field trips this year."

Carol is introducing fair sharing—a rich, real context in which her students can generate and model for themselves mathematical ideas related to fractions. When children are given trivial word problems, they often just ask themselves what operation is called for; the context becomes irrelevant as they manipulate numbers, applying what they know. Truly problematic contexts engage children in a way that keeps them grounded. They attempt to model the situation mathematically, as a way to make sense of it. They notice patterns, raise conjectures, and then defend them to one another.

"Turn to the person you are sitting next to and talk for a few minutes about whether you think this situation was fair," Carol continues.

"It's fair," several children comment. "It's one less sandwich than kids each time. It's three subs for four kids, so when there are five kids, they gave them four. For eight kids, they gave them seven."

"Yeah, but it wasn't fair for the Planetarium group. They had five kids and they only got three subs." Jackie is adamant as she comes to their defense. "The Museum of Modern Art group had five kids, too, and they got four sandwiches!"

"But you could just cut them in different pieces, like fourths or fifths," John offers.

"But the pieces would be different sizes. It's not fair."

"What do you think about her argument, John? Did everyone get the same amount?" Carol inquires, interested in whether John thinks the pieces would be equivalent. He shakes his head, acknowledging that the pieces would not be the same size. Another student raises his hand. "Michael?"

"But the others *are* all the same." As Michael advances this common misconception, several of his classmates nod in agreement. "You keep adding one child and one sub. Three for four is the same as four for five."

"If the Planetarium group had another sub it would all be the same," Aysha says, verbalizing what most are thinking.

Carol has succeeded in making their initial ideas visible. Now she wants to create disequilibrium. "Well, let's investigate this some more. I suggest we work with our math workshop partners and check out two things." She writes the questions down on a large piece of chart paper as she talks. "How much did each child in each group get, assuming the subs were all shared equally in each group? And which group got the most?"

Several students continue to voice their agreement with Aysha and Michael. "I think they all got the same except for the Planetarium group."

"Well, let's check it out and see. Let's investigate a bit, prove your ideas, and we'll have a math congress after we've worked on it some. Use any materials you want, or make drawings to help you prove your thinking. We'll share our thinking when everyone feels he or she has had enough time to work on this."

The children set to work investigating the problem. Some take out Unifix cubes; most draw the subs and show how they would cut them. Carol moves from group to group, ensuring that everyone is busy and clear about the problem. She sits down with Jackie and Ernie for a moment.

"There were three subs for four kids," Jackie explains, "so we cut two subs in half, then the last in fourths. So everybody in that group got one half plus one fourth."

Ernie, her partner, explains their work for the Ellis Island group. "And we're doing the same thing here. See—we're giving each person a half sub first. That is four subs. One sub we're cutting into eight pieces, and the other two into fourths."

"So how much does each person in the group get?" Carol inquires.

"One half plus one eighth plus one fourth."

"And you're going to continue like this with the Planetarium and the Museum of Modern Art groups?" Jackie and Ernie nod yes. Carol notes their strategy: they are making unit fractions—fractions with numerators of one.

Nicole and Michelle, whom she visits next, have worked on the three-subs-four-kids situation very similarly. But for the four-subs-five-kids situation they have changed their strategy. Michelle explains, "We divided these subs up into fifths, because there were five kids."

Carol sees that each of the four subs is drawn and cut up into fifths. "So how much of a sub did each child get?" she asks.

"One of these, one of these, one of these, and one of these." Nicole points to a fifth from each sub. "That's four fifths of a sub for each kid because it is four times one fifth."

"Oh, that's interesting, isn't it? Four subs for five kids ended up being four fifths of a sub." Carol attempts to point up the relationship, but Nicole and Michelle seem uninterested, and they go back to using unit fractions for the seven-subs-eight-kids problem. Carol debates whether or not to suggest that they try the same strategy they used for the four-subs-five-kids situation but decides against it. They are very involved in the context and they (as well as Jackie and Ernie) are cutting up the subs in ways that make sense *within the context*. They can imagine subs cut up into halves, fourths, or even fifths. These are reasonable sizes. Eighths are not, unless they become necessary at the end to share a last sub fairly. The realistic nature of the context enables children to realize what they are doing, to check whether it makes sense.

Working within a context also develops children's ability to make mathematical meaning of their own many lived worlds. There is much to be investigated yet. Asking children to adopt multiplication and division shortcuts too soon may actually impede genuine learning. As the well-known mathematician George Polyá (1887–1985) once pointed out, "When introduced at the wrong time or place, good logic may be the worst enemy of good teaching." Historically, unit fractions were used for a very long time before common fractions were accepted. As the children explore fair-sharing situations with unit fractions, they will have experiences comparing and making equivalent fractions. These experiences will bring up some big ideas and support the development of some powerful mathematical strategies. Let's return to Jackie and Ernie at work to witness this process.

Jackie has drawn four subs, and she and Ernie are deciding how to share this amount fairly among five kids—the ones who went to the Museum of Modern Art. "Let's give everyone a half again first. That leaves one and a half subs left."

"So let's cut the whole one up into fifths." Ernie draws four lines, making five equal parts, as he talks.

"Okay, so now every kid has one half plus one fifth," Jackie continues, "and now we have to cut up the last half into fifths. So it's one half plus one fifth plus—one fifth? That can't be—these are just slivers." She points to the small pieces resulting from cutting up the half sub. "These slivers are only about half the size of those fifths. So what do we call these?"

Jackie and Ernie are struggling with a big idea. To resolve their puzzlement they must grapple with the heart of fractional relationships. One fifth of a half sub is smaller than one fifth of a whole sub. What is the whole? And what is the equivalence of this piece to the whole?

"You're right—two of these fifths [the slivers] are about the same as one of those fifths," Ernie ponders. "So maybe it's a half of a fifth. But what is that?"

"We know it is a fifth of a half of a sub—"

"Yeah, but it is also one half of a fifth—see." Ernie points out the relationship of the sliver to the fifths that resulted when one sub was cut into five equal pieces. He is noticing that $1/2 \times 1/5 = 1/5 \times 1/2$. This relationship is a specific example of the commutative property of multiplication, although for him at this point it is probably not generalizable.

"Well, if it's a half of a fifth, then it must be a tenth," Jackie offers.

Ernie ponders her suggestion and then finds a way to prove it. "Oh, I get it—look. If this half is cut into fifths to make the slivers, then the other half could be too. And then—you're right—there's ten pieces in the whole sub. So one fifth of a half *is* one tenth."

"So now the Planetarium group is easy. Everybody gets a half plus one tenth!" Jackie draws the subs for the last scenario, showing the fair sharing. "Now all we have to do is compare them!"

David Hilbert (1897), in his book *Report on Number Theory*, wrote, "I have tried to avoid long numerical computations, thereby following Riemann's postulate that proofs should be given through ideas and not voluminous computations." As they set out to compare the four scenarios and prove which group got the most, Jackie and Ernie could add up the fractional parts and make common denominators, but they don't. Working with unit fractions has allowed them to hit upon a brilliant strategy to make the problem simpler.

"Everybody, in every group, got a half. So we can eliminate that," Jackie suggests.

"So all we have to do is compare the remainders," Ernie finishes her thought. "So we have one fourth for the Museum of Natural History group, one fifth plus one tenth for the Museum of Modern Art group, one fourth plus one eighth for the Ellis Island group, and one tenth for the Planetarium group.

"The Ellis Island group got one eighth more than the Museum of Natural History group."

"And the Museum of Modern Art group got one fifth more than the Planetarium group."

"But how do we compare the others?"

Ernie grabs some Unifix cubes. "I have an idea! What's a good number to use?" He ponders for a moment, then clarifies for Jackie, "I'm trying to think of a number that we could use to build the subs—a number that five and four and ten would go into—"

"How about twenty?" Jackie offers.

"Yeah—that's good." Ernie counts out twenty cubes and builds a stack with them to represent a sub. "Okay—so the fourth is five cubes, the fifth is the same as two tenths . . . and one tenth more, that's three tenths." As they begin to combine amounts and use 20 as a common denominator, they make a first attempt at generating common fractions. Jackie continues, "Ten times two is twenty, so two, four, six—three tenths is the same as six twentieths. That's more than five twentieths!"

At first the eighths stump them: 8 does not go into 20 evenly. But Ernie returns to their drawing. Using his fingers, he points to each eighth and says, "Two of these make a fourth—so the Ellis Island group got three eighths."

Jackie excitedly finishes the comparison. "Eighths are bigger than tenths. We're comparing three eighths to three tenths. If you cut up a sub into tenths, those pieces are smaller than if you cut it up into eighths. The threes are the same on the top"—referring to the numerators—"so the Ellis Island group got the most—three eighths of a sub!"

"Plus the half," Ernie reminds her. "And the Planetarium group got the least. One tenth is the littlest because if you divide a sub into fourths or fifths or tenths—the more pieces you have the smaller the piece is! They only got a half plus one tenth!"

What Is Revealed

This glimpse into Carol's classroom reveals a very different approach to mathematics from the one most of us experienced in our past schooling. Traditionally mathematics has been perceived as a ready-made discipline to be handed down by a teacher skilled in the art of transmitting, or explaining, clearly. In the classrooms most of us have attended, teachers stood at the chalkboard and explained fractions as shaded parts of a whole. They taught rules for making common denominators. They demonstrated procedures for operations with fractions, like invert and multiply, and students practiced them over and over. Some teachers may have used fraction bars or pattern blocks to demonstrate, hoping to develop understanding. But the premise was always the same. The teacher was the fountain of wisdom who understood that mathematics was a discipline thought to comprise facts, concepts, formulas, and algorithms, and this discipline could be transmitted, explained, practiced, and learned if teachers were well versed in it and learners were diligent. Most students in mathematics classrooms did not see mathematics as creative but instead as something to be explained by their teacher, then practiced and applied. One might call this traditional approach "school mathematics."

Mathematicians, on the other hand, engage in quite a different practice. They make meaning in their world by setting up quantifiable and spatial relationships, by noticing patterns and transformations, by proving them as generalizations, and by searching for elegant solutions. They construct new mathematics to solve real problems or to explain or prove interesting patterns, relationships, or puzzles in mathematics itself. The renowned mathematician David Hilbert once commented that he liked to prove things in at least three or four different ways, because by doing so he better understood the relationships involved. At the heart of mathematics is the process of setting up relationships and trying to prove these relationships mathematically in order to communicate them to others. Creativity is at the core of what mathematicians do.

Interestingly, the sculptor Henry Moore described his work in much the same way Hilbert did. He said that before he sculpted something, he always drew the figure several times to learn more about it. In fact, we all find ways to make meaning from our interactions in the world. The process of constructing meaning *is* the process of learning. We create our knowledge; we do not discover it. Writers make meaning when they formulate stories and narratives, when they construct characters and plots, when they play with words and metaphors. Scientists make meaning by wondering about scientific phenomena; by hypothesizing, designing, and performing experiments; and then by proposing explanations that fit their results. Musicians hear cadence, rhythm, harmony, discordance, and melody as they interact in their world. Artists see color, form, texture, and line.

In fields other than mathematics, we've understood this constructive nature of learning. We teach students to become good writers by involving them in the process of writing. In science, we engage learners in actively inquiring, in formulating hypotheses, and in designing experiments. We teach art by allowing learners to create their own "masterpieces." Have we traditionally been teaching mathematics in our classrooms or only the "history" of mathematics—some past mathematicians' constructions and their applications? Is there any connection at all between "school mathematics" and "real mathematics"?

The vignette from Carol's classroom is evidence of a different view of mathematics—one more closely akin to the process of constructing meaning, one that might better be termed *mathematizing*. Children are finding ways to explore situations mathematically, they are noticing and exploring relationships, putting forth explanations and conjectures, and trying to convince one another of their thinking—all processes that beg a verb form. This view of mathematics was put forth by the well-known 20-century Dutch mathematician Hans Freudenthal (1968) when he argued that mathematics was a human activity—the process of modeling reality with the use of mathematical tools.

To generate such mathematizing, Carol immerses her students in an investigation grounded in context. As they examine the fair-sharing situation and develop their own strategies for dealing with it, they find ways to simplify the numbers by pulling them apart. They notice relationships. Then they explore these relationships and try to figure out why they are happening. They raise their own mathematical questions and discuss them in the mathematical community of their classroom. But is this only process? What about content? Do all the children construct an understanding of fractions? Is this the goal that day for all the children? What does it mean to "understand" fractions?

Back to the Classroom

Let's return to Carol's classroom as she continues to visit with and question her students. Three children—Michael, Gabrielle, and Ashleigh—are sitting on the floor with big chart paper in front of them, on which they have drawn big subs. Carol joins them. "So tell me what you're doing. How are you guys thinking about this?"

"Our drawing shows how we cut up the subs," reports Ashleigh. "It wasn't fair. The cafeteria staff did make a mistake. Now we're trying to figure out which group got more."

Teachers often confuse right answers with understanding. Right answers are of course important, but they are not sufficient. Carol probes further, "And how are you thinking about that?" she asks.

Michael explains, "We were thinking that if we gave everybody half a sub, then we could tell." At first Carol thinks their strategy is the same as Jackie and Ernie's, but as Michael continues she realizes that they are not completing the division—they are not thinking relationally. "When we get rid of the halves, the Ellis Island group has three subs left, the Museum of Natural History group has one left, the Museum of Modern Art group has one and a half subs left, and the Planetarium group has only half a sub left. Three is the most!"

Carol realizes that although their answer is correct—the Ellis Island group did get the most—their thinking is not. "But how do you know that three subs is more—don't the remainders get shared too? Don't the three subs have to be shared with the eight kids? The one-and-a-half subs only have to be shared with five kids, and here"—she points to the three-subs-four-kids scenario—"you have one sub left to share with four kids. Eight is more people, so how do you know which is more?" Michael looks puzzled as he realizes Carol's point.

Gabrielle comes to his rescue, but her thinking is not solid either. "One sub for four people, that's one fourth, and here"—she points to the one-and-a-half-sub remainder—"one sub for five people is one fifth. One fifth is more than one fourth." This misconception is common when children begin to explore fractions. The whole number five is more than four, so why wouldn't one fifth be more than one fourth? One of the benefits of exploring fractions using a fair-sharing situation is that this misconception is easily dispelled.

Ashleigh disagrees. "No, one fourth is more than one fifth."

Now Gabrielle looks puzzled. "No." She shakes her head, continuing to ponder the subs being cut. Then, realizing that Ashleigh is right, she slowly agrees. "Oh—yeah."

"Convince me," Carol challenges Gabrielle.

"When you share with five people the pieces are smaller than with four." Gabrielle is clear.

Carol continues probing. "What about this half sub remaining in the Planetarium group? It still has to be shared with five people. How much will they get? Is that one fifth too?"

All three children are at first quiet as they puzzle over Carol's question, but Ashleigh thinks it through. "No, it is one fifth of half a sub. That's one tenth."

"Can you prove that to us, Ashleigh?" Carol continues to push for mathematical thinking—to go beyond just answers.

"If you cut the other half into five pieces too, the sub is cut into ten pieces. So each of the fifths of one half is one tenth of the whole thing." She points to the pieces as she talks, and Gabrielle and Michael are convinced by her explanation. Carol concurs and then suggests that they continue exploring which group got more. She moves on to Jennifer and John.

These two children have modeled the problem like Nicole and Michelle did in the four-subs-five-kids situation, but they have done so consistently. Jennifer explains, "We cut up every sub into the number of people. See. Three subs for four people was three fourths, and four subs for five people was four fifths."

Carol asks, "Show me how you got three fourths for each child."

"It's just one fourth out of each sub, and there's three subs."

"And this worked every time?" Carol pushes for generalization. "Wow, what a great shortcut! Can you come to math congress being able to prove that this procedure would always work—that the number of subs divided by the number of people is how much of each sub everyone will get?" They nod enthusiastically, pleased with their solution, and they set out to find a way to prove it to their classmates.

TEACHING AND LEARNING AS DEVELOPMENT

As she moves from group to group, Carol's questioning changes in relation to what the children are investigating and the ideas and strategies each child is in the process of constructing. Although the connection between fractions and division is an overall "horizon"—an overall goal purposely embedded in the context—each child is at a different place developmentally, and therefore the context is open enough to allow for individual exploration and divergence.

Carol continues to support and encourage development as she leads the subsequent *math congress*. In a math congress, the whole class gathers and children present and discuss their strategies and solutions with one another. Just as mathematicians work out formal proofs to convince their fellow mathematicians of the relationships they have been exploring, Carol's students defend and support their thinking as Carol guides their discussion to reveal important mathematical ideas and strategies. The math congress is much more than just sharing; it is a critical part of the math lesson. As children prepare to present their work, and as they think about how they will communicate their work and anticipate their classmates' questions, their own understanding deepens.

As Carol plans for the math congress, she thinks about how she will structure it, which group she will start with, on which ideas she will focus, how she will make sure that everyone is challenged. Not everyone will share. There is not enough time, nor is that the goal. Carol will use the congress to focus on a few critical ideas. Should she just have a group share that can explain their thinking well? A group with an elegant solution? A group she didn't get to, so that she can see what they did? Would any of these pedagogical strategies support development? How *will* she continue to support development?

The Math Congress

"Gabrielle, Michael, and Ashleigh, please start us off." Carol decides to have this group share. Their solution is similar to most: it will prompt a good discussion of equivalence. But she also chooses to have this group share, rather than Jackie and Ernie, *because they have struggled*. Carol hopes that the process of *explaining their thinking* to their classmates will develop even further clarity for them.

The group members come to the front of the class with their chart and post it on the chalkboard with small magnets. Ashleigh begins. "We gave everybody a half first. In the Planetarium group—three subs, five kids—we were left with half a sub. We had to share that, too, so we cut that up into five pieces. Each of those was one fifth of one half. That was one tenth. So in this group everyone got one half plus one tenth."

Ashleigh has been confident and clear. Carol looks around and sees that everyone appears to agree. To check she asks, "How many of you can put in your own words where they got the one tenth?" Many hands are up, since this was an idea that many of the children had grappled with as they worked. Carol asks Christina, a child she did not get to as she moved around the room, to paraphrase, and Christina is able to do so clearly.

Gabrielle continues with the next situation—three subs, four kids. "We did the same thing here. We were left with one sub, which we cut into four pieces. Everyone in this group got one half plus one fourth, or three fourths."

Michael, explaining the equivalence, adds, "Right. See—two of these fourths make one half, so one fourth more is three fourths." Once again their classmates nod agreement. When the group moves on to the Museum of Modern Art situation—four subs, five kids—however, a spirited discussion ensues.

"Everybody in this group got four fifths of a sub. We cut each sub up into fifths, and each person got four times one fifth," Ashleigh explains. As they were preparing for the congress, they redrew this scenario. Their drawing looks very different to Ernie, who has also used an "elimination of halves" strategy. He thought he was following the discussion. Now he is puzzled. "I don't understand," he blurts out. "You just have numbers floating all over your drawing. What do they represent?"

Christina also is confused. "I don't get it either," she declares, "if each person gets one fifth of each sub, isn't there four fifths left over?"

"You gave them each five pieces," another student argues provocatively. "There's two ones in the first sub, and then three more ones. That's five pieces!"

Carol realizes that the numbers on the chart refer to the pieces, not the children. They are counting the pieces each child gets, not distributing pieces to children. As they drew the picture to get ready for the congress, it took on a different meaning. It represents the result of an action that for them is now almost mental. It represents their answer rather than the process of the distribution. To help clarify this Carol asks, "Where is the fifth child in your drawing? Why don't you use a marker and circle the children for us."

Ashleigh circles groups of four fifths, and it now becomes apparent to her classmates what the numerals in the drawing represent.

"Oh, I get it!"

"Oh, yeah."

"But how did you know it would be four fifths?" Ernie wonders.

Michael explains how they went from eliminating the halves to the representation they are now discussing. "We started with a half and we were left with one-and-a-half subs that we still had to share with five people. We cut up the whole into fifths, and then the one half into fifths. But those pieces were really tenths—because they were fifths of one half." His classmates appear to be following his thinking, so he continues. "The one half is between the two and the three." He points to the picture. "One half is equal to two-and-one-half fifths. It's in the middle. Another tenth makes it three fifths, and then plus the last one fifth. So it is four fifths." A few students still look puzzled; others are intrigued and amazed.

Ashleigh continues to clarify, shading in the one half with the marker she still holds, answering her own question. "Where is the half?"

"Oh, in between!"

"Two-and-one-half fifths!"

"Oh, I get it!"

"And the one tenth makes it three fifths."

Their thinking awes Christina. "And so how did you decide which group got the most?"

"We thought it was between the Ellis Island group, which got one fourth plus one eighth plus the half, and the Museum of Modern Art group, which got one tenth plus one fifth plus the half," Michael explains. "We knew the halves could be removed, so we just compared the rest. One fourth is more than one fifth, and one eighth is more than one tenth—because you are dividing by more people. The more pieces you cut, the smaller they have to be to fit in the whole sandwich."

Michael, Ashleigh, and Gabrielle have made a huge jump in thinking as they have worked through this investigation. Starting with eliminating halves and comparing remainders as whole numbers (not in relation to the number of children), they progressed to unit fractions. As they attempted to represent their thinking, they combined the unit fractions into common fractions. They are now solid on understanding that the bigger the denominator, the smaller the fraction. The thinking apparent as they communicate and prove their strategy to their fellow classmates is remarkably different from their thinking an hour before.

Carol has successfully used the math congress to support these students' growth. But she has also used this discussion to bridge the unit fraction strategy with the use of common fractions for the class as a whole. As she continues with the congress, the scaffolds she provides—the way in which she supports development—become even more apparent. "John and Jennifer, your strategy was quite different. Would you share next?"

John and Jennifer describe how they cut each sub into a number of parts that matched the number of people. They show how each piece times the number of subs results in how much each person gets.

Jackie notices the relationship before they can finish. "Hey! Their answers are the same as the numbers in the problem. It's just the number of sandwiches divided by the number of people!"

"Oh, wow!"

"So weird!"

"Will that always work? Why is that happening?" Carol pushes for generalization. "It's just division!" Jackie exclaims. "Twelve subs shared by four people is twelve divided by four equals three. Four subs shared with twelve people is four divided by twelve. It's one twelfth, four times!"

What Is Revealed

By varying her questioning as she monitors the congress, Carol allows her students to think further about their strategies and gives them a chance to "stretch" mathematically from wherever they are developmentally. By constructing their own strategies and defending them, all the children are immersed in an investigation that involves mathematizing. But mathematizing should not be dismissed simply as process. Mathematizing *is* content. Children are exploring ideas—fair sharing, equivalence, and common denominators; the connection between fractions, division, and multiplication; common fractions—in relation to their own level of cognitive development. As children learn to recognize, be intrigued by, and explore patterns, and as they begin to overlay and interpret experiences, contexts, and phenomena with mathematical questions, tools, and models (such as the fair-sharing one in this problem), they are constructing what it really means to be a mathematician. They are learning to organize and interpret their world through a mathematical lens. This is the essence of mathematics.

Carol supports her students by posing questions and offering rich contexts for mathematizing. This approach enables children to take the next step in the learning process. The development of the children seems to guide Carol's teaching. But development can be nothing more than a catchword. No one would disagree that development is important. Educators have talked about developmentally appropriate practice for years. But what does development mean *in relation to mathematics learning and teaching*?

Carol's teaching reflects her appropriate understanding of development. But she does more—she employs a different framework. Her teaching is grounded in the development of *mathematical ideas*—in her knowledge of the structure of mathematics. But there is still more. She understands the paths and the horizons of the landscape of this learning; she knows how children *come to understand* different mathematical ideas. She thinks about how to employ mathematical contexts as a didactic—how to use them to facilitate mathematical learning. She knows and recognizes important landmarks along the way—strategies, big ideas, and mathematical models—and she designs her contexts with these landmarks in mind. Different contexts have the potential to generate different models, strategies, and big ideas. In Carol's framework, learning and teaching are connected. She works on the edge between the structure of mathematics and the development of the children; the value she gives one or the other differs with what happens in her classroom.

STRATEGIES, BIG IDEAS, AND MODELS
IN A TEACHING/LEARNING FRAMEWORK

Strategies as Schemes

The mind is never a blank slate. Even at birth, infants have organized patterns of behavior—or schemes (Piaget, 1977)—for learning and understanding the world. Beginning as reflexes (grasping and orienting, for example), these initial schemes soon become differentiated and coordinated. Children learn to crawl and then walk to objects to be grasped, felt, sucked, and explored visually. Grasping is refined to include pushing, pulling, hitting, and other forms of exploring with the fingers. Sucking is differentiated into chewing, biting, and licking. New strategies for exploration are constructed.

Children attempting to understand "how many"—how many plums there are in the grocer's box, how many stairs they have climbed after going up ten flights, how many boxes are needed to hold 296 candies, how much of a submarine sandwich everyone got—use various assimilatory schemes. They count by ones or skip count by groups. They work with familiar pieces first (how many 10s in 100, for example). They cut up the subs and share them and turn the ratio of subs to people into unit fractions—a *unit fractioning* strategy. These strategies in turn evolve into efficient *strategies for equivalence* (making common fractions) and *strategies for computation* (operations with fractions).

Developing all these strategies is no mean feat! The progression of strategies, or "progressive schematization," as Treffers (1987) calls it, is an important inherent characteristic of learning.

Big Ideas as Structures

Underlying this developmental progression of strategies is the construction of some essential big ideas. What is a "big idea" and how is it different from a strategy?

Big ideas are "the central, organizing ideas of mathematics—principles that define mathematical order" (Schifter & Fosnot, 1993, p. 35). As such, they are deeply connected to the structures of mathematics. They are, however, also characteristic of shifts in learners' reasoning—shifts in perspective, in logic, in the mathematical relationships they set up. As such, they are connected to part/whole relationships—to the structure of thought in general (Piaget, 1977). In fact, that is *why* they are connected to the structures of mathematics. As mathematical ideas developed through the centuries and across cultures, the advances were often characterized by paradigmatic shifts in reasoning. These ideas are "big" because they are critical to mathematics and because they are big leaps in the development of children's reasoning.

For example, *the greater the denominator, the smaller the fraction* is one big idea we saw children grappling with in Carol's class. Another was the idea that *the whole matters*—one fifth of one half is one tenth of a whole sub. Still another is that *fractions are connected to division and multiplication*—four fifths is four divided by five, or one divided by five four times. To construct these ideas, children have to grapple with new perspectives, new ways of interpreting relationships—realizing that fair sharing can be represented as unit fractions or as common fractions, for example. This is a huge shift in thinking for children and, in fact, was a huge shift in mathematics that took centuries to develop!

Models as Tools for Thought

Language was constructed to signify meaning. When we construct an idea, we want to communicate it: through time and across cultures humans have developed languages as a way to do so. Initially, language represents ideas and actions; it is *a representation of thought*. Eventually it serves as *a tool for thought*.

Numerals were developed to signify the meaning of counting. Operational symbols like × and ÷ were constructed to represent the actions of combining and portioning equivalent-size groups. Ratio tables, rational numbers, decimals, and percents were developed as ways to signify relation. While these symbols were initially developed to represent mathematical ideas, they become tools, mental images, to think with.

To speak of mathematics as mathematizing demands that we address mathematical models and their development. To mathematize, one sees, organizes, and interprets the world through and with mathematical models. Like language, these models often begin simply as representations of situations, or problems, by learners. For example, learners may initially represent a situation with Unifix cubes, as Jackie and Ernie did when they represented the sub with 20 cubes, or with drawings that show the fair sharing and equivalent parts. These models of situations eventually become generalized as learners explore connections between and across them.

Teachers can use models as a didactic to transfer learning from informal solutions specific to a context to more formal, generalizable solutions—to bridge models *of* thinking with models *for* thinking (Beishuizen et al., 1997; Gravemeijer, 1999). For example, using ratio tables or double number lines or open arrays to represent children's computation strategies can enable children to develop a sense of "number space"—a mental image of number based on relationships and operations (Lorenz, 1997).

Walking the Edge

Carol walks the edge between the structure of mathematics and the development of the child by considering the progression of strategies, the big ideas involved, and the emergent models. Ultimately what matters is the mathematical activity of the learner—how the learner mathematizes the situations that Carol designs. But learning—development—is complex. Strategies, big ideas, and models are all involved—they all need to be developed as they affect one another. They are the steps, the shifts, and the mental maps in the journey. They are the components in a "landscape of learning."

Strategies, big ideas, and models, however, are not static points in a landscape. They are dynamic movements on the part of a learner in a journey of mathematical development. From this perspective they need to be understood as schematizing rather than as strategies, as structuring rather than as big ideas, and as modeling rather than as models (Freudenthal, 1991). Teaching needs to facilitate this development. Only then can teaching and learning be seen as interrelated—for the connected teaching/learning framework that it is. This is the framework behind Carol's decision making.

SUMMING UP . . .

Reuben Hersh said, "It's the questions that drive mathematics. Solving problems and making up new ones is the essence of mathematical life. If mathematics is conceived apart from mathematical life, of course it seems—dead (1997, p. 18)." When mathematics is understood as mathematizing one's world—interpreting, organizing, inquiring about, and constructing meaning through a mathematical lens—it becomes creative and alive.

Traditionally mathematics has been taught in our schools as if it were a dead language. It was something that past, mostly dead, mathematicians had created—something that needed to be learned, practiced, and applied. When the definition of mathematics shifts toward "the activity of mathematizing one's *lived* world," the constructive nature of the discipline and its connection to problem solving become clear.

When we define mathematics in this way, and teach accordingly, children will rise to the challenge. They will grapple with mathematical ideas; they will develop and refine strategies as they search for elegance; they will create mathematical models as they attempt to understand and represent their world. Because this process of mathematizing is constructive, teachers need to walk the edge between the structure of mathematics and the development of the learner. This edge is a journey across a landscape of learning comprising strategies, big ideas, and models. From the perspective of mathematics as mathematizing, it is the mathematical activity of the learner that ultimately matters; thus, strategies, big ideas, and models need to be understood as schematizing, structuring, and modeling. Teaching needs to be seen as inherently connected to learning.

Children, in learning to mathematize their world, will come to see mathematics as the living discipline it is, with themselves a part of a creative, constructive mathematical community, hard at work.

NOTE

1. Although this investigation was embellished and situated in the context of field trips by Carol Mosesson, the kernel of the activity—fair sharing of submarine sandwiches—comes from Mathematics in Context, Encyclopaedia Britannica Educational Corporation.

REFERENCES

Beishuizen, M., Gravemeijer, K.P.E., & van Lieshout, E.C.D.M. (1997). *The role of contexts and models in the development of mathematical strategies and procedures.* Utrecht, Netherlands: Utrecht University (CD-B Series on Research in Education; 26).

Freudenthal, H. (1968). Why to teach mathematics so as to be useful. *Educational Studies in Mathematics, 1,* 3–8.

Freudenthal, H. (1991). *Revisiting mathematics education: The China lectures.* Dordrecht, Netherlands: Kluwer.

Gravemeijer, K. (1999). How emergent models may foster the constitution of formal mathematics. *Mathematical Thinking and Learning 1*(2): 155–177.

Hersh, R. (1997). *What is mathematics, really?* London: Oxford University Press.

Hilbert, D. (1897). *Report on number theory.* Amsterdam: Zalbericht.

Lorenz, J. H. (1997). Is mental calculation just strolling around in an imaginary number space? In Beishuizen, M., Gravemeijer, K.P.E., & van Lieshout,

E.C.D.M. (Eds.). *The role of contexts and models in the development of mathematical strategies and procedures* (pp. 199–213). Utrecht, Netherlands: Utrecht University (CD-B Series on Research in Education; 26).

Piaget, J. (1977). *The development of thought: Equilibration of cognitive structures.* New York: Viking.

Schifter, D., & Fosnot, C. T. (1993). *Reconstructing mathematics education: Stories of teachers meeting the challenge of reform.* New York: Teachers College Press.

Treffers, A. (1987). *Three dimensions: A model of goal and theory description in mathematics instruction.* The Wiskobas Project. Dordrecht, Netherlands: Reidel.

CHAPTER 11

A First-Year Teacher Implements a Literature-Based/Whole-Language Program in a Fourth–Fifth Grade

Susan Cowey

In 1991 I was offered a one-year position at Wightwood School, a small private school, grades pre-K through 8, in Branford, Connecticut. This was to be the first year I would call a class my own. Prior to that, I student taught in a third–fourth classroom and had been an assistant in a fourth–fifth classroom. It would be my first opportunity to structure a program consistent with my constructivist beliefs, one that would maximize learning. To begin, I turned to my experiences as a fellow in the Center for Constructivist Teaching/Teacher Preparation Project at Southern Connecticut State University. During our coursework, the fellows had had a week of all-day sessions as part of a seminar in language arts instruction. Rather than being taught "language arts instructional strategies," we were asked to participate as "learners" of language arts; we wrote, read, and engaged in spelling investigations. Afterward we were asked to construct our own pedagogical philosophy of learning from our reflections and to write a paper synthesizing our ideas. Two questions were posed to the fellows to frame our reflection: (1) What have you learned about how students learn language arts? (2) What have you learned about the teaching of language arts? The following are excerpts from the paper I wrote that summer:

> Learners are developing skills in language arts from the moment they are born. Language evolves from the utterance of simple sounds to the

expression of very abstract ideas. In our discussions this week, in our writing, each learner brought the whole of her experience to each task. We shared a desire to express these thoughts and feelings even when we had not yet developed words to do so. It is the embrace of that struggle coupled with the motivation to share that results in ever more sophisticated communications. Thoughts come unbidden and unedited. The examination of these ideas through writing and sharing, the very act of converting the abstract mental process to a form that others may perceive, demands organization, so that we may speak or write about them and so that others may see and hear them as we originally conceived of them. As we have seen this week, a learner who is unstimulated by an idea, or who attempts to edit the idea as it is forming, is often unmotivated to communicate it. The audience is paramount in the development of language art skills. It provides the motivation for expression, while also providing the challenge to organize and speak, or write, in a coherent way.

Looking back at my words, I asked myself, "What personal pedagogy have I constructed?" and "What would I do to implement it?"

Learners must write from a need to communicate and therefore have a choice of their topics. My students would need an environment that invites and stimulates discussion, and plenty of time to reflect, not only on any given piece of writing but also on the process of writing.

What would I do? I would immerse my students in rich literature. I would help them construct what they needed to communicate and model that struggle with my own work. I would provide time to write and read and an audience with which to share. I would ask them to constantly reflect on the process. I would do this daily. But how would I begin?

THE FIRST STEP

The Writing on the Wall

It is hard to plan without the students—like defining the null set. I knew I wanted to establish immediately that our room was a place to celebrate and develop literacy. At first I thought some posters with writing process slogans would be decorative and instructive. But this had little to do with valuing writing. When I asked the teacher from the year before if he had any samples of the children's writing, he produced a book with beautiful pieces of poetry from each of the students. For two new students, I took writing samples from their interview materials. It was my first introduction to the children and an opportunity to evaluate their writing schemes. I chose a wall that was visible from the entrance to the room and mounted their writing on colored paper under a sign that read, "The Writing on the Wall." It was my way of saying, "I'm already your audience—I celebrate your writing." The first day the children went to the wall and asked me where I had gotten the writing. They began to compare pieces and reminisce about the events that had inspired them to write. Some remarked on the new students' writing, and it became a point of conversation from which the new students could begin to connect with the others. I began right there at the wall to model the comments and questions I hoped they would later make and ask of one another.

Creating an In-Room Library

Creating an in-room library was not necessary at Wightwood. The room came stocked with a wonderful library, including biographies, reference materials, magazines, fiction, anthologies of poetry, and multiple copies of age-appropriate materials for literature groups.

Wightwood emphasizes thematic teaching, and for my initial theme I had chosen China. Choosing a "theme" presented a dilemma for me. I felt the choice of study must arise from the students' interests. I had written to the students over the summer and had asked them to come to school with three things about which they had always wondered. These questions gave rise to rich and varied investigations of a scientific nature. I wanted to engage the students in a similar investigation of culture, and I thought that researching a common culture would provide opportunity to develop cognitive structures defining what is integral to any culture. Thematic teaching provides opportunity for integration of knowledge in a common context and enhances the community of discourse. However, by definition it limits choice. It was my hope that the selection of such a sprawling, multi-ethnic, and ancient culture would provide ample breadth to address the varied interests of my group.

My group's best resource for literature was the Wightwood parent body. One parent owned a bookstore and was constantly bringing us literature to support our theme. Because of her generosity, we had beautiful picture books and age-appropriate fiction from such authors as Laurence Yep and Amy Tan. In addition, the school library was stocked with wonderful selections of general literature should the in-room library not suffice. Despite the difficulty and time it takes to create an in-room library, it is, to me, an absolute necessity to the whole-language classroom. Without it, the option of choice is lacking and the flexibility to respond to interest and needs is missing.

MEANINGFUL TIME TO MAKE MEANING

Structuring the Day

The structure of the day was very important to me. Scheduling at Wightwood is extremely flexible, as the curriculum is developed primarily by the teachers. Since the children would have Spanish and morning meeting (a schoolwide activity) in the morning, I decided to pursue language arts in the afternoon. From noon recess on, the day was comprised of language art activities. The children would return from recess to read for 45 minutes. During this time, which we termed "readers' workshop," each child selected a book from the room, the school library, or one he or she had brought from home and settled in a comfortable spot to read. There were cushions and pillows that the students moved about to nestle down on to read. Often I would dim the lights just slightly, and the room would fall silent as they became absorbed in their reading. I provided the children with a reading journal in which they made an entry during the last 10 or 15 minutes of the period. The journal was a tool for both the student and me to evaluate reading progress. A typical entry involved logging the title, the page number at the beginning of the reading session, and the page number at the completion. It also included a narrative about their impressions of plot and character. At the back of the journal the children kept a chart of the titles and made note of whether the book had been easy, comfortable, or challenging to read. Sometimes the children would write a letter in their journal to a classmate and exchange it for a return letter. I tried to conference with three students daily, listening to them read, performing my own stylized miscue analysis, discussing the material, and reviewing their journals. A miscue analysis is a technique for analyzing the reader's errors to determine the reader's schemes for making meaning of print. By noting and examining what the reader actually said, versus what was printed, I could determine why he or she was making errors and focus the conference to address specific areas. For example, one of my students struggled to read and was noticeably avoiding reading. After examining my miscue analyses from a few conferences with him, it became clear that he saw reversals and therefore struggled to decode. At the close of our conference, I would leave a written question in the journal for the student to answer.

Every student also participated in literature groups, which were smaller groups of children who read a selected novel and met to discuss it.

After "readers' workshop," we would then move into "writers' workshop." This progression was deliberate, to maximize the reading/writing connection. Most children understood the rhythm of the workshops, having progressed through Wightwood. Wightwood has used writing process for years, and its children produce exceptional pieces of writing. Yet every teacher has a style of his or her own. My workshop was based on Calkins' (1986) and Graves' (1983) work and emulated the styles I had seen modeled in other classrooms. Usually it began with a mini-lesson, which, to my dismay, originally was often seen by my students as a delaying tactic to keep them from writing. I appreciated their enthusiasm for writing and, after a period of struggling to interject mini-lessons beforehand, I began to use a "share time" to "seize the moment" and address an area of writing on the spot.

The children wrote quietly for at least 20 minutes, often longer, before they were allowed to peer conference. After 40 to 45 minutes, we would come together in the meeting area in a circle on a rug to share. The class was an ideal size, only 14 students, so management of sharing was quite easy. Usually the children were inspired to share and prepared to share in a steady rotation.

"Story time" followed "writer's workshop" and was also a special time for the children. They spread out on a rug as I read to them for half an hour. Most of our Chinese theme was introduced through literature, usually at this story time. Sometimes the story would be a short picture book, sometimes a full-length novel. The images and philosophy of the Far Eastern culture began to emerge as I read to them. They drew pictures as they read, a technique I had learned from another teacher at Wightwood. As the children drew the images the words called forth, they were often, in turn, inspired to write. One day, in fact, they decided to adapt one of the stories, Yeh-Shen, the 1,000 year old precursor to Cinderella, into a play. The children incorporated Chinese expressions from the stories into the dialogue, and the images they saw into the scenery. They designed costumes from illustrations and descriptions in the literature. Knowing what using a computer for word processing had done for my willingness to write and edit, I set up the computers at one end of the room as a small center. By the end of the year, however, the children had spread out to use the computers in the middle school and a computer loft as well. The computers were essential to the children as they combined their collaborative efforts at playwriting into a single script.

DECIDING WHAT TO TEACH

Learning About My Learners

To begin teaching using an approach based on a constructivist view of learning, a teacher must understand literacy as a developmental process.

During our teacher preparation instruction, we collected the writings of children from preschool to early adolescence. Using the work of Graves (1983), Calkins (1986), and Fosnot (1989), we examined the children's pieces for their strategies and their developing "big ideas." In truth, examination of a beginning writer's work is like an excursion into a foreign language. A teacher who is reading a child's first piece of writing, with invented spelling, can well appreciate how the beginning reader feels decoding words for the first time.

As my students began to write and share their pieces, I tried to take particular notice of the perspectives and schemes they were employing and the "big ideas" with which they were grappling. The levels of writing were diverse, due in part to the integration of fourth and fifth graders. The levels were not strictly divided across grade levels, however, with some fourth graders showing more advanced writing than some of the fifth graders. Many students wrote short narratives and poems that sometimes were compilations of lists of words with a common theme. The stories were event-driven, with many "and thens." They lacked a climax and focus, were often a mere description of the past night's events, or were patterned after a favorite fairy tale or poem.

Others manipulated events for effect, incorporating dialogue, suspense, effective paragraphing, metaphor, and simile; these showed evidence of a distinct "style." However, even these pieces were emulations of what the children were mostly used to hearing and were rarely a result of the need of personal expression.

The children loved to share their pieces, which were attended to by careful listeners who asked questions that I often wished I had thought of; but the writers seldom revised their work in response to the expressions of confusion from their audience. The need for detail and clarification was becoming apparent, even to the writers who wished only for celebration at first.

As I grew to know each writer, I saw separate needs to address. Janet needed to take some risks. She was writing "list poems" and attempting to rhyme everything, no matter how tortured the words. Eric had creative ideas for characters, but plots evolved almost of their own accord, an unbroken string of events that arose and were resolved from sentence to sentence. Todd could envision a story, but all of his leads began with "One day," which seemed to prompt him to tell a story with minute-to-minute detail. I felt that many of the issues were best addressed in a one-to-one conference with the students, but some were clearly topics for mini-lessons to benefit the whole group.[1]

Todd had been writing on a theme for a while—"One day" stories. He began his stories with "One day" and created a character to "sally forth" from this well-known and overused point in time. He began many a story with leads that would dissatisfy him and cause him to begin anew. Examples of his leads can be read in Figure 11.1. Todd, like many of his fifth-grade peers, had mastered the fundamentals of writing and was experimentlng with the development of a written voice. Often he would fall in love with a first draft, preferring to abandon it and begin a new piece rather than violate the first draft with revision.

While researching for a class in my teacher preparation program, I had interviewed some fifth graders about this aspect of their development. One girl tried to help me understand this tendency: "When I write, it's about me, and my feelings. It's the way I feel, I can't revise my feelings." It is truth and must be told as is governed by the event. Todd was not the only child leading his stories with "One day," or "Once upon a time." It seemed to be a rut into which most of the students had fallen. Knowing that the students probably would not respond to criticism of their leads from others, it became necessary to have the children construct their own sense of what was or was not a strong lead for a story. I tried to examine the model on which they had based their leads. Sitting at night reading to my own daughter, I was amazed to find how many children's books begin with this lead. It made sense to me that children emerging from early childhood books into young readers would carry this mundane model into their writing. It was a familiar and comfortable beginning that offered a truncated setting so that one could get on with the story.

This called my attention to their current choices for reading, and I began to guide them to select beautifully crafted writing, even with picture books, which we were sharing as a group as part of our theme for China.

The Horse
Once I was walking along a country road.
When I looked into a pasture I saw a horse...

The Horse from Hell
One day I was walking into a desserted [*sic*] barn but there was a horse...

(Untitled)
One day Gosh called me and invited me to go to play tennis...

The Monster
One night after I watched MacGyver I whent [*sic*] in my room,
there was a alien...

FIGURE 11.1. Opening lines from a few of Todd's stories.

For many of the children, their attempts at higher-level writing skills were based on imitation. Since this was a strong meaning base for them, I knew that examination of other authors' leads would prove powerful for them.

Plunging In

"When you finish your entries in your reading journals, please bring the book you are reading to the meeting corner for a short discussion before writing." We were in transition from reading to writing time when I presented the idea of leads. The children finished their entries and progressed to the meeting area, books in hand, looking wary and puzzled by this out-of-the-ordinary instruction at writing time. Once they had settled and compared covers and opinions of their books, I began.

"I'm going to ask you to read the first sentence of your books; we will go around the circle; please listen carefully. Show us your book, and then read the title and the first sentence." I purposely avoided framing my specific intention. I wanted them to judge the effective openings of themselves. Eric began.

"Call me Ishmael," he read from *Moby Dick* in a quiet voice. I smiled but only nodded to the next child to read. Her book began with a bit of dialogue. The next child's book began with a dark and brooding setting, described with ponderous detail. And so it went, around the circle. To my amusement, one book started with the "One day" opening! Some were humorous and some were solemn. When the last opening line was read, the classroom was uncharacteristically quiet.

"I'd like you to take a minute to think about which opening line you remember most, and why. When you are ready to share your thinking, raise your hand," I instructed.

Hands shot up immediately, and then tentatively lowered and raised again. The second part of the question required some thinking. After sufficient "wait time," I called on one girl whose hand had been up for a while.

"I like the first one, 'Call me Ishmael,' because it tells you to do something right away," she explained.

A chorus of "Yeahs" were muttered and I nodded. "You're not the only one that finds that opening line effective," I told them. "It's a pretty famous line!"

"It's short and to the point," another student observed.

"Yeah, and you don't waste time having to know who said it, that comes afterwards."

"Well, Eric, were you lost after that?" I asked. "Wasn't it important to know who was talking first, before you heard what was said?"

"No, I found out," he observed.

Another girl piped up, "When a character talks to you, you feel like you're already in the story."

"How about another person; anybody remember a different line?" Hands went up. I called on Todd.

"I remember the line that began with dialogue."

"How was that effective?" I asked.

"Well, I don't know. I guess you find out about the characters from what they say," he observed.

"Anybody agree with Todd?" Several children nodded.

"Do you see any similarities to what we said about Eric's opening line?" I asked.

"Well, it places you right into the story because you hear someone speak," allowed another boy.

"Any other memorable lines?" I probed further.

"I like the one with the descriptive opening," explained Marilyn.

"Why?" I challenged.

"Well, you really get a picture in your mind," she replied.

"What do you think the author was trying to do with that opening, Marilyn?"

"I think the author was trying to set the mood for the story," she explained. The others agreed. After about five lines were cited, the consensus and the ability to cite lines dropped off.

"Why are the other lines difficult to recall?" I asked.

"They weren't very catchy," began one of the students. "They didn't grab your interest."

"Who could tell us what is needed for a catchy, strong lead line?"

The children began to list what they felt was important. I jotted down what they were saying.

"When you begin writing today, perhaps you could review some of your prior stories for opening lines, and revise them."

The children started to disperse around the room. Ryan went straight to his folder and found a piece he had written about a witch. He pulled it out and reread it. Later I found him rewriting the story. Todd sat thoughtfully, having chosen a seat in the meeting area apart from the others. He wrote furiously for a while and then paused to reread his work. I saw him smile and call Ryan over to hear what he had written. It began:

> "Can you see Phil's head?" Ryan said to me. We were climbing the tree, and when you climb a tree in after-school you don't want to be caught by Phil.

Todd had constructed a very different idea of what an opening line should be. He had found dialogue to be a hook for him as a reader and decided to try to use it in his own writing. In the past, Todd would have begun this piece, "One day I was in After-School and Ryan and I were playing. We got in trouble." In addition, his attention to this lead provided a context for him to control the events of the story for some effect. His story continued.

> Uh-oh, Phil's walking over the bridge. Ryan scrambled down. I wrapped around the branch and froze. When I saw him walk away, I climbed down a couple of branches. I looked at Phil. He was staring straight at me.

His story began with the characters up in the tree. Had he employed his earlier scheme for writing opening lines, he would have described the ascent into the tree first. His attention to his lead centered on his audience and the audience's perception of his characters. The story, the character's relationship, and the setting are all told through the dialogue in his opening line. This represented a stretch from his earlier writing to the more controlled, stylistic writing for an audience. It was a "big idea"—a new perspective on the purpose of writing—to hook the audience rather than to give a verbatim description of an event that he had experienced.

The children were particularly focused on their openings for some time after that. I have found that this kind of instant response to a mini-lesson is the exception, rather than the rule. Usually the lesson percolates for a while, until the proper writing context arises in their stories. The mini-lessons become a reference to which we return during our conferences. For example, when looking at a particular skill, such as punctuation, I might ask them to recall our discussions and decide which punctuation would be proper in their writing.

To support my specific mini-lessons, I often returned to the literature. Since I read to them everyday, it was easy to model wonderful writing and I would carefully select poems and narratives that demonstrated a concept they seemed to need. During our literature groups, I asked the participants to tell me in their journals, using webs and narrative, what they knew about a character or plot. Then they were to answer the most important and oft-repeated questions: "What do you know about this character (or event, etc.)?" and "How did the author tell you?" This reflection on the author's intent and technique was important for following how the readers made meaning from the text that they read. I could tell from their discussions whether they struggled with dialogue, foreshadowing, innuendo, and other more subtle forms of communication than statement. This focus by the learner also helped them construct new ideas about writing. As they found new ways to gain meaning in reading, they also found new ideas to employ in their writing. For example, during a literature group discussion with Eric and Mary, I asked them what they thought of a character who had declared that she did not need her mother.

"I think she's strong and independent," declared Mary. "She's her own hero."

"Who's your hero?" I asked them.

"I'm my hero," Eric said firmly.

"Why's that?" I was curious. It was the most revealing thing I had heard him say all year.

"Because I have to do everything for myself."

"My mom's my hero," said Mary. "She's alone, doing it all by herself, and she does everything well."

The children had constructed much from the simple piece of dialogue. They attributed personality traits to the character through inference and were capable of relating literature to their own experience. Later in their writing, they used dialogue to convey underlying messages effectively. This examination of the craft of writing became their automatic response and made the techniques available to the young writers as they constructed their own pieces.

IT'S THE AUDIENCE, STUPID!

Choosing the "Big Idea"

I can well relate to the "It's the economy, stupid!" placard used during the Clinton campaign for the presidency. Keeping my own focus as well as that of the students became difficult at times. What did these developing writers need? Audience recognition. Each time I wandered from this central idea, the focus got fuzzy and conferences diffuse. I would wonder what to do with the writer as we looked at a piece together. Finally it occurred to me . . . It's the Audience, Stupid! I needed to help them consider the very idea of audience. For them, at their stage of development, the audience had always been themselves—first as a passive listener to stories at a parent's side, and then as peers, as they listened to each other's nascent writing efforts. To date, the audience was an unsophisticated, undemanding lot. It was not that they did not appreciate higher levels of writing, it was just that they had not entertained the thought that their audience could vary. For example, their intended audience was seldom, if ever, an adult. Their poetry had the sound of Dr. Seuss and Shel Silverstein; their stories often had the cadence of fairy tales. I wanted to expose them to the possibility of other audiences.

I felt that a more sophisticated audience would stretch them to accommodate and use their highest writing skills. Figure 11.2 shows examples of some of the poems and writings of Maya, Melinda, and Mary.

It was clear to me from working with these students that they were capable of more sophisticated pieces. It was then that we began to talk about the audience. Two girls were sharing a piece that they had collaboratively written about cats. The following is an excerpt from that piece, which was lengthy:

What You Should Know About Your Cat

Sometimes when cats wear hats they look like bats. When a bat is fat, it looks like a hairy mat. When a cat has fangs, it likes to wear bangs. If it has nails, it has to have a tail.

After sharing they looked up to accept the praise of their peers. The standard "I like your poem because it rhymed" comments began. The fact that the words were forced concerned no one, as they were all delighted to hear so many words with similar sounds. I thought the time was ripe for a discussion about audience.

"For whom did you write that piece?" I asked them. They looked confused for a half-minute.

The Monster
The monster is pruple [*sic*]
and very big
it has a big nose
and a pruple wig
its eyes are blue and
its ears are red
it sleeps on the floor and
walks on the bed.

Pain
I got a bee sting I wounder [*sic*]
why?
When I got it I thought I'd die.
Then I got that bee sting I thought I'd cry
I got a bee sting I wounder why.

FIGURE 11.2. Poems by Maya and Melinda, respectively, before audience awareness.

"For the group," one girl answered.

I rephrased the question: "Which group here at Wightwood would enjoy your piece the most?"

"Oh, I think the ABC Group would like it the most," one girl answered quickly. The class agreed. Our ABC Group is our pre-kindergarten group.

"Is that the group that you thought you'd share it with?"

"No, we thought we'd share it here." I had to be careful not to discourage their efforts, so I suggested that they might share it with the ABC Group later that day. That excited them.

"You seem excited to share your piece with the audience that would enjoy it the most. What kind of writing is appropriate for *this* group?"

"Older writing," one child responded.

"What is older writing?"

"Harder words?" asked another.

"I think when you write for older people you write about things that are important to them," offered another.

"What's important to this audience?" Some of them looked surprised and perplexed.

"That depends on the person," they laughed.

Then the discussion picked up. Some offered the standard preteen concerns: school, friendships, appearance, and so forth. I asked them next to think of different types of audiences. Our discussion continued with my suggesting different audiences and their brainstorming the ways the writing would respond.

"When is a good time to consider your audience?" I asked them.

"Before you begin," said one of the boys. "That way you can use the right words and style."

"When you begin your writing in the future, this may be an important consideration as you draft," I suggested. They dispersed to begin writing, excitedly planning their next piece.

Thereafter, one of the things that we commented on at "share" was audience. It was subtle at first, but their desire to share with one another and their awareness of audience affected the quality of writing.

Introducing them to different possibilities sometimes involved sharing my own writing. I noticed that poetry, for many of the children, required a sing-song rhyme, as seen in the children's writing in Figure 11.2. I know that when I was young, poetry had to rhyme or I was not happy with it. I thought sharing some of my own writing, and the transition I had made from rhyming to nonrhyming poetry, might be liberating for them. I began a writing time with a share of my own. First, I read a short poem I had written that rhymed. Without asking for comments, I went on to share another poem, which used no rhyme at all. I looked up at them and explained.

"I can't decide which poem is best. I was hoping, as I read, that I created some images and feelings in the listener. Which poem did that best?" Hands went up.

"They both did," said the first child. "They just did it differently."

"Was that second one a poem?" asked one of the children.

"Did it have a rhythm?" I asked.

"Well, yes," he answered hesitantly. "It wasn't a story; yeah, I guess it was a poem."

"They're both good," said Janet. "Poems don't have to rhyme."

"Poems that do rhyme have different cadences," I said. "The rhyme can vary. Let me read you some that other writers have written." I shared some Robert Frost, including "The Road Not Taken," one of my favorites. It was a beautiful fall day and the poem, with its metaphor of forced choice, seemed particularly well suited to the moment.

Our room opened out onto a small porch that overlooked the woods. After we dispersed for writing, Maya, who had been writing about purple monsters, asked if she could sit outside to write. I told her it was fine as long as she stayed just outside the door, which I propped open. She sat quietly and peacefully writing, periodically looking up and around and returning to her work. Melinda joined her and they worked steadily until I called them for "author's chair." "Author's chair" was a time of sharing, following our writing time. A child who was prepared to share a piece with the whole group would sit in the author's chair and read the piece, soliciting questions and comments. Without collaborating, the two girls wrote the pieces of poetry shown in Figure 11.3.

When Maya shared her piece, there was noticeable awe on the others' faces. They seemed disquieted and yet amazed that Maya had written such a . . . poem! The comments began.

"I really like the way you wrote that poem."

"Was this written for the ABC Group?" I asked facetiously.

"Definitely not!" came the instant response.

"It sounds like real writing!" one child exclaimed.

Maya was beaming. She knew, before sharing, that she had written something quite different. Her share was followed by Melinda's. Of late her writing had taken a noticeable shift. She had strong audience recognition and was groping for a written voice. Her musing on the cycle of life, coupled with the looping images in her poem and the wistful contemplation, certainly seemed not the stuff of a 10-year-old! Both girls had considered their audience. They understood that the images they held in their minds were not shared with their audience until they painted them there. They strove

The Changing Leaves

It is fall, goodbye most likely green trees,
now welcome the red, orange, yellow, brown, purple
and even green needles from those very beautiful
evergreens, my favorite.
I rake up a pile of leaves as tall as the trees and I
jump into it, like I jump into a pool.
The wind is blowing, the trees are rustling like
a deer running away.*
The yellow butterfly lands on a small plant, it blends
in with the yellow leaves, with red stripes on it.
A bird tries to land on a tree, but the bird can't, it
is too windy.
Ahh, it is night, almost winter. I can still see some
little bright red, blue, and purple leaves.

Fall

Fall is a time of dancing through the trees.
Hearing crows crow. Listening to children playing in
the leaf piles. Crickets humming.
A gust of wind comes by, leaves fly everywhere, then
all is silent.
Dragon flies float by doing loops. Some people think
plants wither and die in the fall, but I personally
think that plants are born form a tiny seed and life
just slips away.
And I admire the beautiful colors on the pretty leaves
of such magnificent trees. Trees swaying with a whirl
of wind.
A time when dreams finally seem to be answered. And
you wonder about all the places you've never gone to
but maybe someday will. The grass sways. The sun
beams. I know it's fall.

———

*Maya acknowledged the "influence" of Robert Frost on this particular line!

FIGURE 11.3. Poems by Maya and Melinda, respectively, after audience awareness.

to use language to paint that picture, understanding the implicit messages that accompanied their words. This was a shift from event-controlled writing. Once again the class was subdued, and yet almost simultaneously excited, that one or two among them was writing in this manner. "Real writing," in their words, was attainable; was within their reach.

We began to talk about our individual "highest and best" writing attempts. The children began to use comparative language when discussing pieces at "author's chair." A standard question became, "How did your writing change?" or "How did so-and-so's writing change?" The reflection on their development became a time of synthesis for them, a point from which to make shifts in thinking and to develop new writing goals.

The Need to Say Something

Although Maya and Melinda were beginning to play with language, many others were still writing what Lucy Calkins (1986) has called "safe, correct little pieces." The lack of personal stories and pieces with emotional quality was interesting to me. Some of the children were intense about their writing; for example, Mary and Stan always chose topics that followed their interests. Stan wrote stories with medieval topics; Mary wrote wonderful mystery stories and poems. No one seemed to write about feelings, even in stories with events that should have inspired some emotion. Knowing that they were at a self-conscious age (early adolescence), I did not find it particularly unusual that they did not bare their souls before the group, even though it was clear that there was a lot of trust among the members. I wondered if they would risk working through and sharing some of the issues that I saw arising among them or that I knew were ongoing in their lives. Knowing that this kind of writing is indeed a risk, I decided that it required some modeling. I would take the first risk and share a piece of my own. The piece I chose was a story about my father's heart attack. It was written during the summer institute at the Center for Constructivist Teaching after hearing Catherine Fosnot (my instructor) read *Love You Forever*, a children's book about a mother's love. The story had triggered much emotion in the room, and we had written intensely for the better part of an hour. During "share" there was tremendous catharsis, as people shared their pieces about the loss of a child, the death of a relative, the rift between mother and daughter. I came away impressed by the quality of the writing, the power of raw and unedited first drafts.

From this institute I knew that writing to say something was important for the children as well. I decided to share the piece, even though I seldom got through it without crying.

Before I shared, I briefly explained the circumstances during which the story was drafted and that my father had survived the heart attack and was now well. I also explained that the story was hard for me to read but was important to me. They encouraged me to try, urging me to begin. As I read, they laughed at the appropriate places and watched my face with close scrutiny. They seemed surprised when I got a bit teary at one point, but they remained intent on the story and not on each other. At the end, they applauded and then began to ask questions.

"I'm sorry about your dad," one child offered.

"Is he okay now?" another asked.

"Yes," I assured them.

"Were you scared?" one girl asked.

"Oh, yes," I replied. "I was still scared when I wrote the story that it would happen again. What was interesting to me, though, was that, after I wrote it, I was less scared. I really felt better. When I wrote, I worked through a lot of those fears. What did you think of the writing?" I asked.

"It was really good," one child responded.

"It made you think," said another. "It made you feel sad. One minute you laugh, then you feel sad."

Not wanting to dissect the story, but rather to leave an impression about the power of affective writing, I told them to get started on their own writing.

Janet, who had been writing list poems, had also had some emotional issues in her life. She walked away thoughtfully. She had been experiencing separation anxiety and fears that would overwhelm her. At times she would panic and become afraid she would be sick. She had been working very hard at controlling her feelings and developing self-reliance. "I have a poem in my head," she said.

She went straight to her writing folder and wrote without lifting her pencil from the paper.

"Listen to this," she said during our conference, and then read:

MY FRIEND

> I have a friend
> I have a friend, no one knows her like I
> She has a heart, a heart that never stops beating
> She has a mind, a mind that thinks only wonderful thoughts
> She has eyes, eyes for only her to see through
> She has a mouth, a mouth that only speaks truth
> She has ears, ears that listen to life
> She has a nose, a nose to sense happiness
> For I am she
> I do have a friend

Every teacher has moments that he or she can recall when a child takes a leap. Janet's poem was a triumph for her. It said so much about her capacity to understand and help herself. The piece was later "published" in a class book entitled *Stories and Poems from the Heart*, a title suggested by Janet, and presented, along with the other children's pieces, at an Authors' Tea for parents.

As the children became more comfortable using writing as a tool to work out emotional issues, it even became a place to vent feelings about disputes at recess. Mary and some of the other girls had been having difficulties that arose from the telling of secrets. They all agreed that at times they needed private space, but that secrets seemed to result in hard feelings. Mary's poem, "Secrets," was her poetic ode to the destructive nature of secrets.

SECRETS

A whisper, silent . . . passing through sound
Walking upon air, and not ground
Misunderstandings, lies and a melody so dark
For words are so bare and stark
Empty, evil, a world without light
So cloaked, so covered like the night
So ruined are friendships who are true
So ruined, are people a lot like you
And this because of something called
(Whisper Next line)
A secret

REFLECTIONS

My first year solidified much of my thinking and strengthened my constructivist beliefs. I had learned to focus on learners' needs, to examine their emerging "big ideas," and to help them construct new concepts of writing. They had been given the ownership of their writing, the time to nurture it, and an audience with which to share it. They had been immersed daily in literature and had benefited from modeling. They had reflected on their growth and their own thinking. The shifts in their writing were truly remarkable.

Now as a third-year teacher, but for a first grade, the "big ideas," the areas of concern, have changed. I am addressing different developmental needs, younger writers. Yet they have already shown me that they, too, have a need for expressing their concerns. Their constructions involve the most elementary notions of print and writing, yet their words, their hopes, fears, and stories differ little from those of the older students. Their ideas about writing are best constructed from their own investigation of literature—by reading and writing and beginning again, by being and using an audience, by listening and reflecting, by breaking down old ideas and constructing new concepts of writing.

NOTE

1. Children's names have been changed, throughout the chapter, as well as within pieces of writing that refer to the children by name. Dialogue cited within the chapter is based on my best recollection and not on a transcript or recording. I have made my best effort to accurately recount the dialogue and identify the speakers.

REFERENCES

Calkins, L. (1986). *The art of teaching writing.* Portsmouth, NH: Heinemann.
Fosnot, C. T. (1989). *Enquiring teachers, enquiring learners.* New York: Teachers College Press.
Graves, D. (1983). *Teachers and children at work.* Portsmouth, NH: Heinemann.

CHAPTER 12

The Project Approach in Reggio Emilia

George Forman

Reggio Emilia is a city in northern Italy, about halfway between Milan and Bologna, that has, under the leadership of Dr. Loris Malaguzzi, developed an early education pedagogy that exemplifies constructivism. I have had the good fortune to become a member of this community through numerous trips to Reggio and through several focused projects (Forman, 1992, 1993).

Constructivism can be seen in the manner that these schools encourage children to dialogue among themselves, to experience one another's perspective, and to build a group understanding of a theme. Teachers wait for the child to venture forth with an idea, a hypothesis, a conclusion and then encourage the children to scrutinize these initial propositions for coherence and feasibility. This chapter presents a case study of these practices.

Instruction in these schools comes most often in the course of a long-term project that the children have designed themselves with teachers serving as facilitators. The teachers offer the children a variety of media (such as drawing, clay, and recycled materials) to represent their plans and ideas. These media are treated as fostering multiple symbols for the same general concept. For example, how a water wheel works may be studied through drawing, clay, and wood and wire constructions. As children compare these various representations, they confront new possibilities and generate new questions that would not have occurred had they used only one medium. The following describes some of the work at La Villetta, a preprimary school in Reggio Emilia.

AN AMUSEMENT PARK FOR BIRDS

A Project Begins

In February 1992, Amelia Gambetti, one of the co-teachers for the 6-year-olds, convened the children, about 20 of them, in the center of the room, a space with risers, a veritable Italian forum common in all of these schools in Reggio. She begins:

Amelia: What do you remember about the project that the 6-year-olds did last year out in our yard?

Ilaria: There were bird houses and there were trees. And also there was a straw hut [*an observation blind the children built last year in their playground*].

Andrea: There was a small lake [*a hole the children dug and filled with water*].

[*After more comments, Amelia asks another question.*]

Amelia: Who built the bird houses?

Georgia: The big children [*last year's 6-year-olds*].

Agnese: The children made them for the small birds.

Andrea: Right; if there were small birds and it rained, they could go under cover.

Alice: And go inside when it was cold.

The children continue to revisit their memories from last year. They recall the small lake that became so dirty and discuss ways to keep the water clean. They discuss enhancements to the lake—water wheels and fountains.

Filippo: But why don't we make a small lake, a long small lake with an engine that makes the water go to the right or to the left. We have to have some current. Otherwise the water is still.

Simone: We can place a pipe in the middle of the lake. We can place electrical wires; we can place a wheel that turns inside the water. There it makes wind, and the wheel will move to the right or to the left. If you place a pipe where there are electric wires, and you place a wheel under in the water, it will turn, make wind, and the water will move to the right and to the left.

After about an hour the children decide, as is their custom, to retire to their tables to draw some of their ideas with markers on paper. Their ideas grow richer and more interrelated as they talk with one another on the second day. The teacher asks for volunteers to talk about their drawings.

Andrea, who drew an elevator for the little birds, starts: "I made an elevator. I made it to help the small birds go up, for the ones that cannot fly." (The children often find baby birds in the spring that have fallen from their nests.)

As the children talk, the topics flow from last year to yesterday to the future. The children become concerned with how to keep the water clean if they are to build another lake. Where does the water come from? Is the water already dirty or does it become dirty later? What about a fountain that can clean the water? Where does water from a fountain originate? How does the water get up into the fountain? Should we have some little boats in the small lake? How about other things that are just for fun? By degrees the children expand their plan beyond making bird houses for hungry birds or a lake for thirsty ones. They project their own joy into the life of a bird and decide to make amusements for the birds. Thus the theme of this long-term project was born from the gradual construction of interconnecting topics during these large group meetings in which children talked and drew. Figure 12.1 shows one such drawing, a diving ladder for the birds to use in the lake the children plan to make.

Revisiting

The children in these municipal preprimary schools have learned from age 3 both to express their own ideas and to listen to the ideas of others.

FIGURE 12.1. A drawing for the amusement park for birds.

They do this by a process the teachers call *revisiting*. The children will recall a prior event, adding their collective memory to the here and now as they talk. Their concepts are the product of their shared memories of the event, parallel memories from similar experiences, their concern for the birds, and the knowledge that they will be shortly building something defined in these conversations. To help the children revisit their ideas, the teachers have taught them how to make their thoughts more explicit by using representational media—drawing, clay, wood pieces, simulations, cardboard, and, of course, their words.

Revisiting is also accomplished through photography and audio recordings. Each week, the children see photographs of their work from the previous week. They themselves often take photographs as they study an event. For example, in the Amusement Park for Birds project the children went to the park to take photographs of the fountains. These photographs were not placed in an album as a diary but were taken back to the classroom and used as a catalyst to deepen the children's conception of the fountain.

Slides of the fountain were used in at least three ways in this project. First, the slides were projected onto the wall at the children's height. They could "enter" the photograph as a way to make a more emotional connection with the life of the fountain. The image was cast on their body and they felt surrounded by the image. They began to act out splashing under the water's flow, drinking water from its overflow basin at the top, and looking into the fountain image for its secrets, such as the source of the water.

The slides were also used to make color Xerox prints. The children then took the print of the slide, a picture that they themselves had taken, and told the teacher what they remembered about the fountain on the day they took the picture. These words were tape-recorded and also written down by the teacher as the children talked. On the following day, the children returned to this same Xeroxed print, pasted to a much larger sheet of paper. The print itself was covered with a sheet of acetate just as large as the print. The children were invited to add to their photograph by drawing on top of it (on the acetate) and next to it.

When the children got stuck and could think of nothing else to add, the teacher would get her notebook and read back to the child his or her comments from the previous day. The revisiting occurs in many cycles, expanding the richness of the children's thinking.

Large-Scale Representations

In one case two boys were brought into a small room (the mini-atelier [studio], as it is called in Reggio). There they saw their slide of the park fountain projected on the rear of a piece of white paper mounted on a large piece of Plexiglas standing vertically (see Figure 12.2), a variation on the

FIGURE 12.2. A representation of the Plexiglas easel used at Reggio Emilia.

Plexiglas easel mentioned in Forman and Hill (1984). These two boys had already expressed an interest in the pipes, tubes, and pumps that must be inside the fountain. To facilitate their thinking, Giovanni Piazzi, the school's resource teacher, had built this easel the previous evening.

The two boys, Simone and Andrea, proceeded to draw the tubes that they speculated were inside the fountain, using the rear projected image as a guide and catalyst. Occasionally Giovanni turned off the slide projector so the boys could inspect their additions to the fountain system.

Simone and Andrea began their drawing at the top of the fountain image, one drawing the right contour and the other the left contour of a hidden pipe. When one bent the other turned. There must have been something about the scale of the easel and the dominance of this huge image that caused them to draw adjacent halves of the same object. After some minutes of working on the right and left side respectively, the boys completed the workings of this fountain's water system. When Simone had an idea to make a pump, Andrea followed with a similar pump on his side.

These types of work spaces are common in the Reggio schools, spaces large enough for two or more children to work on a common representation. A large summer fresco, a large wind-making machine, a gigantic rendering of the wee creatures in a plot of grass, and a huge dinosaur painting 60 meters long are cases of large-scale constructions that I remember.

Compare the social context of learning between these macro-spaces and the paper size space of individual art. Working in a common space requires more planning of the final graphic, more negotiation of process, more attention to the other child's perspective. And more importantly, these macro-spaces encourage the children to seek out the relation among the individual components, a crucial process in the development of knowledge structures.

The spider in the field drawn by Mateo needed to be oriented toward the fly drawn by Agnese. The bird in the sky needed to have a field rendered in a scale much smaller than that field seen by the *grillo* (cricket). Knowledge structures, as defined by Piaget, gain their coherence from special types of reciprocity among facts. This reciprocity makes it possible for the learner to reason beyond the givens of the elementary facts. The social context of learning most certainly accentuates the formal dynamics of reciprocity and thereby deepens the coherence of the concepts under study.

Back in the United States one day, on my way to an appointment, I drove past a typical elementary school. The sun was bright; there was a slight chill in the autumn air. The children were out at recess playing schoolyard games. While waiting at a stop light, I enjoyed watching the joy of these children at play. Behind them, their well-maintained modern school presented a backdrop of a caring place. The large windows of one classroom contained about two dozen autumn leaves, no doubt individually drawn and cut out by the children in this class. The traffic light was still red, so I looked at these leaves more closely. Yes, they were highly individualized. Each child, no doubt, had given some thought to his or her personal expression of this prototypic symbol of the season. But the leaves were arranged on the huge panes of glass in a geometric array similar to the alternating diagonals of a herringbone pattern. The art was an expression of elements, but certainly not the relation of these elements. There were no piles of leaves caught in a drift at the bottom of fence post. There were no pictures of people raking these unique leaves into a common pile. There was no attention to the source, no giant maple tree with vacant spaces where these leaves had released their summer's grasp. I was glad when the light turned green.

My point is not some sentimental plea for an autumn scene. Nor is it a plea for collectivism. My point is that the essence of constructivism is the coherence of the relations among elements. In Piaget's research, it was the relation between water poured from a short container to a taller one, or the relation between the thickness of a rod and its flexibility. It is the relation between elements that children explore when they "play" with the facts. It is the teacher's responsibility to facilitate this play by providing the appropriate spaces, materials, and group dynamics for putting things into relation. Perhaps the teacher could have placed a huge picture of a tree on the window and then asked the children to place their leaves in a way that made sense.

I recall a mural a group of kindergarten children made in an elementary school in Amherst, Massachusetts. The work was inspired by a visit from several educators from Reggio Emilia. This huge mural, which ran the length of the classroom, was completed in two stages. In the first stage the children made a cityscape collage from colored construction paper. There were trucks on the highway, windows that folded out, tall buildings, residential houses, their yellow school bus, and even a snow plow—a virtual Richard Scary poster. This mural remained on the wall for several weeks and became familiar to the children. Then on the appointed day, a team of children, each with a small container of thick white paint, transformed the cityscape into the aftermath of a winter's snow storm.

They briskly discussed among themselves where the snow should go. Should it be only on the topmost ridge of the roof or also on the shingles in the foreground? Should the snow be all over the highway or only under the tires of the vehicles? Should the snow be on inclined surfaces in the same degree as on horizontal surfaces? These children were clearly thinking of the art as a representation of a dynamic system of relations. The mural was a set of hypotheses that they would later check when the snow fell outside (see Forman, 1993).

Representations as Plans for Action

In numerous ways the children in the Reggio Emilia schools draw in order to build something. In the Amusement Park project, the children first drew fountains as a way to consolidate their personal recollections of favorite fountains. Then these same drawings were taken into the atelier, where the children propped them up, studied them, and began to make a rendering of this drawn fountain using potter's clay. Such work is typically done in the presence of at least one other child. The conversation back and forth between the two children at work facilitates their learning in at least two ways: The children are both involved in a process of inventing a symbol for their ideas; and, at the same time, they are engaged in a metasymbolic processing because the other child often asks for an explanation.

In one incident that I remember well, Georgia was looking at her drawing of a fountain with a series of sprays coming from its center. She was trying to render this freeform shape using potter's clay. She had the technical skills, given her three years of work in this school since she was 3 years old. She knew to use wire to give the clay support for the thin sprays of water emanating from the fountain. Her friend for many years, Simone, noticed her progress. A loose translation of their dialogue proceeded like this.

Georgia remarks, having placed three wires in her fountain, "I need seven more wires." Her drawing, before her as she worked, had ten sprays. Simone hears her remark, peripherally, as he works on his clay fountain, and notices that her drawing has ten sprays.

Simone: You need ten, see (*and he counts on the drawing— one, two, three, and so forth to ten*).
Georgia: No, I just need seven. I already have three.

Simone: (*still centered on Georgia's drawing*) Ten, you have ten sprays.
Georgia: (*in the voice of an exasperated parent*) No, I already have three
done and only seven more to go, seven more, not seven all together.
(*Simone shrugs in a sort of face-saving acquiescence to Georgia's logic.*)

The point of this sequence, common in these schools, is that Georgia
learned that she had to take Simone's perspective in order to communicate
her meaning. It was not sufficient for her to tell him what she meant. She
also had to address Simone's interpretation of what she meant, to wit, *seven
more* (her meaning), *not seven all together* (Simone's interpretation). The
meaning appeared to be effective when she identified the contrast in their
two perspectives. Remember, Simone and Georgia are kindergarten age.

It is also noteworthy that the children were using a symbol as a referent
for another symbol, that is, the drawing was the referent for the clay fountain. Thus the clay fountain was a rendering of a plan rather than the rendering of an object. A plan is a symbol that carries implications for the execution
of action. It is more than a representation of static features of an object. The
mental set toward a plan involves translating the drawing into a sequence of
actions, in this case, the execution of the clay fountain. Since the drawing is
perceived as a plan, it presents an entree, for other children, a reason for the
co-construction of knowledge, in this case the difference between total
amount and remaining amount. That is, without the plan Georgia could
have placed as many or as few clay sprays as she wished and there would
have been no reason to debate the precision of her representation.

It is also significant that the clay rendering is not the rendering of a
photograph, even though these children often do photograph objects. That
is, the drawing itself is a representation of their recollections about fountains
at large, a record of their personal experiences—the frozen fountain in winter for one child, the fountain with angles and hearts for another, the fountain with fish in its basin for a third. These drawings are externalized memories, even theories about what makes an object fountain-like.

Then, when they sculpt their drawings in clay, they are confronted with
an interesting problem: How do they capture in clay some of the things that
were so easily drawn with pencil? This challenge forces the children to make
compromises in clay for those things that have too fine a detail. But they
also make discoveries about the fountain in clay that were not revealed in
the drawing. For example, one child constructed a basin at the bottom of
her clay fountain that could physically hold a large quantity of water, while
it was not clear that the basin in her drawing was of sufficient depth.

In summary (see Figure 12.3), the drawing is a representation of their
personal theory about *fountainness*. The drawing becomes a plan when used
as a model for sculpting in clay. The plan is read as a set of instructions for

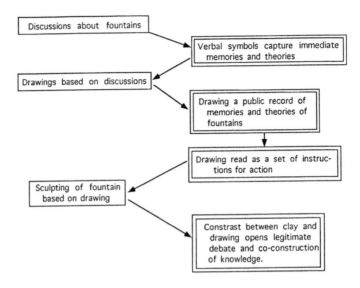

FIGURE 12.3. A representation of the children's theory about *fountainness.*

action, and this allows another child to join into the process of symbolization and discourse with the first child.

THE ROLE OF THE GREATER COMMUNITY

The Amusement Park project continued for several more months and
served as the focal point for the end-of-the-year celebration. The Amusement Park was actually planned, built, and opened on the last day of school.
Eventually, the entire school prepared amusements such as telephones for
the birds, beach umbrellas, channels with flowing water, fountains with
sprays made from recycled materials, tiny elevators so the baby birds could
get back into the trees, and many other real objects that had been discussed
and designed on paper many months before. More that 300 parents, grand-
parents, friends, neighbors, and city officials came to its inauguration. It is a
testimony to the school's belief in emergent curriculum that this inauguration was on the last day of school and the amusements were disassembled
shortly thereafter. The teachers knew that next year's children would certainly design completely different items, if not a completely different project.

These children, from age 3 to age 6, know that these final celebrations
are part of the school's tradition. They remember the previous year when

"the big children" made the lake for the birds. They remember the excitement when the parents came to see the lake last year. These memories have a way of helping the children project themselves into that same situation in the current year. This sense of audience, of someone who will listen, question, and perhaps admire, gives their work purpose. And of course, the birds. The birds did come. The birds did play on the amusements. And the children were delighted at the significance of their work that began in winter and went through to the end of the school year (Forman & Gandini, 1994).

REFERENCES

Forman, G. (1992). The constructivist perspective to early education. In J. Roopnarine, & J. Johnson (Eds.), *Approaches to early childhood education* (2nd ed.) (pp. 102–121). Columbus, OH: Merrill.

Forman, G. (1993). Multiple symbolization in the Long Jump Project. In C. Edwards, L. Gandini, & G. Forman (Eds.), *The hundred languages of children: The Reggio Emilia approach to early education in Reggio Emilia, Italy* (pp. 107–132). Norwood, NJ: Ablex.

Forman, G., & Gandini, L. (1994). *The amusement park for birds* [Videotape for teachers]. Performanetics, 19 The Hollow, Amherst, MA 01002.

Forman, G., & Hill, F. (1984). *Constructive play: Applying Piaget in the preschool* (2nd ed.). Menlo Park, CA: Addison-Wesley.

CHAPTER 13

Teaching Introductory Physics to College Students

Dewey I. Dykstra, Jr.

I am a physicist who holds a constructivist view of the nature of knowledge. By "knowledge," I do not mean facts, which can be memorized and repeated. Parrots can do that. What I am referring to is in the nature of beliefs about the essential nature of aspects of the world and how they work. These beliefs give meaning, significance, and context to facts. The formal definition of velocity, which is stated in a sentence or so in most physics textbooks, is not an example of the kind of knowledge that I mean here. Instead, by "knowledge" I am thinking of something more in the nature of beliefs about the conditions that result in constant velocity or about the nature of velocity as distinguished from acceleration. I call these notions "conceptions." Concerns about the nature of knowledge are sufficiently important that several have written more extensively on the nature of student knowledge and conceptual change in other articles (e.g., Dagher, 1994; diSessa, 1993; Dykstra, Boyle, & Monarch, 1992; Smith, diSessa, & Roschelle, 1993).

I came to this constructivist point of view because of my belief that, as the result of teaching, one's students should have new understandings of the world. I found at the beginning of my career that when I taught as I had been taught, new understandings on the part of the students were not usually the result. Having looked for evidence of new understandings as a result of teaching at a wide range of levels over the past two decades, I have found that this is unfortunately the general state of affairs. I also do not believe that only certain smart people can *do* math and science. Holding these two beliefs has made life difficult, because the first sets up an expectation that is not generally met and the second disallows most common reasons given for why more students do not understand new ideas in science when they leave our classes.

Left with the realization that typical physics instruction results in an unsatisfactory outcome and deprived of the typical ad hoc explanations for this failure, I wrestled in a great disequilibrium for a number of years. In accommodating I have developed a constructivist view of knowledge and come to the conclusion that how I teach physics must be drastically different from how I was taught.

This chapter is an attempt to illustrate what has now become typical of interactions in my classes. Having taught differently for a number of years now, in a manner driven by my students' notions of the phenomena at hand instead of by the text, I notice that each group of students goes through a similar sequence of considerations. The sequence of ideas is so reproducible that often the words they use are similar. What follows is illustrative of my experiences with the students.

We begin in a student laboratory setting. There are 24 students in groups of 4 sitting around large tables.

EXAMINING WHAT WE THINK

Considering Forces and Constant Velocity

While the students are watching, I ask them to consider the motion of a cart as I use my hand to cause it to move at as constant a velocity as possible across a horizontal surface. I repeat this motion several times as I ask the students to consider how the forces that appear to be involved work to result in the motion observed. The class has already used arrows in diagrams to represent forces in a previous class session to illustrate their ideas about the forces that result in an object's remaining stationary.[1] Now they are asked again to represent forces as arrows, illustrating their ideas about the forces acting on an object moving at a constant velocity in a series of pictures of the cart intended to represent the cart at successive equal time intervals. They are asked to make a key for these diagrams to make clear the forces they are trying to represent. They are reminded to adjust the length of the arrows for the forces to represent their thoughts about the relative sizes of the forces involved both in comparison to each other and to reflect any changes that might happen as time elapses. Finally, they are asked to write in prose what they were trying to represent about how the forces result in the constant velocity motion. While they are considering their ideas, some ask "Should we include things like friction?" My response is, "If you think that it is important in your explanation of constant velocity, please do so." A typical student paper contains the elements shown in Figure 13.1.

When it seems that most everyone is finished with this task, I invite them to share the possibilities that seem reasonable to them. I begin with a question that has several safe answers as far as the students are concerned: "What's one of the forces that seems to be acting on the cart while it is moving?" The following is a sample of what typically happens.

Bob offers a safe suggestion: "There's gravity acting down."

I draw an arrow pointing downward on the first picture of the cart and ask: "Does this force act at each of the other times? Is it the same at each time? Or does it change over time, do you think?" I am trying to draw Bob and the class into more participation.

Bob ponders this question, then responds cautiously, "I think that it is acting at each time and that it does not change."

To represent Bob's ideas I use the same size arrow in each of the pictures to represent the gravity force remaining the same through each of the time intervals. I ask, "Are there any more forces acting in this situation?"

This time, Martha volunteers another safe answer: "The table exerts a force up on the cart." This answer is safe since this particular force was the object of class discussion in a previous class session. An example of this discussion has been described by Minstrell (1982).

I ask, "Is this force present throughout the run? Does it change, do you think?" The "do you think?" is specifically intended to shift attention from the notion that I am looking for *the* answer and toward the fact that I am interested in having the discussion revolve around their answers and ideas.

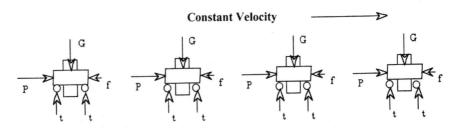

Constant Velocity ⟶

P: the push force   The forces from the table cancel the gravity force
f: the friction force   The push and the friction are constant and P is greater than f
G: gravity
t: the forces from the table

FIGURE 13.1 A typical student pre-instruction response about the forces involved in maintaining a constant velocity.

With some hesitation in her voice, Martha responds with, "Yes, I think it stays the same."

I respond by drawing a force up on each diagram and continue, "Are there any other forces acting on the cart that you think might contribute to its motion with constant velocity?"

Steve suggests, "There's the push."

"Okay, how should I draw this?"

Steve responds, "Draw an arrow acting from behind the cart in the direction of motion in each of the diagrams."

"Does the size of the force stay the same or should it vary?"

Immediately Steve responds, "I think it should stay the same."

As I look around in silent query, it appears, from their facial expressions and nodding heads, that many others agree. I draw the forces according to Steve's instructions and then ask, "Are there any other forces acting?" I am trying to get all the ideas that members of the class might have included, so I will keep asking until no more are volunteered. Because the act of asking again in traditionally taught classes implies that the "right" answer has not been heard, I remind them that we just want to get all the possible ideas out "on the table."

Dwight says, "I included friction."

"How should I draw this friction to represent what you're thinking?"

"Draw a tiny force acting backward on the cart that stays the same in each picture," he replies. I do so.

At this point I ask, "Did anyone have any different ideas from what is drawn on the board so far?"

Bob says, "I didn't include friction; it doesn't make the car go forward."

I respond, "Okay; that's all right with me." Then I ask, "But, if you *were* to include friction, do you think you would do it in the way we have done it here on the board or would you do it differently?"

Bob thinks for a moment and responds, "I guess I would do it as is on the board."

I ask, "Are there any other items that might be included to explain the constant velocity of the cart?" Nobody volunteers.

"So, everyone had one or more of these forces drawn on their papers. If suggestions by your classmates seem reasonable, go ahead and add them to your sketch in your notes. We'll wait a minute or two while everyone thinks about what we have on the board and has a chance to make modifications in their notes." I wait to give them time to do this. I want them to think specifically about what makes sense to them as to what forces are playing a role in this constant velocity motion, because next I am going to ask them what they think the forces must "do" to cause constant velocity.

When it looks like they have finished making additions to their notes, I ask, "How does it seem these forces have to work together or have to *be* in order to result in constant velocity?"

Now Doris says, "I think they have to remain the same."

"Why does it seem to you that they should remain the same?"

After a short hesitation, she replies, "I think they have to remain the same to keep the cart moving at the same speed." There is general agreement.

"What about the friction force? How do you think it fits in here?" I ask the class.

Mike says, "It has to be smaller than the push force."

When I ask, "Why does it seem so?" Mike says, "If it were as big as the push, then the cart would not move." Again, there is general agreement displayed in head nodding and comments.

When I ask about the other forces, typical responses are "The table force just holds the cart up, but does not make it go faster or slower" and "The air pressure is the same." There is some disagreement on this, because, after all, "the air can cause some resistance." Then Dwight suggests that this resistance can be considered part of the friction.

Possibly taking a cue from Dwight, Bob suggests that "gravity keeps the cart on the table, which causes friction, but then we have already taken friction into account."

In summary, there seems to be general agreement that there needs to be a constant force in the direction of motion and, if there is some force working against this propelling force, then the resisting force is much smaller. My intent was to get them to decide on an explanation of constant velocity in terms of forces that makes sense to them. It is *not* important that they decide on the "right" answer here. It is, on the other hand, important that, whatever they decide, their decision is what makes sense to them at this point. What I have described is essentially what every class I have seen has decided, not unanimously in each class, but an overwhelming majority each time. This description of theirs is now prominent in their minds as we move on to think about constant acceleration and then to look at a specific example.

To finish this segment of discussion, I ask the students to consider their answer to this question: "If we were to have the cart moving at twice the speed it was moving before, but still at a constant speed, what differences in our descriptions of the forces would be in order?" After giving them a chance to collect their thoughts and urging them to jot down their ideas, I solicit their ideas.

Dwight volunteers, "If we want the cart to move twice as fast, then we have to push it twice as hard."

Bill asks, "What about friction? If the cart moves faster, isn't the friction larger? Don't we have to take that into account?"

I put on a questioning look and gesture, reflecting the query back to the class.

Mike says with some conviction, "I think we do. The push force has to be twice as much more than the friction force than it was before."

Martha eagerly responds, "Yes, however much greater the push force was than the friction before, it has to be twice as much greater than the friction when we go twice as fast even if the friction is also greater."

I take this opportunity to wait and as I do several of the students with puzzled looks lean to their neighbors to talk. Eventually, there seems to be resolution and general agreement with this notion.

Considering Forces and Constant Acceleration

Next, I use my hand to move a cart with as constant an acceleration as possible across a horizontal table surface as I ask the students to watch and consider a new motion and the forces involved. I repeat the motion several times as I ask the students to consider how the forces that appear to be involved combine to result in the motion. Again, they are asked to represent forces as arrows in illustrating their ideas about the forces acting on the cart. This time it is moving at a constant acceleration. They sketch arrows for the forces in a series of pictures of the cart intended to represent the cart at successive equal time intervals. They are asked to make a key for these diagrams to indicate the forces they are trying to represent. I remind them to make the lengths of the arrows for the forces represent their thoughts about the relative sizes of the forces involved both in comparison to each other and to reflect any change that might happen as time elapses. Finally, I ask them again to write in prose what they were trying to represent about how the forces involved result in the motion in their diagrams. A typical student drawing can be found in Figure 13.2.

When it appears as though everyone is finished with this task, I invite them to suggest the possibilities that seem reasonable to them. I begin by asking, "What's one of the forces that seems to be acting on the cart while it is moving? Should we put gravity in this time?" There is general agreement. I ask, "Does it remain the same at each time?" Again, general agreement is the response.

Bob volunteers, "I think that pretty much the same types of forces are acting in this case, too."

Trying to get everyone to decide whether they agree with Bob, I ask, "Well, what does everyone else think? Does it seem like there are any new forces acting that we need to explain this new motion?" Everyone seems to agree with Bob that the same sort of forces seem to be involved. Again, I am trying to get all the imagined possibilities out in the open. Since no

Constant Acceleration

P: push force   The table forces cancel gravity
G: gravity   The push force gets greater and greater as it speeds up
t: the table forces   If there is friction, the push force still gets greater and greater

FIGURE 13.2 A typical student pre-instruction response about the forces involved in maintaining a constant acceleration.

more forces are suggested, I shift attention to the issue of how these forces work to cause constant acceleration.

"So, how do these forces have to 'work' to result in constant acceleration?"

Now Martha, who seems to be confident in her grasp of the idea that the class seems to be expressing so far, says, "The push force has to get larger and larger."

"Why does it seem like the push force should do this?"

Steve gives his explanation: "To make the cart go faster and faster, you have to push harder and harder." There seems to be general agreement.

"What about the friction force?" I want them to consider the role of each of the forces.

Bob says, "It has to be smaller than the push force."

Mike says, "But if the cart goes faster and faster, the friction gets larger and larger." This is said in such a way that it is fairly clear that this statement is almost a question—"How do we take this into account?"

Martha answers, "It's just like thinking about the cart going at twice the speed. If the friction grows, then the push force has to get even larger. It's how much bigger the push is than the friction; the difference has to get larger and larger for the speed to increase continually." There is a mixture of general agreement and new realization as some are adding the notion of friction into their ideas about forces causing motion.

When I ask about the other forces, the first response is from Dwight: "The push and the friction are the important part here. Gravity just keeps the cart on the table, and the table keeps the cart from falling."

So in general there seems to be agreement that there needs to be a constantly increasing force in excess of friction and in the direction of motion in order for an object to continually increase in speed.

APPLYING OUR NOTIONS TO A SPECIFIC INSTANCE

In the next lab, I invite continued investigation with, "In a previous class session we decided how we think forces explain 'stationary-ness' when we concluded that the forces have to 'cancel each other out' for a stationary object. Just now we have examined our ideas about the role of forces in constant velocity, where it seems to us the push force has to be a constant amount greater than resistance forces, and in acceleration, where it seems to us the push force must constantly increase with respect to the resistance forces to get a constantly increasing speed. Let's consider a specific example and use our ideas to predict what will happen." As the students turn their attention to the apparatus at their tables, schematically described in Figure 13.3, they find a cart attached to a string, which, after passing through some pulleys, is attached to some weights hanging beyond the end of the table.

Up to this point I have been trying to get the students to think about their explanations for motion. This is not a common habit in everyday life, so for many students it seems that there is not a clear, explicit base of expla-

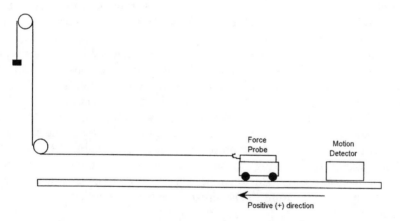

FIGURE 13.3. A schematic diagram of the apparatus used for the forces and motion laboratory activity. The force probe is taped down to a cart and the string holding the weights is attached to the hook on the force probe. This allows the force probe to detect the magnitude of the force from the string pulling the cart while the motion detector records its motion.

nation at hand when they come to class. The previous discussion assists the students in providing this basis for themselves.

My goal ultimately is to maximize the chances that the students will be disequilibrated. The more explicit and detailed their ideas are to themselves and the greater their commitment to these explanations, the more likely the disequilibration when the students decide for themselves that the explanations do not make sense.

I ask them, "If you were to sketch a graph of the force from the string on the cart, a pull force, over time, what do you think it would look like and why?"

There is not consensus. Bob, Mike, Dwight, and others think that the graph should reflect a constantly increasing force because, as Mike points out, "The cart speeds up when you let it go, so the force has to increase to cause this." Theirs is the force graph at the top of Figure 13.4.

Martha, Doris, Steve, and others disagree. "The weight hanging over the side remains the same, so the force has to be constant," says Steve. Theirs is the force graph at the top of Figure 13.5.

Next, because I want them to tie together predictions about forces and the resulting motion, I ask them to imagine what the motion graphs will look like when we make a run with this apparatus, letting the cart go and catching it before it goes off the end of the table. In so doing, I find that they usually make use of the notions expressed in the previous discussion. Bob, Mike, and Dwight produce graphs like the distance, velocity, and acceleration graphs in Figure 13.4. They are predicting constant acceleration. Graphs by Martha, Doris, and Steve look like those in Figure 13.5. They are predicting constant velocity.

Notice that while there are two distinctly different predictions represented in Figures 13.4 and 13.5, both predictions are consistent with the belief about forces and motion agreed upon by the students, which could be expressed as: The force changes as the velocity does. They are all working with the same "big idea" that they brought with them to class—force implies motion. In Figure 13.4, Bob, Mike, and Dwight are saying that since the cart speeds up, the force must be increasing. In Figure 13.5, Martha, Doris, and Steve are saying that since the force remains the same, the speed must remain the same. The differences in the predictions seem to be driven by which specific feature of the situation is being attended to by the students.

Briefly, on Terminology

In much of the science education literature, the term *conception* with various modifiers is used: *alternative conceptions, everyday conceptions, person-*

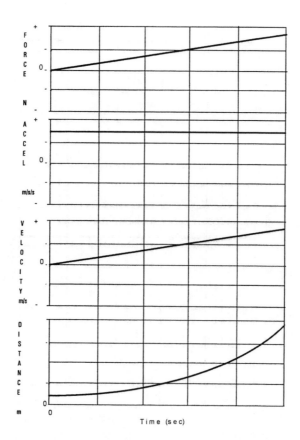

FIGURE 13.4. Predictions of the pulling force on the cart and its motion—constant acceleration. This set of graphs are typical predictions made by students who focus on the fact that they believe the cart will speed up when released, which means to them that the force must increase. The release and catch are ignored here.

on-the-street conceptions, preconceptions, naive conceptions, misconceptions. In the literature there is some debate over what term to use, but this discussion rarely gets to the level of the nature of conceptions. The articles cited in the first paragraph of this chapter are among the few that delve more deeply.

Unfortunately, much of the literature seems to refer to conceptions as the sorts of predictions the students make, as described immediately above. Instruction focusing on this level fails to address underlying notions or beliefs about the world. Left unaddressed, these notions can be expected to be used again by the students. It is this level of notion or belief that ought to

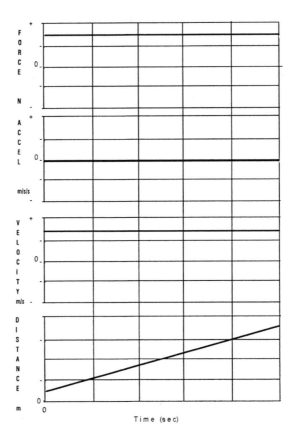

FIGURE 13.5. Predictions of the pulling force on the cart and its motion—constant force. This set of graphs are typical predictions made by students who focus on the fact that they believe the hanging weight does not change as it falls, which means to them that the velocity will be constant and the acceleration will be zero. The release and catch of the cart are ignored here.

be the object of discussion during instruction and that is best called "conception."

Checking Our Predictions

Now that I have received specific, committed predictions as to what will happen, I ask the students to set a computer equipped with motion and force transducers[2] to collect force and motion data during a series of runs. The results of the first run with 100 grams on the hanger are compared with their predictions. There is a mixture of surprise and confidence when the students get results, which are shown in Figure 13.6.

"Look, we predicted that there would be constant acceleration!" Mike and Dwight think the data support their prediction.

"But we didn't predict that the force would be constant!" Bob seems to realize that there is something amiss.

As if she, also, is finding support for her prediction in the outcome, Martha says, "See, we predicted the force would be constant!"

"But we also predicted the velocity would be constant and it's not!" Doris and Steve, like Bob, realize that there is a substantive mismatch here.

They all proceed to collect data on runs with 50, 100, 150, and 200 grams hanging at the end of the string, this time recording the force and the acceleration during each run as indicated on the computer screen. They busily get to work making the runs and recording the data, and as they do, they wrestle with the details of keeping the strings running on the pulleys, catching the carts before they hit something or go off the table, and deciding from what spots on the graphs to take the readings of acceleration and force.

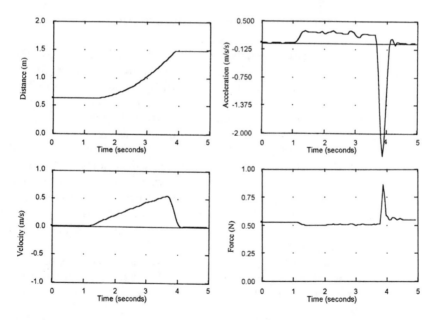

FIGURE 13.6. Graphs from an actual run. Note that this set does not match in shape or form either of the previous two sets. Significantly, while the cart does increase its speed as predicted in Figure 13.4, the force is constant during the motion as in Figure 13.5.

There is additional discussion in the lab groups about the discrepancies between the predictions and the results. At different times toward the end of the lab period, both Martha and Doris come to me and ask essentially the same thing: "There's something missing here. It looks like constant force causes constant acceleration. This 'robs' us of our explanation for constant velocity. So, what causes constant velocity?"

Internally, I am very pleased. This is the exact dilemma in which I hope they will become engaged. Outwardly, I attempt to remain very calm. I want this to be *their* dilemma, not influenced by anything but their consideration of motion and its causes. I want to encourage them in this, so I respond, "What you say makes sense to me. We can't deny what we see in the graphs. This does pose a dilemma. We don't have time now at the end of the lab period to sort this out, but it sounds like we should bring it up next class period. Think about it tonight and be ready to contribute your thoughts when the time comes in class tomorrow."

The time to end the laboratory period has come, and the 24 students in lab scatter to their next classes.

MAKING SENSE OF THE DISCREPANCIES

The next class meeting begins with about 150 students having found seats in the room. I begin by asking questions that review the predictions made. Students can find these answers by looking in their own lab notes. My goal is to get as many of the students as possible back into that state of disequilibration that existed when they realized that the force and motion of the cart were not as they had predicted in lab. I am also trying to get those who were not disequilibrated by the end of lab to be disequilibrated now, too. I try to do this by getting them to review their notes on how they thought velocity and acceleration are related to force and how this entered into the predictions they made about the cart with the falling weight. Because I have been trying to get them to write not only predictions, but reasons behind them, they have something to refer to, which facilitates more people contributing in class.

After asking them what their predictions were and sketching them on the board according to their directions, we find that throughout all of the lab sections there are essentially only two predictions, which are illustrated in Figures 13.4 and 13.5.

"So, did the cart behave according to either of these predictions?" I ask, encouraging them to compare their data with their predictions.

"No, each is half right and half wrong," Steve answers. "The force was constant, which is what one group predicted but the other one did not. As for the motion, the acceleration was constant, which is what the other group predicted. The first group predicted constant velocity instead. For every amount of weight we put on the hanger, the force remained constant, yet the acceleration was constant in each case." Everybody seems to agree; apparently a constant force causes a constant acceleration.

It seems to me that the students have decided that one cannot argue with the data on this issue at this point. They have used the MBL apparatus in previous weeks to study motion, and they trust the apparatus that produces the graphs well enough by now to believe it when it contradicts their hypotheses.

While the class is busy agreeing with Steve, Doris points out, "Wait. There's a problem. If constant force causes constant acceleration, then we don't have an explanation for constant velocity. So, what causes constant velocity?" she says looking to me and smiling because she realizes that this is the time to bring up the questions she asked in lab.

Now the rest of the class is looking at me, too, in silence. The dilemma is just dawning on many. This is a "magic moment" in that my efforts have been rewarded by apparent disequilibration on the part of a number of students. It is as close as I can get everyone in the class at the same time to this dilemma, each with some sense of disequilibration.

I usually have mixed feelings at this point. It is sad that the initial response of the students is to look to me for an answer. This seems to be a response that they learn in school. Hopefully, the more frequently we can create situations in which they create their own answers, the more likely looking to the teacher for the answer will diminish. My response is to get them to think about the possibilities. "So, our previous, seemingly sensible, explanation does not make sense anymore after we have looked closely at the situation. What are some possible alternatives? Let's see if any of them work better."

After some wait time, Bob says, "I heard in a class before that an object stays moving the same way unless an outside force acts on it."

There is silence from the rest of the students, who are looking to see how I react. I respond with a neutral, "Okay . . . Any other ideas?"

Now Martha, who has been thinking about this since she asked about it in lab the day before, says, "I know! It's *no* force, that's what causes constant velocity, *no* force."

Some of the other students smile condescendingly at this. I respond, "Okay, are there any other ideas? We want to get all the possibilities out before we start analyzing them."

Mike volunteers, "Maybe it's a decreasing force that causes constant velocity."

"Okay . . . Are there any *other* possibilities that anyone can think of?" There do not seem to be any other ideas.

"Well, it looks like after having to abandon the constant force explanation, we have as possibilities no force and decreasing force. Why not increasing force? That would round out the possibilities, wouldn't it?" I offer.

Quickly, Dwight answers, "We saw in lab that the bigger the force, the bigger the acceleration. Making the force bigger only makes things worse if we are trying to get constant velocity."

"How does everyone else feel on this issue?" There is agreement with Dwight.

"Okay, so we can decide to rule out increasing force for now. How many think that it might be decreasing force, as has been suggested?"

Several students raise their hands. I look at those students and ask, "Why does this seem like a possible solution?"

Mike answers for this group, "Well, when we look at the distance graphs that we got in lab this week, the beginnings are always curved more tightly and the ends of them are almost straight lines, like constant velocity. So, it takes more force at the beginning to straighten the graph out."[3]

"How many disagree with the decreasing force explanation?" A number of hands are raised in response to my request. "Do you have any response to these comments then?" I ask those students with their hands raised.

Bill says, "It just doesn't seem right. I don't know how to say it. I guess it just seems to me that, if you have a force, there's an acceleration."

Doris, with some excitement, points out, "I think Bill's right. Look at the data we put on the board. We had four different forces and each time we had *acceleration* and not constant velocity." (During the review at the beginning of this class period, the force measured and the acceleration observed for each weight hung over the pulleys was put on the board from the data the students recorded in lab. See Figure 13.7.)

Mike comes back, "What alternative do we have? You can't say that *no* force makes constant velocity. There's never *no* force on the cart. There's always friction on any real cart."

Number of 50 gm masses on hanger	acceleration (m/s/s)	force (N)
0	0.23	0.50
1	0.51	0.95
2	0.71	1.39
3	0.91	1.80

FIGURE 13.7. A typical table of data. The forces and resulting acceleration were generated by hanging different masses on the hanger in apparatus described in Figure 13.3.

Martha comes to Doris' defense. "But, if you look at the data, not only do you always have acceleration for every force, for smaller forces you have smaller accelerations. If the force becomes zero, then so would the acceleration, and zero acceleration is constant velocity. That's why I said *no* force is what causes constant velocity."

Mike says again, "But, how can you have *no* force when there's always some force?" Some students are nodding their heads in agreement with Mike.

Martha does not have an answer but does not agree and frowns, as do a few others.

"What about a rocket in space?" says Bob, as if he had taken a mental side trip and is just now coming back to the conversation. "It's a long ways from anything else, so nothing else affects the rocket. Its engine quits all of a sudden. What does it do? Stop?"

Mike says, "No, it just coasts on, but that's in space where there's no friction!"

Walter, who has not said much until now, says, "You mean that it would not just stop?"

Doris replies, "What's to stop it?"

Walter says, "Hmmm . . . I guess there's nothing out there in space to stop it."

Then Steve says, picking up on the rocket story, "Friction works against you. What if this rocket had an engine in the front to slow it down? If it was firing, that would be like friction. If it was stronger than the engine in the tail, then the rocket would go backwards. If they are exactly equal, then neither could make the rocket go faster or slower when they are both turned on. One force cancels the other one out, *no* force."

"So, you're saying that down here on earth with the cart, when the friction—the front engine—matches the push—the tail engine—then you have no force overcoming the other and the cart neither speeds up nor slows down? I thought that is what makes things stand still," says Jane, another student who has not said much before, but who had obviously been following the discussion.

Bob responds, "But, think again about the rocket. If we turn on the rear engine and get the rocket going at some speed and then, after a little while, we turn on the front engine and adjust to make their thrusts equal, does the rocket stop?"

"Oh, I see, the rocket doesn't stop, it just keeps going at some speed. You're saying the same is true with the cart? Do you see what he's saying, Mike?" says Jane excitedly.

Mike responds, "Okay, I see how what you're saying can work. It sure isn't what I was thinking and I'm not sure it feels right, but I think I see what you mean."

At this point Martha says, with enthusiasm, "This is what I've been saying! *No* force is what makes constant velocity!"

The remaining disagreement with this notion is not strong enough for the discussion to carry itself on. A number of students see how this answer makes sense now. Others, like Mike, may not "feel right" about it, but they see where it "comes from" and how it can explain things. At this point I say, "This is an issue that has occupied people for many years. One of them, Isaac Newton, you know, the guy under the apple tree, thought a lot about it. One of the things he decided made sense to him was this: 'Every object continues in its state of rest, or of constant motion in a straight line, unless it is compelled to change that state by an unbalanced force on it.' Is this what you all are saying?" A discussion on this question follows.

Thoughts on What Happened in the Discussion

Looking back at the beginning of this class session, the notion brought up by both Bob and Martha, for different reasons, that no force was needed for an object to go at a constant velocity (as in what is called Newton's first law of motion), seemed to be such a strange idea to the students that it was ignored. In some classes, when it is mentioned at the beginning of the discussion, the idea is actually considered laughable by some of the students. This, I think, is a measure of either how deeply the notion that "force causes motion" is held or what little sense the "no force causes constant velocity" notion makes to them. In the students' views, motion appears to be translated directly into velocity as they come to differentiate features of motion; hence "force causes velocity" seems to have replaced "force causes motion." The fact that not all of the students seem to find that the new idea "feels okay" is further evidence that the old idea is hard to give up.

This shift from "force causes motion" to "force causes *changing* motion" is all the more difficult because it appears to be dependent on two other shifts in thinking. For many of the students, thinking in terms of continually changing motion is very new, since they have just developed this habit in the previous unit of instruction. One of the key features in the change in thinking about forces is the distinction between motion and changing motion.

The second and less obvious shift in thinking that the students bring into consideration is another aspect in their thinking about the nature of force itself. For many of the students, it seems that things move because a particular force causes the motion. If other forces are present, but the object moves in the direction of this force, then this force seems to be seen as *overcoming* the others and causing the particular motion. It seems that many of the students do not initially view forces as entities that operate simultaneously with the net effect or the totality of the forces determining the outcome, such that equal opposing forces result in an equilibrium. If this were not the case, the dilemma of the meaning of "no force" causing constant velocity would not have been a dilemma and the whole discussion of rockets in space would not be such a regular issue in the discussion, raised by the students in class after class, which is how they resolve the dilemma of the meaning of "no force."

The Status of These Descriptions of the Students' Ideas

These attributions that I have made about the students' ideas are *my* ideas about the students' ideas. Derived from classroom experiences, they are consistent with data collected in individual interviews by researchers and with the classroom experiences of other teachers; nonetheless, they are my reconstructions of the students' notions. These descriptions of the students' ideas only have value or validity insofar as they assist me and other teachers in meeting goals that *we* set, that is, insofar as they are adaptive to our intentions as teachers with respect to the students and they fit *our* experiences with the students. To that extent we can function as teachers as if these ideas do exist in the students, but without this tentative stance as to our understanding of the students' ideas we run the risk of being too rigid and unable to respond well when student behavior is not as we expect.

These descriptions of the students' ideas are not justified because I believe they can be or will be found to actually exist in the students' heads and somehow independently compared to our ideas by some means of understanding other than we have used to decide about them already. I believe this cannot happen. We have already used the only means we have—our existing sense-making capabilities to create this picture of the students' ideas.

While I think we have generated a convincing picture, one that is very useful, we cannot really know what the ideas of others are in an absolute sense. Since we can apparently deal with the world in our role as teachers without this absolute knowledge of the students' ideas, the fact that we cannot have such absolute knowledge does not matter.

A number of students leave the class session just described with a different notion of forces and different notions about themselves and their relationship to knowledge in science. Others are at least aware of the possibility of such differences. I keep working on it the rest of the semester with them.

THE MISMATCH OF GOALS AND METHODS IN TEACHER EDUCATION

We all need to be aware of the role those of us who teach in colleges of arts and sciences play in the preparation of teachers at all levels. If a person teaching methods or philosophy in an Education Department decides that a constructivist point of view is one that they would like their students to understand and be able to use or apply in their teaching, but one or two courses are the extent of the students' exposure to these ideas, then little effect can be expected. The students have had 12+ years of science presented from the transmissionist/realist paradigm, and most likely all the science courses that they take from the "real scientists" teaching in the college of arts and sciences will be consistent with a transmissionist/realist point of view. *How are the students going to teach science when they go out to teach?* Unfortunately it will probably be the way they were taught, not how they were "taught" to teach. After all, this is how the "real scientists" do it and likely how their supervising teacher during their student teaching experience and most established teachers around them at their first position do it, too.

While people *can* and *do* come to teach differently from the way they were taught (examples are in this volume), it is clear that they do not come to do so by merely hearing about alternatives. Examples of teachers coming to teach differently can be found in the work of Schifter and Fosnot (1993) and of Wood, Cobb, and Yackel (1991). These examples share in common disequilibration about learning and an aspect of immersion or long-term exposure and mentoring. One cannot help but think that being taught content in ways consistent with the constructivist point of view, in addition to methods courses, would help in the process of coming to teach differently.

There are many "real scientists" teaching who do not *want* to be bothered with this teaching/educational philosophy "stuff." They do not seem to realize that what students come to believe about the nature of the knowledge involved in the subject, they take by implication from their only source of content knowledge—the treatment of knowledge in science courses. A philosophy of knowledge is implied in this treatment whether or not a teacher intends to imply anything.

In physics the subject is delivered by the professor as given knowledge, organized, hierarchical, and unchallengeable, the implied source of which is the "superior mental capacities" of mostly dead Caucasian European and American men. Now, not all physics professors would agree that this is their picture of knowledge in physics. But they probably would agree that the way physics is typically taught is the best way to cover the subject and demonstrate how it is all interrelated in the time available. Yet the facts that students have no appreciation for the tentativeness of knowledge in science and that they seem to have a fragmented view of the subject are frequently bemoaned by the faculty. *How can one come to know the nature of the knowledge as something constructed and tentative if one never makes some of it oneself?* It now seems to me to be entirely unreasonable to expect that the students have such understandings when we have never shown them anything other than what is typically displayed in school. Emilia Ferreiro (1991) put it well when she wrote: "There is no neutral pedagogical practice. Every single one is based on a given conception of the learning process and of the object of such a process" (p. 46).

QUESTIONING UNSPOKEN ASSUMPTIONS

The overwhelming majority of science courses are conducted knowingly or unknowingly within a transmissionist/realist paradigm. Many good, energetic, thoughtful people have pursued this enterprise for some time. In most human endeavors we find a particular notion that has some status in our thinking and decision making: If a theory or set of assumptions works to explain nearly all of the occurrences that one finds, then the theory is taken as one to rely on. If the theory has to be patched most of the time with exceptions, then it is considered questionable and is abandoned. Studies comparing pre- and postinstruction conceptions of students in physics suggest that almost no change occurs in student understanding as a result of typical science instruction (Hestenes, Wells, & Swackhamer, 1992). Furthermore, this result is found to be independent of the instructor and institution, from public high schools to Harvard University. If one has to invent ad hoc explanations (excuses) for why what one is doing is not working more than 99% of the time, then maybe it is time to start questioning the basic transmissionist/realist assumptions about the enterprise.

SOME BENEFITS OF USING CONSTRUCTIVISM TO GUIDE DECISIONS ABOUT TEACHING

When I started teaching the conceptual physics course a few years ago, I realized that I could not complain about how science is taught in schools unless I did what I understood was the best I possibly could for education majors in the course. I could not deliver lectures and have them do verification labs covering all the major topics in physics in one semester. This "take a drink from a fire hose" approach would not do anything to induce them to challenge their notions about topics in physics, the nature of scientific knowledge, or themselves as future teachers of science to children.

It was time for me to pull together and apply in a whole course the new notions I had been developing over the years as a result of trying to self-regulate over the dilemma described at the beginning of this chapter. I decided that I had to focus on experiences that had the potential for the students to disequilibrate themselves and then give them the "space" to come up with accommodations that fit. This meant that I had to create settings in which it would be safe to be repeatedly "wrong," in which critical examination of one's own ideas and those of others is encouraged and safe, and in which students can collaborate. Covering the whole waterfront could not leave them with anything useful, so I decided to spend time on a few topics on which we know something about possibilities for conceptual change.

The result of acting on the decision to throw tradition to the wind and do what made more sense has been seven years of the most exciting, rewarding, and intellectually stimulating experiences in teaching and learning that I have ever experienced. It has changed my view of what constitutes understanding of topics in my field and how people come to understand them. I have a greater respect for the intellect that is in all of us, and I have been rewarded by the response of a number of students to these insights about themselves.

Of course, there are still those students of college age who just want the answers and who are quite sorry that I have decided to do things differently. But the challenge of understanding *these* students well enough to get inside and facilitate disequilibration in them is also exciting. I am convinced that whether they realize it or not, many of the students have looked deeper into their own ideas and into the phenomena than their peers who have not had a similar course experience. When you have invented an idea for yourself, it is much more a part of you than when you memorize a description of it from someone else.

TEACHING TEACHERS

If there is a key to reinventing our educational system, it lies in what our teachers believe about the nature of knowing. Without a reexamination and change in beliefs about the nature of knowing, there will be no substantial change in the enterprise of education; we will stay in a vicious cycle. Driven by the discrepancy between our students' scores on standardized tests and those of students from other countries, we search for solutions. Noticing that students in other countries spend more time in class on the subjects, we call for our students to spend more time on-task. (Does this sound like some recent national curriculum efforts?) This requires that teachers at earlier grades have more content knowledge. After all, if they do not, how can they transmit it to their students? The response is the call for teachers to major in a *real* discipline. (Does this sound like recent, widely touted recommendations?) The result will be more students taught in the traditional way for more time. If we already turn students off to science in droves now, think what would happen if we had them three or four more years to teach them in the same way!

The flaw in the whole argument lies in the transmissionist and/or realist view of knowledge that underlies this line of reasoning and proposed its solution to our educational crisis. The exams that are used to compare our students test the acquisition of memorizable information or skills, not the conceptions possessed by the students. In fact, the failure of normal science instruction to have an effect on students' beliefs about the world is noticed generally and internationally (Pfundt & Duit, 1994). More time on-task certainly will have an effect, but it must be time on the *necessary* task. It must include the kind of changes in environment and bases for teacher decisions in the classroom that are illustrated in the examples in this volume.

Will making teachers major in a *real* subject create a desirable and sufficient difference in the students? Not in the measures that I think are important. Will making the students spend more time on-task create a desirable and sufficient difference in the students? Why would it, if no time is ever spent on the students' notions about the world? The answers are not so simple as these.

We can only make a difference in the views about knowledge that the students have when they come to college if we can produce a concentrated enough experience in a wide range of subjects in which students are encouraged and supported in the examination of the nature of their knowledge about phenomena. I know that my colleagues in this effort realize this takes more than just a couple of courses in teacher education. Changing how the teachers are taught is one of the necessary steps in breaking the cycle. If we can get teachers to question the unspoken assumptions that underlie current practice, then the practice can change in a substantial way. Faculty in the liberal arts and sciences must begin the process by questioning the unspoken assumptions and then examining their practices in the light of their conclusions.

I close with a quote from Arnold Arons (1990), Emeritus Professor of Physics at the University of Washington:

> I wish to emphasize most strongly that the teachers whose incapacities [to adequately prepare grade school students for later studies] are *not* the ones to be blamed. The [responsibility] resides in *our* hands at the colleges and universities. *We* are the ones who perpetuate the mismatch. . . . *We* are the ones who made the teachers as they are. (p. 324)

Acknowledgment. In addition to many colleagues, I am indebted to the National Science Foundation for support in some of the work that led to the ideas expressed above via grant numbers: MDR-8950313, MDR-9153989, and MDR-9154015. The opinions expressed herein are not necessarily those of the National Science Foundation.

NOTES

1. This previous class session is similar to one that Jim Minstrell (1982) and John Clement (Camp & Clement, 1994) hold with their students.
2. We use transducers and software originally developed as part of the Microcomputer-Based Laboratory (MBL) Project funded by the National Science Foundation (Brasell, 1987; Thornton, 1994). Similar hardware and software is available for most of the commonly available classroom computers.
3. The distance graph that one sees in Figure 13.6 is in the shape of what is called a parabola. It is more curved at the beginning of the graph, as Mike points out. In trying to make the distance graph straighter, Mike is using the fact that a constant velocity shows up as a slanted straight line on a distance graph. He is saying that if we had more force at the beginning, then this curved part would be pulled out straighter and that less force is needed later, as the distance graph tends toward being a straight line later in the run.

REFERENCES

Arons, A. (1990). *A guide to introductory physics teaching.* New York: Wiley.
Brasell, H. (1987). The effect of real-time laboratory graphing on learning graphic representations of distance and velocity. *Journal of Research in Science Teaching, 24*(4), 385–395.
Camp, C., & Clement, J. (1994). *Preconceptions in mechanics.* Dubuque, IA: Kendall/Hunt.
Dagher, Z. (1994). Does the use of analogies contribute to conceptual change? *Science Education, 78*(6), 601–616.
diSessa, A. (1993). Toward an epistemology of physics. *Cognition and Instruction, 10*(2&3), 105–226.
Dykstra, D., Boyle, F., & Monarch, I. (1992). Studying conceptual change in learning physics. *Science Education, 76*(6), 615–652.
Ferreiro, E. (1991). Literacy acquisition and the representation of language. In C. Kamii, M. Manning, & G. L. Manning (Eds.), *Early literacy: A constructivist foundation for whole language* (pp. 31–55). Washington, DC: National Education Association.
Hestenes, D., Wells, M., & Swackhamer, A. (1992). Force concept inventory. *The Physics Teacher, 30*, 141–158.
Minstrell, J. (1982). Explaining the "at rest" condition of an object. *The Physics Teacher, 20*(1), 10–16.

Pfundt, H., & Duit, R. (1994). *Bibliography: Students' alternative frameworks and science education* (4th ed). Kiel, Germany: Institute for Science Education, University of Kiel.

Schifter, D., & Fosnot, C. T. (1993). *Reconstructing mathematics education: Stories of teachers meeting the challenge of reform.* New York: Teachers College Press.

Smith, J. P., diSessa, A., & Roschelle, J. (1993). Misconceptions reconceived: A constructivist analysis of knowledge in transition. *The Journal of the Learning Sciences, 3*(2), 115–163.

Thornton, R. (1994). Enhancing and evaluating students' learning of motion concepts. In A. Tiberghien & H. Mandl (Eds.), *Physics and learning.* New York: Springer-Verlag.

Wood, T., Cobb, P., & Yackel, E. (1991). Change in teaching mathematics: A case study. *American Educational Research Journal, 28*(3), 587–616.

CHAPTER 14

Being There: Middle School Students as Coconstructors of a Classroom Senate

Catherine A. Franklin

Sen. Wright: First of all, I would like to remind you that our bill was not passed in 1990 and it is not the Clean Air Act that you are referring to.

Mr. McCrag (coal miner): It is similar to the Clean Air Act, but in your bill I believe it says that you have to have filters and these filters are relevant. They do cost $100 million dollars and up. . . .

Sen. Wright: But it is tax deductible.

Mr. McCrag: But that doesn't matter. *It is $100 million dollars and up!* [italics to emphasize agitated tone of voice]

Mr. Cart (coal miner): It is a lot of money.

Sen. Santos: What would you say about the 10,000 families who have lost loved ones due to pollution (as a result) of mining?

Mr. McCrag: We obviously don't want air pollution. If there is a way to solve it, we want it, but without having us all lose our jobs.

The senators and the coal miners were engaged in public debate at a congressional hearing on the proposed Clean Air Act. The bipartisan Environmental Affairs Committee sat facing the invited witnesses. Democrats and Republicans sat on either side of the room. Mr. McCrag and Mr. Cart were seated at a table in the center of the room. Mr. McCrag and his associate had been invited by the committee to provide testimony based on their prior experiences with clean air laws. Their West Virginian coal mine had shut down because they had been unable to meet the financial costs involved in complying with the federal clean air regulations of 1990. From time to time, Mr. McCrag paused before responding to a senator's question and poured himself a glass of water from the blue, plastic pitcher in front of him.

This senate hearing was not in Washington, D.C. It took place in an urban elementary school (N–8) in New York City. The senators and the coal miners were actually eighth graders; they had constructed their respective positions within this legislative unit. Tom as Sen. Tom Wright had been working within committee to develop this legislation. Jorge as Sen. Jorge Santos supported this legislation. The two witnesses played double roles; in addition to being senators, they were also witnesses at this hearing. They framed their testimony to reflect the perspective of concerned coal miners. This testimony was based on research investigations that revealed how past environmental regulations had a devastating economic impact on the coal mining industry of West Virginia.

BEING THERE: TEACHING AND LEARNING THROUGH CURRICULUM DRAMA

Students and I, their teacher, constructed this ongoing legislative drama. There were no scripted roles or fixed frames of reference within this experience. Students worked over an 8-week time frame to develop their own legislative voice and position within this political community. Together we investigated legislative issues, terms, and political situations that emerged within this enacted curriculum.

I call this approach to teaching and learning "curriculum drama." Curriculum drama forms a bridge that links the challenge of teaching and learning content to the authentic interests, concerns, and energies of the students. In this way, students can generate complex understandings *as insiders* to the defined unit of study. At the same time, this constructivist approach pulls the class together into new ways of being, knowing, and interacting with one another.

Curriculum drama is different from educational drama and simulations. Curriculum drama is curriculum in action; it allows the "story" to work on the student (Haine, 1985), curriculum, and classroom environment. It is coconstructed by both students and their teacher.

In contrast, both educational drama and simulation research have a teacher-directed, top-down quality about them. Although educational drama may have a more emerging genesis than simulation, both are directed, powered, and shaped by the adult in charge.

In curriculum drama, students are active inquirers in the curriculum.

Not only do participants draw upon their imagination within this context (e.g., generating the position of a senator); students demonstrate learning and reflection (Heathcote, 1984) through language, gesture, and social interactions (Wolf, 1994, 1995).

In this particular case, an eighth-grade class transformed itself into concerned members of an active legislative body. This was one of the three major units in our spring semester study of American Government. With the written consent of the students and their families, I worked as teacher-researcher to examine this 2-month-long unit with this class of 25 eighth graders. This classroom research study became the basis for my doctoral focus and this chapter is drawn from that body of work. Pseudonyms are used to protect student privacy.

Priming the Pump: Developing Background Understandings

The classroom senate demanded student leadership and peer collaboration. I needed to prepare them for this. From the beginning of the year, each student developed practice in facilitating class meetings and in supporting their classmates as leaders. Twice a day we held student-led meetings in the morning and afternoon homeroom period. Each week a different student led the 15–20 minute sessions that occurred at the beginning and end of the day. She or he called on classmates to carry out specific, discrete responsibilities (e.g., reporting on news, taking attendance, reviewing homework assignments).

As the classroom teacher, I supported the weekly leader. If the designated student leader had an effective management style, I maintained a low profile in the meeting. If a student experienced difficulty taking on this public role, I closely mentored her or him. By the time spring came, everyone had led a number of homeroom sessions and the class had developed extensive practice collaborating with peers as designated leaders.

It was also important to build student interest and curiosity about the world around them. From the beginning of the school year to the end, we set aside time during morning homeroom period to discuss the news. Each week I assigned two students the daily task of summarizing national and international events. The rest of the class then added detail and/or points of clarification to the reported news. Students became at ease with voicing their own meanings of the world and interacting with other shared perspectives. Sometimes these reports led to lively discussions and fiery debates. From this daily ritual, the political world became a relevant topic of conversation within the room. Students came in knowing that I expected them to share current news and to actively question the world around them.

Setting the Stage: Developing a Sense of Believability

In the spring, we worked to transform the classroom setting to a legislative environment. We began by examining Article 1 of the U.S. Constitution (legislative branch); this served as the blueprint for organizing our classroom senate. Students then researched and wrote reports on their particular state (e.g., geography, people, and issues), presented their findings in regional meetings, and investigated the voting record of their two U.S. senators. Finally, the class explored the historical background and contemporary status of the two major political parties.

The class divided into two groups, Republicans and Democrats, to reflect the current ratio of political affiliation within the U.S. Senate. At the time of this study, the Republicans were in the majority. As classroom teacher, I determined these groupings based in part on the voting patterns from the state that each student had selected, and I adjusted groupings accordingly for gender balance and group dynamics.

Students were not expected to mimic or adopt the political ideologies from the major parties. However, they could use their earlier study of political parties as a frame of reference. Students in the Republican Party faced a major challenge; most did not want to be in this group! The following dialogue highlights their challenges:

Stan: Are we going to change our views on things?

Jim: Well, I think that a lot people think that Republicans don't care about poor people.

Alex: (*interjecting*) *That's stereotyping!* [italics for spoken emphasis]

Jim: No, Alex, that is not what we should be like, but what I think a lot of people think they are like.

Amanda: Like Democrats . . .

Leah: I don't think that the Republicans—

Stan: (*interrupting*) We *are* [italics for spoken emphasis] the Republicans.

Leah: What I am saying is that practically everyone here is a Democrat.

Jorge: No!

Alex: No!

Stan: We are all Republicans. Right now we are in Washington, D.C. (*The group convulses in laughter*)

Jim: Okay, okay. Eli? (*calling on a person with his hands raised*)

Eli: . . . we shouldn't think of ourselves as Democrats or Republicans. I think that we are not old enough to know about these views. I think that we should just have our own views and not be Democrats or Republicans.

This dialogue showed the raw struggle of a group involved in the social process of building collective meaning and working to create a common frame of reference. Most of them had concerns about being assigned to this party; it went against their own liberal outlook. Stan raised the opening question to the group. He wondered if his colleagues were going to change their views on issues now that they were Republicans. By phrasing the question in an inclusive way ("Are we . . ."), he engaged others in the meaning-making process. From the beginning, the emphasis was on "we." The quest for who they were as a political unit was approached as a collaborative endeavor, not as an individual problem.

The dialogue also illustrates the preliminary resistance that students had with this task. Leah distanced herself from the term "Republican" with her comment "I don't think that the Republicans. . . ." Her comment was interrupted by Stan who playfully argued "We are Republicans," and a bit later "we are in Washington, D.C." Laughter helped to defuse group tension and confusion.

Eli refocused the group. By emphasizing the importance of "having our views," he urged the group to break out of the fixed boundaries of political labels. Genishi, McCarrier, and Nussbaum (1988) speak of collaborative talk as "full of complex zigzags that form unique and interesting patterns" (p. 190). Children needed time to appraise ideas, address stereotypes, and bond through laughter—in other words, to work together to make social meaning.

It took time for the group to create meaning and a common sense of purpose around the term "Republican." It had to make sense to them. They had to move from viewing this term from the third person view of "they" to the more familiar view that it was now "we." Heathcote referred to this as "feeling on the inside" (Wagner, 1976, p. 78). Students had to work through their sense of disequilibrium. They needed time to come up with "big ideas" (Schifter & Fosnot, 1993) about being "Republican" when, as Leah said, "practically everyone here is a Democrat." They had to "break set with old assumptions and construct meaning" (Lambert, 1995, p. 40).

Eventually, the group began to work in a more cohesive manner. Chris, one of its members, reflected upon this process. "CF" refers to the author.

Chris: Well, at first we had a few problems . . . but I think in this last meeting we really pulled together and started to think as one.
CF: What enabled you to then start "thinking as one"?
Chris: Well, I think we opened our minds up a little bit and expanded it. We thought about what the party meant to us . . . It took time to think about it. I mean when we had the first meeting it was right after

we heard what parties we belonged to, and so some of us might have been unhappy about the party and didn't know what to think. So then we had two nights to think about it and again get our characters and expand our views.

The classroom senate did not develop polarized political parties. In fact, this was a rather congenial senate and apart from the fact that one party was in the majority, there was little to distinguish one group from the other. The following section explores the collaborative work that took place within these political groups.

Tweaking Legislation: Probing Questions and Appraising Ideas

The Democrats held a working session on legislative initiatives. Students sat in desks arranged in a circle and their elected party leader facilitated the meeting. Each student presented her or his initial ideas about legislation. Students listened and responded with questions.

Mary, an active and dedicated environmentalist representing the state of Massachusetts, crafted the "Clean Air Act." The following conversation took place when it was first introduced to the Democrats.

Mary: My bill is to keep the air clean from factories and smog. Sixty per-
cent of all factories in the United States will have filtering screens over
their chimneys so that when the smog and smoke come up from the
factories, it will be filtered.
Mike: I'd just like to make a point . . . Within one year they should get a
filter. A lot of pollution can happen in a few years.
Katie: Do you know how much the filters cost?
Mary: I don't know.
Katie: Do you think it will be a big amount?

Students took it upon themselves to scrutinize legislative ideas and to pose questions to their peers. Katie's concern about the cost fact of Mary's bill was genuine. In a subsequent conversation, Katie explained her preoccupation.

We know about our economy and how we are in debt . . . I mean some people might have had their parents lose jobs and know how hard it is to get another one. We realize how hard it is for them. We don't want people to lose their jobs. We are really thinking about this stuff. We are doing this from experience.

The shift from student to senator changed the meaning of their class-room work. It moved from being an academic study to being a situation where the collaborative process of appraising ideas triggered deep personal connections with the world around them. Jorge, the Republican majority leader, expressed a similar approach to the senate. "We are just addressing the issues which seem to be important." The senate experience began to reflect upon the students' understanding of the world.

After initial review within the student's political party, bills were then assigned to a committee. Mary's Clean Air Act went into the Committee on Environmental Affairs. Through the course of a week, the committee met a number of times. The Clean Air Act expanded its initial goal "to help keep the air clean from factory's smoke and smog" to include "making all city buses and garbage trucks electric." Moreover, the detail within this bill became more complex and comprehensive. By the end of the week, this legislation contained nine separate provisions.

Tom, a member of this group, commented upon the committee experience of developing legislation:

> It took a long time thinking about it and deciding what to do in writing it. That was probably the biggest part. 'Cause we actually think our bill is pretty good. It is well thought out. I like the way we really were involved in it.

From this experience, Tom understood that the process of creating legislation took a long time. He valued this work because it was "well thought out." Coming from Tom, this was significant. Throughout the year, Tom typically completed his work in a hurried fashion. In this context, however, Tom was markedly different. Working with his peers in this process, he slowed down and began to pay closer attention to details.

This group drew upon the collective ideas and skills of its members to further develop viable legislation. They continued to negotiate with one another through this process. In the following dialogue, Jesse worked at including aspects of his own bill, "Reducing Smokestack Pollution," into the committee's collective legislation entitled "The Clean Air Act." He took responsibility for writing up the group's recommendations.

Jesse: (*reading aloud from his legislation*) This bill will establish a group of inspectors to go to the plants once a month to make sure the law is being obeyed.

Tom: That's a lot—once a month.

Jesse: Should I say once every two months? (*looking at members of the committee*)

Tom: What about every three months . . . until the filter is being properly used?

Mary: No, because then they should check to make sure the filter is being properly used.

Jesse: Yeh, exactly.

Tom: (*nods his head in agreement*)

Mary: So, once every two months.

Jesse: (*changes original sentence to "once every two months"*)

Overall, the process of creating legislation within committee became an experience that deeply engaged students. As individuals they drew upon the collective resourcefulness of their colleagues to create viable legislation. Furthermore, students felt a sense of realness in their work. Tom explained:

> It seems real because we have to do all this stuff that real senators have to do. I mean it is not that much fun to write bills. [Nonetheless] you can kind of use your own ideas and put down your ideas that you would do if you were a real senator.

For a homework assignment, students wrote letters to their constituents about their committee work. This task provided a new angle to the daily senate reflections that I had been assigning in class. The following came from Mary in the Committee on Environmental Affairs.

> Dear Fellow Americans,
> Here in Washington we are trying hard to come up with an easy, *low-financed* (italics added) way to help the environment. As you already know, many major cities are having problems keeping their air pollution down. . . . Some ideas we've discussed are: putting filters over factory smokestacks and making all city buses and trucks electric. . . . We will be working to come up with ways to put this bill in effect for the *lowest cost* (italics added) to you.

Written for an audience that extended far beyond the boundaries of her eighth-grade classroom, Mary placed herself in Washington, D.C. and addressed the American public at large about the benefits of her committee's legislation. While she did not provide specific details, she did emphasize its affordable cost. Financial cost was a major theme in conversations within both her political party and committee. Furthermore, the extensive use of plural pronouns in this letter indicates how Mary viewed this work as a collaborative endeavor.

Students began to construct this senate experience by engaging in different tasks (e.g., devising legislation, appraising ideas) and participating in various group settings (e.g., political party sessions, committee meetings). This helped to create multiple layers of membership within the classroom senate.

Shaping the Experience: Hearing on the Clean Air Act

The Clean Air Act was eventually scheduled for a senate hearing. To prepare for this experience, the class worked on gathering current news articles from journals and newspapers that related in some way to the Clean Air Act. I paired students and assigned them the task of locating an article that connected to the Clean Air Act. My goal was simply to develop a collective base of understanding around issues and terms that related to this legislation.

Two students, Mike and Amanda, were excited about their research work. They shared the article they found and reported that because of the impact of the 1990 Clean Air Act, 1,000 coal mines had closed in West Virginia. ("East's Coal Towns Wither in the Name of Cleaner Air," 1996). They asked the Environmental Affairs Committee if they could present the article's findings in the form of witness testimony. Although neither had been to West Virginia or to a coal mine, they believed that they could portray the key perspectives of these West Virginian coal miners. The committee agreed to hear their testimony.

Three adult witnesses also agreed to testify. With approval from the committee, I enlisted the support of my colleagues at the school. Three teachers agreed to review the Clean Air Act, as constructed by the students and to write witness statements that reflected the experience base and perspective of one of the following characters: a worker at a chemical processing plant, an environmental scientist, a city bus driver. The Environmental Affairs Committee decided upon the sequence of witness testimony. They decided to have the coal miners provide their testimony first. Tom explained the reasoning behind this strategy:

> Well, I thought that the people who were against Clean Air should go first; all the bad things about the bill could be said. We could then ask the witnesses who were for the bill and have them discuss it. So people would change their minds about it.

The committee took ownership of this hearing. They recognized that there were still flaws in the legislation and that these would be exposed by the testimony of some of the witnesses. At the same time, they believed that witnesses who were in favor of the bill would ultimately make more compelling arguments.

Pivotal Testimony: Perspectives from West Virginian Coal Miners

The hearing opened with the Environmental Affairs Committee sitting in front and the two parties on opposite side of the room. Chris, as Senator King, was chairperson of the committee. He began the session by pounding the wooden gravel on the desk in front of him. He stood up to gain people's attention and spoke: "Today we will hear testimony on the Clean Air Act from John McGrag, who is a former coal miner, and Will Cart, a former foreman."

Mike as John McGrag gave his testimony first. He sat in the center of the room behind a table facing the committee. He began with his prepared statement.

Last December we were shut down by the Peabody Holding Company, the largest coal company in the country for failure to meet the regulations set by the 1990 Clean Air bill. Why did this happen? The 1990 Clean Air Act. One of the provisions said those coal mines producing sulfur dioxide had to get "scrubbers" in their smokestacks to reduce the pollution. These scrubbers cost $100 million or more. We couldn't afford a scrubber, so every person in the mine lost their job.

Students as coal miners did not adapt an accent or a dialect to convey their role as West Virginians. Nor did they alter their clothes or body language. They were not attempting to act as West Virginian coal miners; instead they worked to convey the respective experiences of two individuals who had lost their jobs due to environmental regulations.

After they finished reading their opening statements, Mike as "Mr. McGrag" and Amanda as "Mr. Cart" together answered an array of questions from the senators. Chris, as Senator King, presided over the hearing. He called on senators who raised their hands.

Sen. King (Chris): Senator Wright.

Sen. Wright (Tom): First of all, I would like to remind you that our bill was not passed in 1990 and it is not the Clean Air Act that you are referring to, so that stuff is not relevant.

Mr. McCrag (Mike): It is similar to the Clean Air Act, but in your bill I believe it says that you have to have filters and these filters are relevant. They do cost $100 million dollars and up.

Sen. Wright (Tom): But it is tax deductible.
Mr. McCrag (Mike): But that doesn't matter. *It is $100 million dollars and up!* [italics used to emphasize agitated tone of voice]
Mr. Cart (Amanda): It is a lot of money.

Senator Wright attempted to distance the new Clean Air Act from the one passed in 1990. He was unsuccessful in this attempt. Mr. McCrag pointed out the similarities and noted the cost factors involved in this type of comprehensive legislation. Furthermore, as evidenced by the increasing loudness of his voice, Mr. McCrag became emotionally connected to the facts that he was sharing with the senate. It meant something to him. He was willing to reveal by the exasperation in his voice the extent to which he was connecting to his constructed role as coal miner.

Sen. Santos (Jorge): You said that four hundred people or more lost their jobs.
Mr. Cart (Amanda): In my mine.
Sen. Santos (Jorge): How many jobs were lost in total?
Mr. Cart (Amanda): Well total—including mine and others . . . seven hundred and fifty.
Mr. McCrag (Mike): That is in our county.
Sen. Santos (Jorge): What would you say about the 10,000 of families who have lost loved ones due to pollution due to mining?
Mr. McCrag (Mike): We obviously don't want air pollution. If there is a way to solve it, we want it, but without having us all lose our jobs. If there was any way you could do it, without us losing our jobs, it would be better.
Sen. Santos (Jorge): Better than having people dying.
Mr. McCrag (Mike): I can't make that decision—I just don't want to lose my (Mike) job. Because we don't want air pollution, we are suffering from it too.

Senator Santos, the Republican leader, attempted to frame the discussion within a humanistic context ("What would you say about the . . . families who have lost loved ones . . ."). He articulated a concern for the greater good. Mr. McCrag, however, did not accept that approach. He was not willing to take an either/or position. He admitted that while he was concerned with the health risks associated with air pollution, he was also concerned with keeping a job.

Through the stories of Mr. McCrag and Mr. Cart, and the corresponding statements and questions posed by senators, students confronted the inherent complexities of environmental regulations. There were no easy answers here. This preliminary session set the tone for subsequent testimonies. Students developed an ease for analyzing and questioning witnesses. In doing so, they explored issues related to short-term cost factors and long-term health benefits of this legislation.

Questioning Adult Testimony: Shifts in Power

After the coal miners, the senate then heard from Mr. Leaf, a worker from a chemical processing plant, and Mr. Wilk, an environmental scientist. In actuality, Mr. Leaf was their current math and science teacher, Bob; and Mr. Wilk was their sixth-grade environmental science teacher, Brett. In this school, teachers are referred to by their first names.

Sen. Cape (Jim): Filters are quite expensive; they cost $100 million. Aren't you worried that you will lose your job?
Mr. Leaf: Sure, I'm worried about losing my job, but . . . I'm more worried about the effect that pollution has on the environment.
Sen. Blitz (Mike): A lot of people like the Clean Air idea, but they will be losing their jobs.
Mr. Leaf: Well, I think it is the government's responsibility to help smaller companies stay in business.
Sen. Blitz (Mike): To help these companies costs a lot of money. It is many millions of dollars . . . the government is going to have to pay a lot of money.
Sen. Mix (Kate): What do you think is an appropriate cost of a filter?
Mr. Wilk: Well, since we live in a free market society, it is what the market will bear.
Sen. Mix (Kate): Well, right now they are selling for $100 million dollars . . . Not many factories can purchase these, because the price is so high.

In both of these sessions, it was the students as senators who were informing the adults as witnesses about the current $100 million cost for scrubbers. While the students were respectful of the adults' testimonies and their perspectives on the legislation, they were not necessarily accepting it at face value. In fact, they probed testimony from different angles and from different points of view. Students even went beyond asking questions; they also commented upon adult testimony and in some cases disputed it. This was a complete reversal from the classroom situation where teachers asked questions and students responded.

Of course, not everyone asked questions; most, in fact, listened. Nonetheless, in their decision to listen carefully to the proceedings, they showed in nonverbal ways that the discourse between witness and senators were both relevant and meaningful. Moreover, their collective attention to the dialogue created an additional layer of believability to the situation. At moments when they had private conversations with peers, they spoke quietly and briefly. For the most part, the exchange of ideas between the witness and the senators held their attention and curiosity. The hearing helped to inform them of their own position of the bill.

Shared Suspense: Communities in Motion

While the bipartisan Environmental Affairs Committee supported the Clean Air Act, both parties were divided about the bill. Both Republicans and Democrats expressed concern about the potential loss of jobs as a result of strict environmental regulation. Senators worried about the $100 million cost for scrubbers. Nonetheless, in an informal poll taken before this final session, the party whips determined that most members of the senate supported the bill, 14 to 11.

The students and I engaged in a number of activities to prepare for the senate debate and possible vote. Students wrote speeches articulating their public position on the Clean Air Act. We reviewed the rules for senate debate and voting procedure. I spoke about the use of *cloture* as a way of avoiding a "filibuster"; cloture is a procedure used to limit debate and a filibuster is a tactic used to delay a vote. As we were about to begin debate, these terms became relevant for the senators to understand. I informed the class that two-thirds of the senate needed to agree on cloture; I did the math on the board and with 25 members in our senate, I arrived at the number 16. The actual number should have been 17, but no one contradicted me at the time.

Alex as Republican Senator Koch was the president pro tempore, and he recognized senators that wished to speak at this debate.

Sen. Santos (Jorge): I plan to ratify the Clean Air Act. I feel that the nation's air being clean far outweighs the bill's drawbacks. I yield the floor.

Sen. Koch (Alex): Senator Blitz.

Sen. Blitz (Mike): I plan on voting against this bill. Although clean air is a great and worthy cause, many people who work in factories will . . . get fired in order for the factory to keep their profit margins up . . . The filters would be hundreds of million dollars, and I think that ruining people's lives is not the answer to clean air. I yield the floor.

Sen. Koch: Senator Cape.

Sen. Cape (Jim): I am against the bill . . . the filters for the factory smokestacks are (Jim) way too expensive. This would force many businesses to close and would send the economy into a tailspin. I yield the floor.

The debate continued. People became increasingly vocal. Time was running out. The class period was coming close to an end.

Sen. Straus (Stan): I call for a vote! [italics used to convey shouting tone]
Sen. Koch (Alex): You can't call for a vote without being recognized.
Sen. Vork (Sue): (calling out) Well, then recognize him!
Sen. Koch: I have the floor to call on people and I do not call on you.
Sen. Straus: (calling out) He is breaking the rules.
Sen. Koch: I am not breaking the rules.

Even in the midst of such pandemonium, senate leadership prevailed. Although he was challenged by his peers, Alex as Senator Koch handled the situation. Nonetheless, senators became increasingly agitated; it appeared that Senator Koch only recognized senators who were aligned to his position on the bill. Abigail, one of the quieter students in the class, reflected about this moment:

I felt most like it was a real situation during the harrowing floor debate. I was trying desperately to get a vote happening . . . People were really sticking up for their beliefs and battling it out.

Eventually, Alex called on a senator who formally made the motion for a vote. After being seconded, the senate then decided to vote for cloture. By a public show of hands, 16 senators indicated their support for cloture. They were the ones who were fed up with the debate and wanted to move the process closer to a vote.

At this point, one senator did the math and loudly proclaimed that cloture needed 17 votes and not 16. On her own accord, she went up to the chalkboard and explained her calculations. This moment was greeted with relief for those who opposed the bill and did not want the legislation to come to a vote.

As the classroom teacher, I intervened. I expressed my wish for wanting the process to move forward. I felt they had gone as far as they could with the senate debate and I thought it was worthwhile for them to experience a vote.

In a loud, determined voice, someone cried out, "Let's walk out. That way we won't vote on it." Students began to leave the room. Some stomped off alone, others left hesitantly with friends. They waited outside the doorway and gathered together in the hallway. They looked both bewildered and exhilarated. This was their first protest action. I peered out at them and noticed that nearby teachers were poking their heads out from their own classrooms, surprised at the commotion in the hallway.

Back in the room, there were 13 hopeful senators left. This was just enough for a quorum. The majority leader took over and called out the names of the senators. When their names were called they announced their supporting vote for the bill. Midway through this process, one of the senators decided to leave. This ended the quorum and voting was suspended.

Debriefing

In our debriefing about this experience, students had a variety of explanations for their actions. Those who were opposed to the Clean Air Act felt that if they remained in the senate for the vote, there was a chance that it might pass. By engaging in a dramatic protest action, they calculated that it might attract the undecided to join in. Those who had stayed in the senate were in favor of the legislation and had joined in solidarity with one another.

This was an awakening experience for us all. The class did not act as one in this event. There were multiple perspectives, interpretations, and actions. Students admitted being influenced by the words and actions of their peers. Others revealed their commitment to their constituent base and how this guided their respective positions on the bill. There were still others who revealed the difficulty of making decisions when they were not ready to take a stand. This compelled students "to realize that the world everyone sees is not *the* world but *a* world which we bring forth with others" (Maturana & Varela, 1992, p. 245).

REFLECTION: ENVISIONING NEW POSSIBILITIES

The coconstructed curriculum drama was a messy and organic process. Building knowledge and authentically engaging in curriculum can be like that. The classroom senate became a place where students identified issues, appraised ideas, and addressed conflicts. They participated within a "community of practice" (Lave & Wenger, 1991). In doing so, students connected with others to generate complex understandings about the legislative branch of government.

Student energy powered the direction of this curriculum drama. They proposed the legislation they wanted to initiate, they determined the meaning of political labels within their respective parties, they posed the questions to the witnesses at the senate hearing, and they decided what position to take on the Clean Air Act. Working in various communities within the senate, students developed diverse frames of reference from these different groupings. For instance, within committee students focused on developing a key legislative issue. Within the larger group of a political party, students worked to develop an inclusive political agenda and platform. In formal senate sessions, students made public speeches and supported, or argued, key legislative issues. As they learned to cope within a complex "web of relationships" (Lambert, 1995), challenging tasks and unpredictable situations, their engagement in the senate deepened.

Students developed partnerships with one another. They had to. Students were new to the idea of constructing legislation and being senators. No one had prior experience with developing a political agenda. This situation propelled students to explore new ways of being with the world and new ways of interacting with their peers. In an environment of trust, they worked together to share experiences, skills, and understandings. Political parties, and committees in particular, became support structures for individual students. It was within these settings that students developed reciprocal partnerships. They shared and reflected about their experiences within the senate. They sought counsel from one another to prepare for upcoming legislative events.

Success hinged on the ability of a group to collaborate. Nowhere was this more apparent than in the final moments of the classroom senate. Opponents to the Clean Air Act acted not as students resisting a teacher's authority, but rather as senators inflamed at the attempt to limit debate. They knew they had the freedom and the authority to walk out of a senate proceeding. They were not cowered by fear of disciplinary reprisals or academic suspensions. Perhaps even more amazing, was the other contingent of senators who resisted peer pressure and remained in the classroom to vote for the Clean Air Act. They identified with and believed in the long-term benefits of this bill. The success of either group depended upon its ability to remain unified. In the end, the protestors' efforts were more successful, so the legislation did not pass. As their teacher, I applauded both groups' actions. It was evident that through their experiences in the curriculum drama, students began to develop a sense of autonomy and deep ownership with the senate.

The classroom senate was about opening up to new possibilities of being in the world. Students as senators enacted new ways of knowing and understanding. Within their community of legislative practice, they developed a powerful sense of agency. In the senate hearing, they became skilled at asking penetrating questions to expert witnesses, even adult witnesses. In the senate debate, they showed their position on the Clean Air Act through their public decision to either stay or leave the classroom. Their actions went beyond simply committing to an answer on a worksheet or a test. Instead, the situated demanded a mind-body connection. Students had freedom of movement; they were not expected to sit passively. In this constructivist classroom, students envisioned new possibilities, became invested in new topics of conversation, and engaged in productive ways of taking action within the classroom setting. Curriculum drama was about "being there."

REFERENCES

East's coal towns wither in the name of cleaner air. (1996, February 15). *New York Times.*

Genishi, C., McCarrier, A., & Nussbaum, R. N. (1988). Research currents: Dialogue as a context for teaching and learning. *Language Arts, 65,* 182–190.

Haine, G. (1985). In the labyrinth of the image: An archetypal approach to drama in education. *Theory into Practice, 24*(3), 187–192.

Heathcote, D. (1984). Drama and education: Subject or system? In L. Johnson & C. O'Neill (Eds.), *Dorothy Heathcote: Collected writings on education and drama.* Evanston, IL: Northwestern University Press.

Lambert, L. (1995). Toward a theory of constructivist leadership. In L. Lambert, D. Walker, D. Zimmerman, J. Cooper, M. Lambert, M. Gardner, & P. Slack, *The constructivist leader.* New York: Teachers College Press.

Lave, J., & Wenger, E. (1991). *Situated learning: Legitimate peripheral participation.* Cambridge, UK: Cambridge University Press.

Maturana, H., & Varela, F. (1992). *The tree of knowledge.* Boston: Shambhala Publications.

Schifter, D., & Fosnot, C. T. (1993). *Reconstructing mathematics education: Stories of teachers meeting the challenge of reform.* New York: Teachers College Press.

Wagner, B. (1976). *Dorothy Heathcote: Drama as a learning medium.* Washington, DC: National Education Association.

Wolf, S. (1994). Learning to act/acting to learn: Children as actors, critics, and characters in classroom theatre. *Research in the Teaching of English, 28,* 7–44.

Wolf, S. (1995). Language in and around the dramatic curriculum. *Journal of Curriculum Studies, 27,* 119–137.

CHAPTER 15

Teachers Construct Constructivism: The Center for Constructivist Teaching/Teacher Preparation Project

Catherine Twomey Fosnot

"How do I view the process of teaching? Part actor, part salesman. You have this body of knowledge that you have to get across to the kids, but most students really don't want to be in school, so you have to sell them on this education kick." John, a graduate of a traditional teacher certification program, is being interviewed at the completion of his first year of teaching. At the probing of the interviewer, he continues describing his pedagogical philosophy:

> You have to sell this body of knowledge to them, but if you don't make your presentation good and you're not a good actor, they're not going to buy. . . . You know, I mean it's easy to reach your scholastically minded kids; however, out of a classroom of thirty, how many of them do you have? Three, four? You cannot reach 100%, and anyone who thinks it's possible is living in a fantasy world.

John's beliefs about the teaching/learning process are quite similar to those of most prospective teachers when they enter a teacher preparation program (Fosnot, 1992; Hutcheson & Ammon, 1986). Because these teacher candidates have been learners themselves for many years in classrooms where teachers have frequently lectured, they have constructed a view of learning as the acquisition of specific facts, rules, and attitudes that are picked up by exposure and a view of the teacher's role in the process as showing and telling students what they need to know (Hutcheson & Ammon, 1986). Although John has completed a certification program, and most likely has learned much about teaching materials and instructional strategies in the several methods courses he has taken, sadly his beliefs about pedagogy have remained unchanged. What needs to occur in teacher preparation programs to enable beliefs to shift, and what does the process of constructing constructivism look like?

CONSTRUCTING CONSTRUCTIVISM

Facilitating Shifts in Beliefs

If understanding the teaching/learning process from a constructivist view is itself constructed, and if teachers tend to teach as they were taught, rather than as they were taught to teach (Jones, 1975), then teacher education needs to begin with these traditional beliefs and subsequently challenge them through activity, reflection, and discourse in both coursework and field work throughout the duration of the program. Most importantly, participants need experiences as learners that confront traditional views of teaching and learning in order to enable them to construct a pedagogy that stands in contrast to older, more traditionally held views. Further, field experiences need to allow for investigation and experimentation in child development, learning, and teaching; and schools used as partnership sites for field experiences need to approach curriculum in an integrated, learner-centered fashion with emphasis on learner investigation, reflection, and discourse. Last, to ensure that newly constructed beliefs can be actualized in practice when graduates get their first jobs, a mentor program (connecting the university and the elementary school) needs to be in place throughout the first year of teaching, with faculty visiting and supporting graduates and collaboratively teaching—and thereby helping them to put into practice strategies stemming from their newly constructed beliefs about teaching and learning. In other words, a large percentage of teacher education coursework needs to occur directly in field sites, emerging from learners' questions.

In the fall of 1989, with the assistance of federal funds (Federal Funds for Innovation in Education, Department of Education), the Center for Constructivist Teaching/Teacher Preparation Project was established to design and subsequently provide a theoretically consistent teacher education program based on constructivism. A two-year (45-credit) graduate certification/M.S. program was designed based on the principles outlined previously. Five field sites (K–6 programs) centrally located across the state of

Connecticut, representative of public and private institutions as well as suburban and urban environments, were chosen to be partners in the project.

Constructing Pedagogy from an Analysis of One's Own Learning. In August 1990, 15 cooperating teachers from the partnership sites enrolled with 30 preservice teacher candidates (graduate students already holding undergraduate degrees in liberal arts) in a three-week intensive summer institute, which would serve as the first course in a two-year program for the teacher candidates. This institute, Teaching and Learning I, was team-taught by education and liberal arts faculty. In this institute, participants were involved in constructivist-based learning experiences (on the adult level) in order to provide them with shared opportunities to analyze their own learning and thinking.

Week 1 focused on mathematical problem-solving experiences, with manipulatives provided as tools, and computer classes with LOGOwriter. Participants worked collaboratively in small groups solving problems and then returned to whole-class "math congresses" (Fosnot, 1989; Schifter & Fosnot, 1993) to share the patterns they had explored and the solutions, formulae, and algorithms they had constructed. Participants were encouraged to argue and defend their own ideas to the group, rather than having the faculty acknowledge solutions as correct and/or complete. For example, investigating how many handshakes would be possible in the group if they only shook hands with each person once, participants constructed several formulae for permutations, explored the patterns in the progression, set up tables and diagrams for their data, and constructed triangular numbers; working as geographers in a simulation exploring the area of rectangular plots of land, they investigated quadratics and constructed their own algorithms for factoring; using base-5 blocks and working collaboratively, they constructed their own number systems and then defended them to the group of the whole (for details on the session on number systems, see Fosnot, 1989, or Schifter & Fosnot, 1993).

Week 2 involved participants in language arts activities, such as writing workshops, cooperative reading and discussion groups, the writing of double-entry journals, and investigative spelling activities regarding phonic patterns and language roots (see Fosnot, 1989). Word-processing, bookmaking, and newspaper-layout software was used in the computer class.

During week 3, participants worked on a project in science or social studies. The week began with a simulation. Participants were asked to be architects in a design company that had been requested to propose bridge designs in a rainforest area of Brazil. Along with the physics involved as they tested their designs, social science issues were processed and heightened when the "disgruntled environmentalists" in the group and the minority group of males were fired as the company administration (faculty) became progressively more autocratic. Science and social science questions arising from the simulation formed the basis of project work that participants engaged in during the remainder of the week. Computer classes entailed on-line search via the program Bibliomation to enable participants to gain research skills in accessing information for their projects.

In order to illuminate and thus challenge beliefs about pedagogy, participants in the institute were subsequently asked to reflect on how the instructors facilitated learning and on the specific aspects of the experiences that were conducive to thinking. On Friday afternoon of each week, the group came together as a whole—a community of discourse—to propose and discuss pedagogical principles that were an outgrowth of the reflection on participants' own learning. Every attempt was made in the discussion to process contradictions to old traditional schemes, such as "teaching is telling." Participants also kept journals during the institute and were asked to write a final synthesis paper at the end of the institute describing the processes of learning and teaching. An excerpt from Leah's paper discussing her perception of mathematics education provides a window into the type of reflection most participants experienced:

> I had always believed that the purpose of mathematics, for the student, was to get the correct answer and the purpose of the teacher was to provide the directions on how to arrive there. I now see what an incorrect and narrow definition of mathematics learning I had! I have come to believe that the process of arriving at an answer is of equal, if not greater, importance than the answer. I also now see the teacher as a very intricate and important facilitator in this process—providing support, guidance, allowing for further investigation and deeper understanding through questioning and probing. This allows the learner to truly come to terms with the process.

Leah goes on to discuss the importance of ownership and active learning:

> I would like to discuss the importance of discovery and ownership of the solution. During our problem-solving sessions I found the most positive and beneficial learning experience was when I could understand the discovery (mine or someone else's) in my own terms. The "ah-hah" that occurred was a very empowering feeling, one that I had never associated with math before. I've come to realize that it is very important that the learner feel a part of the process, not just a processor of facts and rules to get an answer that is correct for the teacher.

And last, she discusses the power of group learning:

> Another important idea I learned this week is the power of group learning. The group work facilitated learning because the interaction of ideas provided an opportunity for reflection . . . and the experience of sharing ideas allows the learner to see that there are many different ways of looking at a problem. When I look back on my early math experiences, I can only wish that I had the opportunity to work collaboratively. Instead I remember just seeing a bunch of heads bent over, scribbling away to get the answer!
>
> This institute has left me feeling excited and empowered as a learner (exhausted, too!). I feel that I am developing some very new ideas about my learning, how others learn, and the important role of the teacher in this process. I know I will never forget these experiences. I will be synthesizing all of this for a very long time!

Constructing Pedagogy from an Analysis of Children's Thinking. During the following fall semester and winter intersession, the 30 teacher candidates investigated the learning and thinking of elementary children using clinical interviews, videos, case studies, and collected samples of children's work from the partnership sites. Rather than separate methods courses for each discipline, a few specific topics were explored in depth to enable participants to construct the developmental nature of construction and to focus them on children's ideas rather than on predetermined curriculum and instructional strategies. Topics explored were place value, division, fractions, literacy, invented spelling strategies, ideas regarding pulleys and balance, notions about friendship and family, self and society, and artistic development. Every attempt was made to attach meaning to children's ideas and actions, to their "conceptions at the start" (Duckworth, 1987). In a sense the participants were asked to become developmental psychologists and epistemologists and to then construct an emergent curriculum from these observations. Ellie's synthesis paper, at the end of these explorations, exemplifies their impact:

> My understanding of the process of learning has changed over the last few months. As I studied the way children come to know, I also became clearer about how I come to know. The one thing that has impressed me most is the idea that we simply don't see things the way they actually may be. As we learn, we differentiate more variables or aspects of an event. It is this new vision that once again causes disequilibrium to occur and continues the cycle of coming to know. Not only is learning a natu-

ral process, a self-regulating process; it is a process which occurs by virtue of our existence. I am, therefore I learn.

This understanding of my own learning process has allowed me to
better understand and respect the knowledge of young children. The
process of learning literacy, or number, is as complex and complicated
as any adult endeavor. Through my study of the way children know, I
have come to see a few patterns, patterns that seem to repeat throughout our lives. When the child first experiences something, be it internal
or external, she [seems to] experience the whole picture. Through her
interaction with herself and the world she begins to see that this whole
thing actually consists of separate things. As she explores these parts,
she integrates them back into the whole and better understands. The
idea that a person can know "it" and be done seems absurd in this
context. . . . The process of teaching, within this understanding, becomes the process of facilitation.

Because Ellie has formulated a pedagogy firmly grounded in an analysis
of learning, she is able to critically evaluate the teaching process and design
teaching activities to promote learner construction. A later journal entry exemplifies her developing pedagogy:

In a classroom I visited, a teacher was doing a lesson about air and water
balloons. I was not satisfied with the presentation and thought about
how I might change it. First of all, why do this activity? What science
are the children learning? Are we exploring the concept that air has
volume? Are we looking at the properties of water and air? Are we going
to see how the balloon changes as we blow it up? I became curious
about the explanation children might have for the balloon increasing in
size.

I would start the activity with a simple invitation. "I was at a birth-
day party last weekend. The decorations were red and blue and everyone
got to bring a few balloons home. I began to wonder why balloons get
bigger when we blow into them. Does anyone have any ideas about
this?" This might lead to a question like, "I wonder what else we could
do to make the balloon bigger?" Then we could actually start to do
things with the balloons. As the teacher, my job would be to be certain
that everyone was participating and that everyone understood the problem. My next step would be to help direct and clarify thinking by asking
good probing questions and helping children paraphrase their thoughts
and ideas. I would also be looking for strategies children were employing and planning an order of group presentation when we come back
together as a whole to present findings. As the teacher, I help children

see how each group attacked the problem and I give them [scientific] vocabulary for their ideas.

Cooperative Field Work in the Sites. During the following spring semester, the 30 teacher candidates joined the 15 teachers, who had previously participated in Teaching and Learning I, two to a classroom, for cooperative field work. Cooperative field work is a full-time team teaching situation in one of the partner sites. Although this type of field work on the surface may appear similar to traditional student teaching experience (and in this program, it took the place of it), it is distinctly different in that it is cooperative in nature, rather than imitative. In the traditional student teaching experience, students usually begin with small-group work, are responsible for designated lessons, and then eventually take on the role of the "master" teacher with responsibilities for the whole class. The expectation exists that the student will be able to carry on the work of the "master" teacher smoothly, in a similar fashion to that of the "master" teacher—in that sense, it is imitative. The perspective advocated here was instead a cooperative venture, where participants could brainstorm, plan, and implement together with "master" teachers. The focus was on creative and critical thinking in relation to pedagogical decision making. Faculty were on-site and held seminars once a week.

An excerpt from Kate's journal, written halfway through the cooperative field experience, is illustrative of the type of brainstorming and reflection that occurred, continuing to provide new connections between curriculum and development, learning and teaching, and thus a deepening understanding of pedagogy:

> Phrases like "teacher-as-researcher" and "teacher-as-learner," though understood in an abstract sense, became very concrete for me this weekend. Teaching math has been a struggle for me and Jim [her fellow student teacher].

Here Kate is referring to the fact that she and Jim had been attempting to teach a unit on angles. At first they had begun by assessing each child's knowledge of the correct use of protractors—then their plan was to engage the children in measuring the interior angles of several polygons and to hold a whole-class "math congress" to share their discoveries. They quickly learned, however, that most of the fourth and fifth graders did not understand how to measure with the tool; and even with much explanation from both of them on its use, the children were still confused about where to place it on the figures. Further questioning of the children revealed that they believed they were measuring a linear distance between the line segments, rather than the degrees of a turn. During seminar that week (which was held on-site), Jim and Kate shared what they had learned about the children's conceptions and their own struggles about what to do next. The group of eight student teachers at that partnership school and I brainstormed together several activities they might try, such as having the children use LOGO (which they were already familiar with) to draw shapes and then having them invent a measurement tool that could be used to figure out the amount of each turn in the drawing if the procedures had been erased. Kate and Jim tried these activities over the next few weeks and reported that the children had constructed several measurement tools, some of which, interestingly, approximated the protractor. They then used this experience to explain the protractor. Although they felt they had finally succeeded in teaching the concept of measurement of angles, they remained dissatisfied with the progression of the unit and believed they had resorted to too much "telling." Kate's journal entry continues:

> We decided to refocus our "investigations." I use the term "investigation" subjectively because, for me, some of the activities we did were not true investigations, but "telling experiences." And we did not know where to go next. We met with Deanna [the cooperating teacher who was committed to teaching in a constructivist fashion due to her participation in the summer institute, but who was also just learning to structure investigations in place of using a math text]. She suggested we look through a series of books from England dealing with math concepts. Reading these further enhanced my framework of a "whole-to-parts" pedagogy I've been constructing for myself. I think I ran into trouble before because I fell back on my own original ideas of teaching that I had seen my teachers use, a "parts-to-whole" theory: explanations of theorems and proofs first, then application.

As Kate struggles to clarify for herself this new pedagogy she is constructing—"whole-to-parts"—she focuses her reflection on trying to ascertain what the "whole" is that she wants to focus investigation on. She continues:

> Bring the kids back to reality, I thought, back to the concrete. For me, punctuated by the reading, this was "shapes." Forms are seen everywhere and they can be investigated by exploring their angles, vertices, etc. So now the task became to think of what the "big ideas" were that I wanted them to grapple with—no small task.

"Big ideas" (Schifter & Fosnot, 1993) is a term we use during the coursework when we try to understand the meaning the child brings to the experience. We ask, "What are the big ideas the child is grappling with?" The purpose is to focus teachers on content ideas that often require structural shifts in thinking for children, rather than on skills or behavioral objectives. Kate continues:

I kept thinking about "ontogeny recapitulates phylogeny." As with the angle-measuring devices, the need to measure arose from the problem posed—experimentation, followed by questions, followed by hypothesis testing, followed by experimentation. But what is the need for investigating shapes, angles, and volumes?

In this excerpt Kate herself can be observed grappling with some "big ideas." What is the connection between teaching and learning? What form should investigations take so that learners will be engaged, raise questions, and construct concepts? Because of her experiences in the summer institute, where she constructed pedagogy by analyzing her own learning, she attempted to answer her questions by putting herself once again in the learner's role. Her journal continues:

One activity I had seen in the English series dealt with conservation of volume. It asked the student to construct houses of blocks using 36 blocks each time upon three different base floorplans. I suppose the student would eventually see a pattern of conservation and I guess compensation—what I took off the top, I put on the side—but how boring . . . what will they own from this activity? Keeping within the confines of a given floorplan only means following directions and counting. That certainly is not a "big idea." Thinking about those houses set me on a line of questioning, though. Only three examples for floorplans were given: Were there any more? I began to draw out on graph paper all the combinations of 36 I could think of. I found my level of excitement increasing. My investigation led me to find that area of a face of a house is related to the depth. Hmm, I thought, what other combos are there and what combo gives you the most perfect cubed house—3 by 3 by 4, because it is closest to 3 cubed. I continued with my investigation and found a systematic way of coming up with a total of ten designs for 36 blocks. I found that area is related to depth and both are related to volume. I found a relationship between designs.

Kate concludes:

How intriguing. As a learner trying to satisfy my need for discovering some possible "big ideas," I've learned that I need an open-ended kick-off investigation for my students to engage in where they can raise their own questions.

Reflective Field Experience. After completion of the cooperative field work, teacher candidates remained in the field site for four more weeks to engage in reflective field work, a focused observation and/or research study on a pedagogical issue of interest to the teacher candidate. A professional conference was held as a culminating experience for students to present their research, with cooperating teachers and administrators invited.

Observational work is not new to traditional education programs; however, it usually occurs at the beginning of the program. Teacher candidates, at that point in their career, have little notion of what to look for and thus often gain little from their observation. During cooperative field work, however, many important personal questions arise. Reflective field research not only gives prospective teachers the opportunity to study in depth a question of their own but also serves to further develop their ability to evaluate the teaching/learning situation. Faculty supervisors have traditionally done all the evaluating; student teachers have been asked to design and implement lessons, then been assessed as they performed. Reflective field research engages prospective teachers in the evaluation process instead by having them observe other teachers involved with children in a learning situation.

Integrative Field Experience (Clinical Fellowship Year). After completion of the reflective experience, participants received their initial teaching license from the state, allowing them to seek a paid teaching position. To ensure that innovations would be implemented by the novice and that the novice teacher would receive support if the school climate was not conducive to change, a faculty mentor from the project visited one day a week, serving as a resource and support, and often engaged in collaborative teaching. A seminar was also held one night a week back at the university.

Sara began her first year with an immediate goal of putting a writing workshop and a literature-based reading program in place in her second grade. Within a few weeks, a few vocal and influential parents began to complain that skill pages from workbooks were not coming home. They called the principal, who immediately scheduled an observation and conference with her, subsequently demanding that she use the basal reader and the spelling text as well as demonstrate use of praise and reinforcement. By November Sara was in tears most of the time, and she was panicked that she would lose her job. I scheduled a meeting with her principal, and we discussed the practices she was trying to put in place. He shared his needs resulting from pressure he was receiving in the district, and we worked out a compromise: Sara would not need to use basals everyday, but she would be responsible for their content and they needed to be incorporated into her reading instruction in some fashion. Sara and I then planned a record-keeping system and a management system to deal with his requests. We also simultaneously planned a parent open house to explain her writing program and then held several Author Teas where the children could read their published pieces to an audience of parents. Center faculty also offered four in-service days focused on constructivism, literacy, mathematics, and project work to administrators who hired novice teachers from the program. The purpose of these sessions was to provide administrators with an understanding of the innovations novice teachers were implementing. It was hoped that novices would then be more likely to receive support and change would be more permeating and lasting. These sessions were highly successful, with administrators requesting that other teachers from their school attend with them. Sara's administrator attended these sessions and began to get quite excited by the new ideas.

By February Sara had turned the tide: Parents and administrators both began to support her practice; colleagues began to seek her out for new ideas; and the local public television station even filmed her class during a writing workshop and an Author's Tea. In fact, her administrator recently commented that he now saw Sara as one of the leaders in the school.

Developing Teachers as Change Agents. In the summer of the second year of the program, participants enrolled in the final institute, entitled Institutions, Schools, and the Change Process. In this course based on the foundations of education, participants explored how institutions are inherently connected to society and discussed various methods of creating change in schools. In this way we hoped to empower them as change agents. On successful completion of this course and the first year of teaching, participants in the program received a master's degree in elementary education.

The mentoring component of the program, the support it provided, and the emphasis on the change process in schools were crucial to the successful implementation of the novice teachers' new visions for practice. Without faculty working with them during their first year of teaching, many would have floundered as they struggled with all the overwhelming issues of classroom management, curriculum, administration's demands, and parental demands that burden the first-year teacher. Mentoring of first-year teachers is not a new idea, but most often mentors are other classroom teachers in the school. Thus the mentoring tends toward ensuring current practice rather than innovation. Further, since teachers who base their practice on constructivism are being asked often to "invent" curricula, having an experienced resource who shares the vision, and who can thus plan accordingly with the novice teacher, is necessary to ensure innovation. Teachers with such support can make the best of even traditional school settings. In fact, their belief in constructivism only deepens. Sara's journal, written during her first year of teaching, attests to this fact:

> I've learned that there are two needs I must fulfill. There's the school's curriculum and, most importantly, there's each child's needs. I've concluded, more soundly, how much better time is spent teaching what the child needs when she/he needs it. Though times I've felt pressured, even forced, to "teach" what I know is meaningless to a child, I've learned this is not meaningful teaching, and it definitely does not result in meaningful learning. For example, the basal test may be passed, but there is no evidence that such skills have been incorporated into the child's daily writing.
>
> Students learn to write by writing to fulfill their own needs and desires to communicate. They learn to read by reading interesting books and print. They learn about "neighborhoods and communities" by investigating their own neighborhoods and community. This doesn't happen by reading all about them on social studies book pages, or by being told, but it happens through constructive meaning-making.

CONCLUSION

Just as young learners construct, so, too, do teachers. Teacher education programs based on a constructivist view of learning need to do more than offer a constructivist perspective in a course or two. Teachers' beliefs need to be illuminated, discussed, and challenged. Teachers need to be engaged in learning experiences that confront traditional beliefs, in experiences where they can study children and their meaning-making, and in field experiences where they can experiment collaboratively. Only through such extensive questioning, reflecting, and constructing will the paradigm shift in education—constructivism—occur.

REFERENCES

Duckworth, E. (1987). *"The having of wonderful ideas" and other essays on teaching and learning*. New York: Teachers College Press.

Fosnot, C. T. (1989). *Enquiring teachers, enquiring learners*. New York: Teachers College Press.

Fosnot, C. T. (1992). Center for Constructivist Teaching/Teacher Preparation Project. Final Grant Report, FIE #R 215A93232.

Hutcheson, B. P., & Ammon, P. (June, 1986). *The development of teachers' conceptions as reflected in their journals.* Paper presented at the annual meeting of the American Educational Research Association, San Francisco.

Jones, E. (1975). Providing college-level role models for the socialization of elementary level open classroom teachers. *California Journal of Teacher Education, 2,* 33–51.

Schifter, D., & Fosnot, C. T. (1993). *Reconstructing mathematics education: Stories of teachers meeting the challenge of reform.* New York: Teachers College Press.

EPILOGUE

Constructivism Revisited: Implications and Reflections

Catherine Twomey Fosnot

The last century brought with it many scientific and technological advances. As we enter the 21st century, the models we currently use to describe and explain our world have dramatically changed: from Cartesian coordinate systems and Newtonian mechanics to relativity; from quantum mechanics to chaos, complexity, and string theories.

The fields of biology, neuroscience, cognitive psychology, and epistemology have been affected no less, and these changing models have, in turn, dramatically affected the way we now understand the interrelated acts of teaching and learning. In the early part of the 20th century, "a change in behavior" was thought to define learning. Thus, teaching was characterized as clear communication with appropriate learner practice, reinforcement, and motivation. Disciplines were broken down into skills and concepts, sequenced from what was considered simple to complex tasks, and assessments were designed to measure changes in behavior. We thought of the mind as a muscle in need of exercise and affected by practice. Today we know such models to be insufficient. Teaching and learning are far more complex; they are about interaction, growth, and development. Today we see "mind" as the result of the human construction of coherence, of explanation within communities of discourse as problems are posed and solved (Brown, 2001; Deutsch, 1997; Maturana & Varela, 1998).

When this book was initally conceived, the expressed purpose was to explicate and illustrate the educational implications of an emerging and controversial new theory in cognitive science: constructivism. Ten years later, the theory is no longer controversial. Most contemporary neurobiologists and cognitive scientists agree: Knowledge is actively constructed. The implications of constructivism for *education*, however, remain controversial. In the last 10 years schools have been engaged in a flurry of reform initiatives encompassing new curricula, new forms of assessment, new stan-

276

dards, and professional development. But various interpretations of constructivism abound, often equating it with "hands-on" learning, discovery, and a host of pedagogical strategies. Resulting confusion and misinterpretation has resulted in public attacks by the media, by parents, and even at times with various groups in the academic community. Thus it seems appropriate in this epilogue chapter, written nearly 10 years later than the first edition of this book, to reflect on the biological and cognitive science evidence and to provide further implications for an application of the theory to education.

REVISITING THE THEORY

The Biological Foundation—Cells as Open Systems

What were the changes during the last century in biology? As Perry and I described in Chapter 2 of this edition, current biologists no longer speak of simple genetic determinism, where new cells are produced from naked DNA. Instead they describe whole cellular networks—cellular structures as open systems—living, evolving systems that are organizationally closed but materially and energetically open (Capra, 2002). Cells need to feed on continual flows of matter and energy from their environment in order to stay alive. The Nobel laureate Ilya Prigogine (1996) describes these cellular structures as dissipative, to emphasize the interplay between maintaining the organization of the structure of the cell on the one hand, and the flow and change (dissipation) on the other. When the flow of energy increases, the system may encounter a point of instability, known as a "bifurcation point," at which point an entirely new form of order may emerge. Capra describes the importance of this new biological model:

This spontaneous emergence of order at critical points of instability is one of the most important concepts of the new understanding of life. It is technically known as self-organization and is often referred to simply as "emergence." It has been recognized as the dynamic origin of development, learning, and evolution. In other words, creativity—the generation of new forms—is a key property of all living systems. And since emergence is an integral part of the dynamics of open systems, we reach the important conclusion that open systems develop and evolve. Life constantly reaches out into novelty. The theory of dissipative structures, formulated in terms of non-linear dynamics, explains not only the spontaneous emergence of order, but also helps us to define complexity. Whereas traditionally the study of complexity has been a study of complex structures, the focus is now shifting from the structures to the processes of their emergence. (2002, p. 14)

Cells are now understood as being a part of an *autopoietic, nonlinear system*. An autopoietic system undergoes continual structural changes while preserving its weblike pattern of organization. The parts of this system continually produce and transform one another in two distinct ways: (1) by self renewal (tissues and organs replace cells in order to maintain a pattern of organization); and (2) by creating new structures, which are developmental and a consequence of the coupling of the organism's cells with environmental influences. In other words, as living systems couple with their environments, recurrent interactions eventually result in structural changes. A cell membrane continually incorporates substances from its environment into its metabolic processes. An organism's nervous system changes its connectivity with every sense perception, but it also attempts to preserve coherence. This pattern is nonlinear, and most importantly, the environment only triggers the structural changes; it does not produce them.

This current biological model of the emergence of novelty has become recognized as an explanation of the dynamic origin of development, learning, and evolution. During the last 25 years, the study of "mind" from this systemic, biological perspective blossomed into the rich, new interdisciplinary field of cognitive science—a field that integrates and transcends the traditional frameworks of child development, psychology, neurobiology, and epistemology.

The Cognitive Science Foundation

Early work in cognitive science focused on Cartesian views: dependent and independent variables, linear change models, and feedback loops. But as the field began to come into its own, and as research accumulated, these models were seen to be inadequate to explain the complexity of learning. More promise appeared in models characterizistic of autopoietic systems. Researchers began to talk about the behavior of an organism as being determined by its structure—structures that are themselves formed by a succession of structural changes (Maturana & Varela, 1998; Piaget, 1987).

Humans seek coherence and meaning. They act on and within their environments with strategies, or schemes, as they seek to make their world similar and maintain their organization (their understanding of it). When puzzled—when new problems emerge that contradict earlier notions, or when new problems make earlier strategies insufficient (or at a minimum inefficient), "bifurcations" result and new structures evolve. It is now commonly understood that human organisms act on their world, coupling with it, interpreting every experience. They do not simply take in, or absorb, information. They interpret it, organize it, and infer about it with the cognitive structures they have previously constructed. Thus, consciousness progressively evolves (Malerstein, 1986). It requires a level of cognitive abstraction that includes the progressive ability to hold and use mental images. These mental images allow us to formulate values, beliefs, goals, and strategies. And representation of these ideas with language and mathematical symbols for explanation and justification within social communities of inquiry and discourse is what learning—epistemological evolution—is all about. This is a constructivist model of learning.

REVISITING THE IMPLICATIONS FOR EDUCATION

Constructivist Pedagogy versus Constructivism as a Learning Theory

As constructivism began to take hold among cognitive scientists as a viable model to explain epistemology and behavior, it began to have an effect on models of education. A constructivist pedagogy began to be formulated and major reform began taking place. Classrooms soon became workshops, with teachers as facilitators, rather than transmitters of knowledge. The role of questioning, disequilibrium, learners paraphrasing each other and discussing ideas in learning communities, the importance of think time and pair talk, and the role of problem-solving and inquiry all began to be descriptive of the "new" classroom.

Although educators now commonly talk about a "constructivist-based" practice as if there is such a thing, in reality constructivism is not a theory of teaching; it is a theory about learning. In fact, as we shift our teaching toward trying to support cognitive construction, the field of education has been left without well-articulated theories of teaching. Reformed practice has been attacked as fuzzy and relative. Major questions loom around *what* should be taught, *how* we should teach, and *how best to educate teachers* for this paradigmatic shift. The problem is that reform-based pedagogical strategies can be used without the desired learning necessarily resulting. This is because constructivism is a theory of learning, not a theory of teaching, and many educators who attempt to use such pedagogical strategies confuse discovery learning and "hands-on" approaches with constructivism.

The intended purpose of both editions of this book has been to look deeply at the question, What is constructivism? What implications does this theory have for teaching? How is it different from discovery learning? From a constructivist perspective, we cannot direct learning to get everyone to the same "ah ha" at the end of the lesson. We can only facilitate "coupling" with problematic situations, help raise questions and puzzlements, and support discourse and development. Learning—deep, conceptual learning—is about structural shifts in cognition. It is about self-organizing at moments of criticality. These changes are complex and nonlinear, and they are the result of interacting, autopoietic systems.

From a constructivist perspective, meaning is understood to be the result of humans setting up relationships, reflecting on their actions, and modeling and constructing explanations. The reality of a cat is a different one than the reality of humans because cats' and humans' minds organize and infer differently. An infant has a different reality than an adult. The infant "knows" the world through sensorimotor schemes, in contrast to the adult who has highly developed mental imagery and logical structures of thought. Even among two adults, realities are different because they are based on interpretations that are the result of past individual experiences and beliefs that formed different neural networks and pathways. Within our human communities we test our models, construct explanations, and prove our thinking. In a sense, we negotiate meaning until we come to believe that we all mean the same thing. Thus constructivism is not to be confused with solipsism. However, as von Glasersfeld makes clear in Chapter 1, we do not and cannot "share" meaning. The best we can do is discuss our ideas in communities until we believe that we agree, until the meanings seem "taken-as-shared" (Cobb, 1996), until our ideas are justified and accepted as explanations by the community. Since these individual constructs are built from reflection on strategies (schemes), on ideas (structures), and on models (representations), learning needs to be understood as the individual development of strategies, "big ideas," and models, but within a cultural, social community of discourse.

The Dutch Version of Reform: Realistic Mathematics Education

While all of this reform work in education based on constructivism was going on in many parts of the world, the Dutch were involved in reform, too—most specifically, in the field of mathematics education. But they were taking a slightly different tack. Hans Freudenthal, a Dutch mathematician, was invited by Bruner to participate in the Woods Hole conference on new math in 1960, but declined the offer. He argued against structuralism, saying that mathematics should be thought of as a human activity of "mathematizing"—not as a discipline of structures to be transmitted, discovered, or even constructed—but as *schematizing, structuring, and modeling the world mathematically*. Thus, even as early as the 60s he took a contemporary constructivist view on education and began to work with Dutch mathematics educators and researchers to develop what he called "Realistic Mathematics Education." Volumes of research and curricula were developed after extensive research, much too much to present coherently here. In 1995 when the first edition of this book went to press, I had just begun to shift my work solely to mathematics education and to collaborate with the Freudenthal Institute at the University of Utrecht. The didactics of RME, that is, the use of context and models, intrigued me and caused me to seek funding for our now ongoing collaboration. In this revised edition, the original chapter on mathematics education was substituted by a more recent chapter (Chapter 10) that is reflective of that collaboration.

The Role of Context

In the United States, as we worked to reform mathematics education from a constructivist perspective, we were using good problems—at least, we were attempting to! We knew rich exploration and conversation around big ideas were important to mathematical learning. But it is not enough to just come up with good problematic situations, because these only bring forth *initial* schematizing. The teacher's responsibility is to foster growth over time *beyond* the student's initial attempts. The Dutch were employing context as a didactic to accomplish this. They were building in constraints and potentially realized suggestions to actively promote disequilibrium, reflection, and development. They were designing contexts that had the potential to perturb.

To take a simple illustration, the pictures in Figures E.1, E.2, and E.3 show ways that contexts might be used to foster progressive mathematizing around multiplication. When children are engaged in investigating "how many," the context of fruit trays (see Figure E.1) allows for counting by ones, but the array arrangements support the construction of skip counting and/or using doubles. In contrast, the context of window shades supports the development of doubling and the use of the associative property (see Figure E.2) simply because one curtain is pulled back; and the context of tiled patios with furniture covering some of the tiles might support the development of the distributive property because some tiles are obscured and cannot be counted (see Figure E.3). By choosing and designing situations that have the potential to perturb learners' initial strategies, teachers can employ context as a powerful didactic that supports the development of big ideas (structuring) and strategies (schematizing). [Author's note: Similar pictures can be found in the Dutch curriculum, Rekenen and Wiskunde (van Galen et. al., 1995)].

The Role of Models

A second important aspect of the RME didactic is the use of models, such as the open number line, the ratio table, the double number line, and the bar model. Rather than using models as a visual or hands-on material as

FIGURE E.1. Fruit arranged in an array: How many apples?

we had done in the United States in the early days of constructivism, within RME they are developed initially with contexts such as measurement (for the open number line), recipes and fair sharing (for the ratio table), and population bars and racetracks (for the bar model and double number line). In Chapter 10, Carol Mosesson introduced fair sharing and the ratio table within a context of submarine sandwiches. After the models are developed, they are then employed by teachers as a community tool to represent students' strategies for computation. Eventually these mathematical models become tools with which learners think. Figure E.4 shows an example of a child's work where the number line has become a tool for mathematical thinking.

Limitations

Employing the use of context and using models didactically were important pieces of the puzzle that early math reformers basing their practice on constructivism had not thought much about. While we planned problems as the starting point of instruction and we engaged children in rich discussions, we had not thought carefully about scaffolding and supporting development over time. The Dutch had. On the other hand, the Dutch had a model of

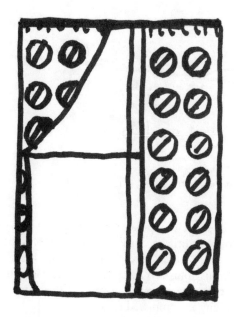

FIGURE E.2. Curtains: How many balls?

FIGURE E.3. Patio: How many tiles?

$$127 + 42 = 169$$

FIGURE E.4. Using the open number line as a tool.

learning that was linear. They spoke of learning lines and planned sequences that were crafted very tightly to move the whole class along this "line." They characterized learning as the development of progressive schematization. The problem with this approach to teaching is that learning is not linear. As Perry and I tried to make clear in Chapter 2, it is complex and nonlinear. Mathematical thinking is comprised of a landscape of big ideas (structures), strategies (schemes), and mathematical models, as Dolk and I described in Chapter 10. It requires the interpreting and explanation of part/whole relations and transformations (structures), the refinement of strategies and procedures (schemes), and the emergence of ways to mathematically model problems. The Dutch seemed to have an important *didactic* employing context and models, whereas in the United States we had developed a reformed *pedagogy*, turning classrooms into workshops and facilitating communities of discourse to facilitate development. In our collaborative project in New York, Mathematics in the City, we tried to combine the strengths of each.

MATHEMATICS IN THE CITY

Mathematics in the City began in 1995, funded by the National Science Foundation—a collaboration between the Freudenthal Institute and the City College of New York. It is primarily a professional development (inservice) project in mathematics education; although as we worked in classrooms with elementary teachers helping them to reform their practice, we researched several sequences employing context for the development of number and operation K–6; we developed mini-lessons using the open number line, open arrays, and double number line; and we developed what we came to call landscapes of learning. Rather than perceiving of scope and sequence as a learning line of progressive schematization, we perceived of learning as a nonlinear journey comprised of many paths toward a horizon. The journey incorporates landmarks of big ideas, strategies, and models. Readers interested in more detailed descriptions are referred to Fosnot and Dolk (2001a, 2001b; 2002).

Assumptions Regarding Mathematics

Rather than a discipline or body of knowledge (concepts, skills) to be transmitted, we defined mathematics along the lines of Freudenthal's (1991) notion of "mathematizing"—the activity of interpreting, organizing, and constructing meaning of situations with mathematical modeling. But we expanded it to include mathematizing as a way of making meaning in the world. To us, it is a constructive process, which includes noticing patterns in special cases, analyzing why they are occurring, expressing them in some form of generality, and searching for elegance in the creation of strategy or proof. This "mathematizing" involves the setting up of quantifiable and spatial relationships, the constructing of patterns and transformations, the proving of them as generalizations and models, and the searching for elegance of solution. It involves the interpreting of one's "lived" world, mathematically. Mathematicians *create* mathematics to solve real-life problems or to explain or prove interesting patterns, relationships, or puzzles in mathematics itself—in a sense, they even mathematize their mathematical activity (Gravemeijer, 1997). They define problems and raise questions.

Constructing mathematical ideas is not only a cognitive activity; it is also a social one. Being a mathematician means being mathematical within a mathematical community. Mathematicians prove their ideas to each other. Ideas hold as accepted truths only insofar as the mathematical community accepts the proofs. Paul Cobb's chapter, Chapter 3, provides a theoretical explanation for this coordination of perspectives.

Assumptions Regarding Teaching

If mathematics is defined as "mathematizing," then what implications does this have for teaching? Learners need to be given the opportunity to search for patterns, raise questions, and construct ideas, strategies, and ways to mathematically model their "lived" worlds; and they need to be invited to defend their thinking to others in the community. The classroom, in a sense, becomes a *workshop* as learners investigate together. It becomes a mini-society—a community of learners engaged in mathematical activity, discourse, and reflection. Learners must be given the opportunity to act as mathematicians by allowing, supporting, and challenging their "mathematizing" of particular situations. The community provides an environment in which individual mathematical ideas can be expressed and tested against the ideas of others. Learners share perceptions with each other and with the teacher, and their ideas become modified, selected, or deselected, as common (taken-as-shared, Cobb, 1996) meanings develop. This enables learners to become clearer and more confident about what they know and understand.

Frameworks for Learning and Teaching

Linear Frameworks. Only focusing on the structure of mathematics will lead to a more traditional way of teaching, one where the teacher pushes the children toward procedures or mathematical concepts. In this framework, learning moves along a line. As Perry and I described in Chapter 2, historically curriculum designers employed such a framework. They analyzed the structure of mathematics and delineated objectives and goals along a line. The small ideas and skills were assumed to accumulate eventually into concepts (Bloom et al., 1971). Many teachers held similar frameworks of learning and teaching. Each lesson, each day, was geared toward a different objective, a different "it." All children were expected to understand the same "it," in the same way, at the end of the lesson. They were assumed to move along the same path; if there were individual differences it was just that some children moved along the path more slowly—hence, it was thought that some needed more time, or remediation.

Learning Trajectories. As educational reform based on constructivism has taken hold, curriculum designers and educators have tried to develop other frameworks. Most of these approaches are based on a better understanding of the learning of children and of the development of tasks that will challenge them.

Simon (1995), for example, describes a learning/teaching framework that he refers to as a "hypothetical learning trajectory"—hypothetical because until the students are really working on a problem, we can never be sure what they will do, or whether and how they will construct new interpretations, ideas, and strategies. The teacher, however, expects the children to solve a problem in certain ways; in fact, expectations are different for different children. Simon uses the metaphor of a sailboat.

> You may initially plan the whole journey or only part of it. You set out sailing according to your plan. However, you must constantly adjust because of the conditions that you encounter. You continue to acquire knowledge about sailing, about the current conditions, and about the areas that you wish to visit. You change your plans with respect to the order of your destinations. You mod-

ify the length and nature of your visits as a result of interactions with people along the way. You add destinations that prior to the trip were unknown to you. The path that you travel is your [actual] trajectory. The path that you anticipate at any point is your "hypothetical trajectory." (pp. 136–137)

As Simon makes clear, teaching is a planned activity. Teachers do not walk into their classrooms wondering what to do. They have a lesson planned and they anticipate what the children will do. With responses from children, teachers acknowledge the differences in thinking in children's strategies, and they adjust their course in relation to these interactions.

Landscapes of Learning: Steps, Shifts, and Mental Maps

In our original work with teachers, we too used the terminology of a hypothetical learning trajectory—even though we described it in terms of knowledge of models, strategies, and big ideas. But this terminology now seems too linear. Learning—real learning—is messy business. We prefer instead the metaphor of a landscape (Fosnot & Dolk, 2001a, 2001b, 2002).

Learning and teaching are more a journey across a landscape than a trajectory, or learning line. The big ideas, strategies, and models—the structuring, the schematizing, and the modeling—serve as important *landmarks* for teachers to use as they plan, and as they journey with their children. As teachers design contexts for children to explore, the goal is to enable children to mathematize—to act on, and within, the situations by mathematically using the landmark strategies. These progressive schematizations are the *steps* in the journey. The environment—the context as well—is designed to facilitate discussion around big ideas because these landmark ideas are major shifts in perspective—major shifts in structuring. As children model and represent their strategies, and as they develop generalized mental models of the part/whole relations for situations and operations, they construct *mental maps* that can eventually become tools with which to think. For children, the landmarks epitomize their struggles in their journey to "make sense of" the world—they characterize the steps, shifts, and mental maps in the development of mathematizing. Teachers have horizons in mind when they plan—horizons like place value, or addition and subtraction. These appear from a distance and the journey thus seems to be a perpendicular line, a goal to be reached (a hypothetical trajectory), but in reality the journey is made up of many landmarks, and there are many ways to get to the horizon. The paths to these landmarks and horizons are not necessarily linear. Nor is there only one. As in a real landscape, the paths twist and turn; they cross each other and are often not direct. Children do not construct each of these ideas in an ordered sequence. They go off in many directions as they explore, struggle to understand, and make sense of their world mathematically. Strategies do not necessarily affect the development of big ideas, nor the reciprocal. Often a big idea, like unitizing, will affect counting strategies; but just as often, "trying out" new counting strategies that they have seen others use (like skip counting) will affect the development of unitizing. Ultimately, what is important is how children function in a mathematical environment (Cobb, 1997)—how they mathematize.

The Role of the Teacher

Viewing learning and teaching as a journey across a landscape makes teaching very difficult. The investigations must be rich and provide opportunities for many levels of mathematizing. Teachers must have an in-depth knowledge of the landscape in order to facilitate the journey. This means they must understand mathematics to be the *activity of mathematizing*. And they must also understand the *development* of the landmarks—they must understand that learning is the result of autopoietic structures—of assimilation and accommodation. Often Piaget's notion of assimilation has been misunderstood—assimilated, itself, with behaviorist beliefs. It has been described as a "taking in" of new information as long as learners are developmentally ready to understand it. From this perspective, learning is nothing more than the association of new concepts with prior concepts, and the cognitive reordering to build this connection. In contrast, Piaget describes assimilation as the "acting on" a situation with initial organizing schemes—to make the situation "similar" to the present cognitive structures of the learner. This gets to the heart of constructivism. We know the world *through* the schemes and structures we use to explore it. Perturbations to these assimilatory schemes cause cognitive reordering (accommodation). These perturbations can come about when learners reflect on their actions and infer them to be insufficient or inefficient. They can come about when a cognitive structure is perturbed; or when two ideas seem to be contradictory. Thus, teachers need to become facilitators, provocateurs, and questioners. They must turn classrooms into workshops and structure discussions around big ideas and efficient strategies. And of course, pedagogical strategies need to be aligned with the process of learning, rather than with transmission.

Teacher Development

When learning and teaching are viewed from the perspective of a landscape, new models of pre-service and inservice education must be formulated. One viable model was offered in Chapter 15—work that my colleagues at SCSU and I did just prior to the writing of the first edition of this book.

As we move into the 21st century, advances in digital technology are providing new promising possibilities for teacher education. Real teaching is based on visions of past practice, of strategies based on beliefs about learning, about epistemology, and the role of the teacher. Most teacher decision-making is split-second decision-making in the context of the teaching/learning act and is directly connected to the context of the classroom. Digital technology allows the teacher educator to immerse teachers in the context of real classrooms. Just as context is critical in learning to mathematize one's "lived" world for students, the real world context of the classroom is critical to teachers as they learn to teach.

Digital production projects have traditionally used the technology to accompany texts for illustrating examples such as lessons, coaching models, and/or interviews (Carpenter, Franke, & Levi, 2003; West & Staub, 2003), or in other cases for modified lesson study (www.Lessonlab.com). Of exception are a few projects characterized by a more interactive, inquiry-driven approach to learning, such as MILE (Dolk et al., 1996), or the University of Michigan's Space for Teaching and Learning Exploration (SLATE).

Current digital lab environments go even beyond those uses (see Dolk, Fosnot, Cameron, & Hersch, 2004). They are interactive multilevel learning environments for the professional continuum. They bring the context of the classroom to the fingertips of the learner. Users are immersed in the study of children over time in exemplary classrooms; they examine the teacher's didactical employment of context; they can inquire about and analyze the pedagogy; they clip and paste moments from footage and build "landscapes of learning" (trajectories) that show children constructing "big ideas," developing strategies, and/or using mathematical models as tools; they are asked to solve mathematical problems in several ways and anticipate student strategies, which they subsequently examine; they design investigations and mini-lessons for the next day; they examine how the teacher in the environment continues and they subsequently analyze children's work to assess the effectiveness. They can even add clipped footage as hypertext—evidence to support arguments and provide examples in term papers and literature reviews, or as sample evidence of the NCTM standards. The materials are cross-platform, thus enabling users to work at home on assignments as well as in college classrooms, or on the Internet. Inservice and pre-service activities are interspersed to deepen teachers' abilities to analyze the mathematics in children's work, to explore the role of context in teaching mathematics, and to investigate teachers' questioning and choice of problems. Such materials provide a powerful context, an environment for discourse and learning.

CONCLUSION

Constructivism is a theory of learning, not a theory about teaching. But when one analyzes the theory, one can begin to formulate a reformed practice that supports rigor, empowerment, and the construction of genuine understanding. Over the past 20 years, educators have been hard at work to reform the process of schooling accordingly—to bring our educational institutions into the 21st century. It is my hope in providing this second edition that I have updated and extended the theory sufficiently and done justice to the telling of the many attempts of reform, thereby contributing in some small fashion to the promises and possibilities of tomorrow.

REFERENCES

Bloom, B., Hastings, J., & Madaus, G. F. (1971). *Handbook on formative and summative evaluation of student learning.* New York: McGraw-Hill.

Brown, S. (2001). *Reconstructing school mathematics: Problems with problems and the real world.* New York: Peter Lang Publishing.

Capra, F. (2002). *The hidden connections: Integrating the biological, cognitive, and social dimensions of life into a science of sustainability.* New York: Doubleday.

Carpenter, T., Franke, M., & Levi, L. (2003). *Thinking mathematically: Integrating arithmetic and algebra in elementary school.* Portsmouth, NH: Heinemann Press.

Cobb, P. (1996). A Socio-cultural perspective. In Fosnot, C. T. (Ed.), *Constructivism: Theory, perspectives, and practice* (Chapter 3). New York: Teachers College Press.

Cobb, P. (1997). Instructional design and reform: A plea for developmental research in context. In Beishuizen, M., Gravemeijer, K., & van Leishout, E. (Eds.), *The role of contexts and models in the development of mathematical strategies and procedures* (Chapter 12). Utrecht, Netherlands: The Freudenthal Institute.

Deutsch, D. (1997). *The fabric of reality.* New York: Penguin Books.

Dewey, J. (1910). *How we think.* Boston: Heath.

Dolk, M., Faes, W., Goffree, F., Hermsen, H., & Oonk, W. (1996). *A multimedia interactive learning environment for future primary school teachers.* Utrecht, Netherlands: Freudenthal Instituut, NVORWO.

Dolk, M., Fosnot, C. T., Cameron, A., & Hersch, S. (2004). *Young mathematicians at work: Professional development materials.* CD-ROMs and Facilitator Guides. Portsmouth, NH: Heinemann Press.

Fosnot, C. T. (1989). *Enquiring teachers, enquiring learners: A constructivist approach to teaching.* New York: Teachers College Press.

Fosnot, C. T. (1996) (Ed.). *Constructivism: Theory, perspectives, and practice.* New York: Teachers College Press.

Fosnot, C. T., & Dolk, M. (2001a). *Young mathematicians at work: Constructing early number sense, addition, and subtraction.* Portsmouth, NH: Heinemann Press.

Fosnot, C. T., & Dolk, M. (2001b). *Young mathematicians at work: Constructing multiplication and division.* Portsmouth, NH: Heinemann Press.

Fosnot, C. T., & Dolk, M. (2002). *Young mathematicians at work: Constructing fractions, decimals, and percents.* Portsmouth, NH: Heinemann Press.

Freudenthal, H. (1991). *Revisiting mathematics education: The China lectures.* Dordrecht, Netherlands: Kluwer Academic Publishers.

Gravemeijer, K. (1997). Instructional design for reform in mathematics education. In Beishuizen, M., Gravemeijer, K., & van Leishout, E. (Eds.), *The role of contexts and models in the development of mathematical strategies and procedures* (Chapter 1). Utrecht, Netherlands: The Freudenthal Institute.

Kamii, C. (1989). *Young children continue to reinvent arithmetic—2nd grade.* New York: Teachers College Press.

Malerstein, A. J. (1986). *The conscious mind.* New York: Human Sciences Press.

Maturana, H., & Varela, F. (1998). *The tree of knowledge.* Boston: Shambala Press.

Piaget, J. (1970). Piaget's Theory. In P. H. Mussen (Ed.), *Carmichael's manual of child psychology.* New York: John Wiley & Sons.

Piaget, J. (1977). *The development of thought: Equilibration of cognitive structures.* New York: Viking.

Piaget, J. (1987). *Possibility and necessity.* Minneapolis: University of Minnesota Press.

Prigogine, I. (1996). *The end of certainty.* New York: Free Press.

Schifter, D., & Fosnot, C. T. (1993). *Reconstructing mathematics education: Stories of teachers meeting the challenge of reform.* New York: Teachers College Press.

Simon, M. A. (1995). Reconstructing mathematics pedagogy from a constructivist perspective. *Journal for Research in Mathematics Education, 26,* 114–145.

Treffers, A. (1987). Integrated column arithmetic according to progressive schematization. *Educational Studies in Mathematics, 18*(2), 125–145.

van Galen, F., Gravemeijer, K., Kraemer, J. M., Meeuwisse, T., & Vermeulen, W. (Eds.). (1995). *Rekenen and Wiskunde.* Utrecht, Netherlands: Uitgeverij Bekadidact Baarn.

von Glasersfeld, E. (1996). Introduction: Aspects of constructivism. In C. T. Fosnot (Ed.) *Constructivism: Theory, perspectives, and practice* (Chapter 1). New York: Teachers College Press.

Vygotsky, L. (1978). *Mind and society: The development of higher psychological processes.* Cambridge, MA: Harvard University Press.

West, L., & Staub, F. (2003). *Content-focused coaching: Transforming mathematics lessons.* Portsmouth, NH: Heinemann Press.

About the Contributors

Paul Cobb is Professor of Mathematics Education at Vanderbilt University. He has written extensively on the topic of mathematics teaching and learning and is particularly interested in the issue of discourse and community as they relate to constructivism.

Susan Cowey is a first-grade teacher in Branford, Connecticut. Previously she was a Graduate Fellow at the Center for Constructivist Teaching and taught a fourth–fifth combination grade, also in Branford.

Rheta DeVries is Director of the Regent's Center for Early Developmental Education and Professor of Curriculum and Instruction at the University of Northern Iowa. She has authored books on constructivist education, including *Moral Classrooms, Moral Children: Creating a Constructivist Atmosphere in Early Education* (co-authored with Betty Zan).

Maarten Dolk is a researcher and developer of mathematics education materials at the Freudenthal Institute in the Netherlands, where he has been involved in the development of inservice materials for teachers and of multimedia learning environments for student teachers. He has also directed an inservice project in the Netherlands for teacher educators and staff developers. His work in the United States is related to the inservice of primary school teachers.

Eleanor Duckworth is Professor of Education at Harvard University. She studied and worked with Jean Piaget and Barbel Inhelder for over 20 years and served as Piaget's interpreter for his U.S. lectures during much of this time. She was a staff member of the Elementary Science Study and evaluator of the African Primary Science Program. She has published books, monographs, and numerous articles about teaching and learning.

Dewey I. Dykstra, Jr. is Professor of Physics at Boise State University, Idaho. As well as a skilled bagpipe player, he has published extensively and is a frequent workshop leader, both nationally and internationally, on the topic of science teaching and learning.

George Forman is Professor of Early Childhood Education at the University of Massachusetts at Amherst. He is the author of numerous books and articles on Piaget's theory and its application to education. His most recent focus is the Reggio Emilia Project Approach in Italy, which he has described with Edwards and Gandini in *The Hundred Languages of Children* (Ablex).

Catherine Twomey Fosnot is professor of education at the City College of New York and director of Mathematics in the City, a national center of in-service in New York City. She is the past president of the Association for Constructivist Teaching and she has twice received the "significant contribution" award from AERA's Constructivist SIG, as well as the "young scholar" award from the Educational Communication and Technology Journal for her writing on constructivism and educational technology. She is the author of several books and articles on constructivism, among them *Enquiring Teachers, Enquiring Learners,* also published by Teachers College Press.

Catherine A. Franklin is a professor in the School of Education at the City College of the City University of New York. Her research interests include social studies, middle school education, and curriculum design. She has been a classroom teacher in Columbia, Japan, Nepal, and the United States.

June S. Gould, formerly Assistant Professor of Language Arts at the Center for Constructivist Teaching at Southern Connecticut State University, is a language arts consultant to school systems in Connecticut and Westchester County, New York. She teaches the novel and short story in Manhattanville College's Masters in Writing program at Purchase, New York. A novelist, she is also the author of *The Writer in All of Us: Improving Your Writing Through Childhood Memories* (Dutton) and the forthcoming, *Passionate Attention: Reading to Transform Your Classroom and Your Life.*

Maxine Greene is the William F. Russell Professor in the Foundations of Education at Teachers College, where she teaches courses in aesthetics and educational philosophy. Her books include *The Dialectic of Freedom* and, most recently, *Releasing Imagination: Art, Education, and Community.* She is a former president of AERA and is presently developing a Center for Social Imagination at Teachers College.

Candace Julyan has been involved in science and environmental education for over 20 years as teacher, administrator, and curriculum developer. Influenced by her doctoral studies with Eleanor Duckworth, in the past decade she has become more focused on the relationships among the teacher, the learner, and the science content. She developed and directed the elementary science curriculum project—the National Geographic Kids Network—and is currently the director of an elementary level, investigations-based telecommunications project at the Arnold Arboretum and a Lecturer on Education at Harvard University.

Randall Stewart Perry has a Ph.D. in earth and space sciences from the University of Washington with certification in the interdisciplinary studies of astrobiology and early evolution. He is currently a Research Scientist with the Planetary Science Institute and a Research Fellow at Oxford. He is the author of several articles on the origin of life, prebiotic chemistry, and biogeochemistry. Currently he is at work studying the oldest evidence of life on Earth.

D. Kim Reid, Ph.D., is professor of education at Teachers College, Columbia University. As a graduate student, she found constructivism a more satisfying and productive approach to the understanding and instruction of disabled students than the prevailing theories and epistemologies. As a result, all of her subsequent work has been grounded in a constructivist perspective. Her research interests lie in exploring a disability studies perspective in the field of learning, in exposing special education as a tool of institutionalized racism, and in analyzing the ways that humor is used to construct notions of disability in contemporary society.

Deborah Schifter worked at the SummerMath Programs at Mount Holyoke College since their inception in 1982, becoming director of SummerMath for Teachers in 1988. She has also worked as an applied mathematician and has taught elementary, secondary, and college level mathematics. She has authored several books and numerous articles on mathematics teaching and learning and currently works at the Center for the Development of Teaching at EDC, where she directs an NSF funded project entitled "Teaching to the Big Ideas."

Jan Weatherly Valle, a former middle and high school teacher of students labeled "learning disabled," teaches graduate students in special education at the City College of New York. She is a doctoral candidate at Teachers College, Columbia University. Her research centers around parents and families of children with disabilities, parent and professional collaboration in schools, implementation of inclusive and constructivist classroom practice, and disability studies in education.

Ernst von Glasersfeld is known by many as the father of radical constructivism. He has published many articles and books on this topic and currently shares his time between the Scientific Reasoning Research Institute at the University of Massachusetts and the Institute of Behavioral Research at the University of Georgia.

Betty Zan is Research Fellow at the Regents' Center for Early Developmental Education, University of Northern Iowa and a doctoral candidate at the University of Houston. She co-authored *Moral Classrooms, Moral Children: Creating a Constructivist Atmosphere in Early Education* with Rheta DeVries.

Index

Abstraction
  empirical, 45, 47, 48
  See also Reflective abstraction
Accommodation, 16–18, 19–20, 42, 47,
  104, 111, 169, 242, 288
Activities, 41–45, 47–51, 99, 100, 144–46,
  264
Adams, R., 153
Adaptation, 3, 4–5, 43, 45
  and biological aspects of learning, 12, 13,
    14, 15
  and cognitive evolution, 27, 28, 29, 30
Administrators, 272–73
Amarel, M., 64, 100
American Educational Research Association
  (AERA), 152
Americans with Disabilities Act, 152
Ames, L. B., 10
Ammon, P., 263, 264
Amusement park for birds project, 213–21
Apprenticeship, 42, 52
Appropriation, 25, 43, 45
Arithemetical activity, 48–51. *See also* Mathe-
  matics
Armstrong, F., 154
Arons, Arnold, 243
Art education, 112
Artiles, A. J., 153
Arts
  and cognition, 124–25, 129
  and consciousness, 110, 114–15, 116,
    118, 121, 126, 128, 129
  and culture, 113–14, 116, 117, 124, 126
  defining the, 112–13
  and disabled, 153
  and experience, 112, 119–20, 121, 124,
    125, 129
  and meaning, 111–13, 116–29
  and reality, 110, 112–14, 116, 118,
    121–29
  teaching and learning in, 110–31
  and truth, 110, 115, 120, 121, 122, 127
Assessment, 9, 10, 100, 276. *See also* Evaluation

Assimilation, 16–18, 31, 42, 47, 72, 111,
  118, 169, 288
Assumptions, 241, 243, 285–86
Atwell, N., 92
Audience, 194, 203–10, 211, 221
Axel, E., 44

Bak, Per, 11, 16, 33
Bakhurst, D., 41
Ball, D. L., 40–41, 52, 53–54, 85, 92
Balloons, working with, 64–75
Barthes, Roland, 129
Barton, L., 154
Bastable, V., 89
Bauersfeld, H., 43, 44
Behavior, 6, 13–14, 28
Behaviorism, 8–9, 155
Beishuizen, M., 190
Beliefs, 53, 161–62, 175, 264–74, 279
Berger, P., 122
Bernstein, R. J., 42
Bickmore-Brand, J., 24, 25, 103
Biological Science Curriculum Study
  (BSCS), 63
Biology, 9, 11–16, 27–29, 277–78
Bishop, Elizabeth, 116, 117, 119, 126
Bloom, B. S., 9, 286
Blumer, H., 31, 42, 46
Body-parts counting system, 49–50
Bogdan, R., 154
Bordieu, P., 153
Bouck, E. C., 155
Bovet, M., 17
Bowlby, J., 29
Boyle, F., 222
Brain, 30, 31
Brantlinger, E. A., 155
Brasell, H., 244
Brazil bridge problem, 265–66
Bredo, E., 44
Brown, J. S., 39, 42
Brown, S., 276
Bruner, Jerome, 11, 24, 25, 27, 33, 103,
  280